D1520049

Ursula K. LE GUIN

a primary and secondary bibliography

Masters of
Science Fiction and Fantasy

Editor
L. W. Currey

Advisory Acquisitions Editor
Marshall B. Tymn

Other bibliographies in the series:

Lloyd Alexander, Evangeline Walton Ensley, and Kenneth Morris
Leigh Brackett, Marion Zimmer Bradley, and Anne McCaffrey
Samuel R. Delany
Gordon R. Dickson
Andre Norton
Clifford D. Simak
Theodore Sturgeon
Jules Verne
Jack Williamson
Roger Zelazny

Ursula K. LE GUIN

a primary and secondary bibliography

ELIZABETH CUMMINS COGELL

G.K. HALL &CO.

70 LINCOLN STREET, BOSTON, MASS.

Library of Congress Cataloging in Publication Data

Cogell, Elizabeth Cummins.
   Ursula K. Le Guin, a primary and secondary bibliography.

   (Masters of science fiction and fantasy)
   Includes indexes.
   1.   Le Guin, Ursula K., 1929-   —Bibliography.
I.   Title.   II.   Series.
Z8495.88.C63   1983   016.813'54   82-12071
[PS3562.E42]
ISBN 0-8161-8155-1

This publication is printed on permanent/durable acid-free paper
MANUFACTURED IN THE UNITED STATES OF AMERICA

To Evelyn and Cedric,
who taught me to persevere.

Contents

The Author

Elizabeth Cummins Cogell holds degrees from Cottey College and the University of South Dakota. She was a Fulbright scholar at the University of Bristol (England), examining the relationship between seventeenth-century scientific thought and poetry. She is currently writing her dissertation on Ursula K. Le Guin at the University of Illinois at Urbana-Champaign. She has served as treasurer of the Science Fiction Research Association for four years and is currently on the editorial board of Extrapolation. In addition to several articles on Le Guin, she has published a bibliography of library collections of science fiction and an article on Darko Suvin's aesthetics for science fiction. Her teaching specialties at the University of Missouri-Rolla include science fiction and technical writing.

Preface

This volume provides a chronological listing of publications by and about Ursula K. Le Guin. It includes her fiction, poetry, and essays, as well as critical evaluations of her work. I have made every effort to ensure the accuracy of this project by examining all of these works. The few items I was not able to see are marked by an asterisk (*) and followed by the source which verified their existence. All items listed were published in the English language.

The primary bibliography is divided into three parts. Each entry is numbered and identified by the letter of the appropriate section. Within a given year, entries are arranged in order of appearance.

Part A lists all of her fiction--novels, collections, edited anthologies, and stories in magazines and anthologies. Each entry begins with the first publication of a work followed by the major reprints and editions in chronological order. All known appearances of each short story are listed, although only the first edition of any anthology is included. Alternate titles are listed as separate entries and cross-referenced to the main entry. Part A begins in 1961 and is comprehensive through December 1980.

Part B, Section One, includes Le Guin's poetry and miscellaneous publications such as translations, records, and tapes. It begins in 1959, is comprehensive through December 1980, and includes the poetry collection published in 1981. Part B, Section Two, lists adaptations of and creative responses to her work from 1970 through 1980.

Part C includes all of her nonfiction publications and papers. It lists her university theses, essays, book reviews, letters, notes and comments, introductions and afterwords, as well as interviews and responses to questionnaires. It begins in 1951, is complete through December 1980, and contains four 1981 items.

The secondary bibliography is listed in Part D. It includes significant analyses of her work--book reviews, essays, introductions, biographies, bibliographies, and letters. It begins in 1966, is comprehensive through December 1979, and includes numerous 1980 and

Preface

several 1981 pieces. Within each year, the entries are arranged
alphabetically by author's name. Each entry begins with the first
publication, includes reprint information, and is followed by an
annotation describing the contents of the article.

The annotation generally states the main ideas of the essay, indicates the context within which the critic discusses Le Guin's work,
and notes any comparisons made to other authors or pieces of literature. More book reviews are eliminated than any other type of secondary material. Those reviews which are included contain some significant critical assessment and are either at least 100 words long or in
some way indicate the reputation of Le Guin. Many reviews, especially
in newspapers and small or irregular periodicals, lack page numbers
because they were found in Le Guin's clipping files at the University
of Oregon archives.

Two indexes are included: one for the primary bibliography and
one for the secondary.

Reference books and tools in the fields of science fiction, fantasy, and children's literature were used, as well as indexes to
citations, newspapers, book reviews, and essays. The greatest difficulty came in securing fanzine material and in identifying 1980 publications.

There are many people who have assisted me during this project
and to whom I am very grateful. Le Guin herself graciously allowed
me to examine the first editions in her home library and gave me per-
mission to use some of the material in the University of Oregon
archives. Then there are the bibliographers who preceded me--Jeff
Levin, Jim Bittner, and Joe De Bolt. Not only have they made earlier
listings of Le Guin's work, they generously provided me with information when I sought it. Help also came from those bibliographers and
collectors in the field of science fiction--Lloyd Currey and Marshall
Tymn. Many librarians have aided me, but three deserve special men-
tion--Daisy Burton of the Interlibrary Loan Department, University
of Missouri-Rolla; Doris Mehegan, head (as well as curator and in-
dexer) of the Spaced-Out Library in Toronto; and Edward Kemp, Special
Collections, University of Oregon (Eugene). These three people made
me feel at home in their collections and took a personal interest in
my work. The reference librarians at UMR should also be thanked for
helping track down ephemeral publications and noting current references to Le Guin which they saw during their workday.

Virginia Kidd, Le Guin's literary agent, was helpful and encour-
aging at the beginning of this project and the University of Missouri-
Rolla, through the Humanities Department and the Weldon Spring Faculty
Development Fund, made possible my trip to Oregon. Impossible to
name are all the editors, publishers, collectors, and bookstore owners
who provided me with hard-to-find Le Guin material.

Preface

I would also like to thank Roberta McNail and Dan Cogell, not only for their careful work but also for their good humor and patience when entries had to be renumbered. Roberta typed the final manuscript and Dan worked out the two indexes.

Finally, there are those who gave me psychological support for what turned out to be a long project--my colleagues at UMR (especially W. Nicholas Knight and Marvin Barker), colleagues in the Science Fiction Research Association, friends, students, and even relatives. My husband, Wayne Cogell, deserves more than this special note for enduring all the steps of this project. His encouragement was essential for the completion of the manuscript.

Introduction

The Le Guin that can be named
Is not the eternal Le Guin.

I hope I will be forgiven for this plagiarism of the first two
lines of the Tao Te Ching.[1] I have removed the word "Tao" in each
line, the word underlying all Chinese philosophy whose referent is
the ineffable, constantly changing force or order of nature, the
basis of both science and ethics, the source of being and becoming.
In place of this word I have inserted the name of a writer of science
fiction and fantasy, a Portland housewife, a late twentieth-century
Taoist sage sans robe, forest hermitage, and flowing beard.

The substitution is justified by more than just the fact of
Le Guin's interest in and use of Taoist philosophy. The lines express, on the simplest level, a literal truth about names. This
author is also a Kroeber. She wrote poems, short stories, and novels
as Ursula Kroeber; she wrote a senior honors thesis and an M.A.
thesis as Ursula Kroeber. Moreover, the Kroeber lifestyle and the
activities of her parents have been shaping influences. Her biography reminds us that when as readers, teachers, scholars of her fiction we speak of "Le Guin" meaning the "author," we are generally not
thinking of all the other strands of her days--daughter, wife, mother,
friend, Washington Post book reviewer, observatory newsletter editor,
caretaker of cats, gardener of geraniums, cook, dishwasher, editor,
amateur photographer, landowner, artist with pen and ink, translator,
tv movie consultant, rider of Portland city buses. . . . Trying to
name them all is like trying to name all the parts of the sea in the
world of Earthsea. The task is made more difficult by her insistence
on her own and her family's privacy, which I respect.

Even if we use the term "Le Guin" to refer only to the author,
however, the stolen lines are still applicable. No discussion, no
matter how detailed, no matter how precise its vocabulary and minute
its dissection, ever equals even a single story, poem, novel, review,
or essay which is being analyzed. Translating her metaphors (her
"lies" as she calls them) into critical prose means that something is

always lost--all the nuances cannot be named, cannot be gathered up in one armload of paragraphs. Le Guin has made such a comment about her choice to write fiction: "If I could have said it non-metaphorically, I would not have written all these words, this novel" [The Left Hand of Darkness].[2] Furthermore, she is an author who dwells on the ambiguous, who delights in Taoist paradox, and who experiments with the genres of the fantastic.

The most important reason why these lines are appropriate is that Le Guin is a contemporary, active author. She is currently writing poems, novels, short stories, reviews, essays and submitting them for publication. It is inappropriate to speak of the "Le Guin opus" because there is none--there is no completed, final body of work. Each new piece changes our perspective on the previous pieces. She has directly expressed a desire for "perpetually inventing new people" in her poem, "Ars Lunga"; and in her longest poem, "Coming of Age," the speaker/writer recognizes that certain dreams and fantasies must be relinquished and new ones, initially painful, must take their places.

Therefore, "the Le Guin that can be named / is not the eternal Le Guin." This bibliography should be viewed as a record of a process to date; the process of writing is unfinished and so is this text. Appropriately, this introduction will highlight those elements of the process which will be most helpful for using the material in this book and about which I can provide new information.

It has four topics:
1. Selected biography
2. Publishing career
3. Non-fiction essays
4. Critical reception

I hope that the independence of these topics will allow a reader to read thoroughly, browse, or even skip a section that seems dull or irrelevant at the moment.

1. Selected biography.
It is fitting that our primary source of knowledge about this author's parents is their writing for they, too, protected their family privacy. The best single book is her mother's biography of Le Guin's father, Alfred Kroeber: A Personal Configuration (1971). Although not a family chronicle, it is a clear picture of personal presence--warm, intelligent humanists who enjoyed their work and flourished on cultural anthropology.

Le Guin's mother was Theodora Kracaw Kroeber (Denver, 1897--Berkeley, 1979). Her best known work is Ishi in Two Worlds (1961) which was in its fifteenth printing at the time of her death. Although she titled it a "biography," she more often referred to it as a "story" and her retellings of it through various approaches[3] indicate her fascination with the California Indian, the lone survivor of his Yahi tribe, who wandered into civilization 29 August 1911, and lived four years and seven months in the twentieth century, most of it under the care of the staff (which included Alfred Kroeber) at the University of California's Museum of Anthropology. Her book emphasizes Ishi's remarkable ability to cross from one world into another and back again. Le Guin, also, is taken with the crossing of limits and borders: such crossings provide narrative, anthropological, and ethical situations that produce dynamic tensions. In the Earthsea trilogy, Ged crosses the ultimate borderline into the land of the dead and returns; most of her Hainish novels depict a protagonist moving from his own society across space and time into an alien or remotely related society. As with the Ishi story, survival and the nature of being human are primary concerns. The greatest mystery of the Ishi story is that his twentieth century friends never learned his own name, a fact Theodora Kroeber often mentioned in prefaces and interviews. So also Le Guin is concerned with naming in her science fiction and certainly in the Earthsea magic where knowing the true name gives the knower power over the thing or person.

Theodora Kroeber's first book was The Inland Whale: Nine Stories Retold From California Indian Legends (1959). It, too, suggests factors that entered into Le Guin's imagination and her attitude toward art. Theodora Kroeber's awareness of the female character is reflected in her dedication: "This Book is dedicated to the ancestors and descendants of its nine heroines." The collection demonstrates and discusses the importance of storytelling, especially in the oral tradition. The reader receives each story through at least three people: the story's protagonist, the informer who told the story to Theodora Kroeber or others, and Theodora Kroeber who is now telling the story to the reader. As she commented in her introduction, "A work of art has more facets than are turned to the light at one time."[4] This heritage appears in Le Guin's concept, best expressed in the opening paragraph of The Left Hand of Darkness: "I'll make my report as if I told a story, for I was taught as a child on my homeworld that Truth is a matter of the imagination. The soundest fact may fail or prevail in the style of its telling" (7). The oral tradition supplies us with the story that constitutes the first volume of Le Guin's Earthsea trilogy. The dynamic quality of the text, of the important relationship between teller and listener/reader is discussed in one of her most recent essays, "It was a Dark and Stormy Night; or, Why Are We Huddled about the Campfire?"

The accomplishments of Alfred Kroeber (New Jersey, 1876--Paris, 1960) in anthropology are impressive, in part because so much of what he did was on the borders of a new field--he earned the first Ph.D. in anthropology at Columbia University and founded the Department of Anthropology at the University of California (1901); he was the last "of the great American anthropologists whose Indian informants--or at any rate the older ones--had still, as young men, followed a traditional way of life."[5] He wrote the first general textbook for the field (Anthropology, 1923). Because the field was new, he could afford to be a generalist. Thus he studied ethnography, kinship relations, and linguistics; he worked in the field as an archaeologist and was a practicing psychoanalyst in San Francisco for a while.

It is impossible to speak to his hundreds of publications. What is valuable is to note how his work pervaded the household, a situation that Le Guin herself has mentioned. She has spoken of the influence of his study and his writing:

> He taught and traveled and dug up ancient pots and lived
> with Indians, and did all the neat things that anthro-
> pologists do, and he also wrote a great deal. So I grew
> up with the notion that science and writing were normal
> human activities, like dancing or whistling. I didn't
> show promise as a scientist, but have written poetry and
> prose all my life (I can't dance worth a hoot, but can
> whistle pretty well).[6]

As an ethnographer, Kroeber lived and worked in alien cultures, the experience of many of Le Guin's characters--Rocannon, Falk, Genly Ai, Lyubov. Kroeber's specific findings on the significance of naming or the activities of dreaming have to be reckoned as influences. Certainly his observations on the interrelationship among environment, culture, language, and people affected the way he and his family viewed the world. Le Guin has commented on this in a general way:

> The people that I met as a kid--that generation trained
> by Boas, and the next generation--they were exciting
> people. They had this intense interest in individuals
> and individual cultures, and then also this kind of
> broad range of trying to put large ideas together.
> They were not culture-bound types, I must say, they
> were pretty free souls, those anthropologists. They
> loved the variety of mankind, they just ate it up![7]

Kroeber's Handbook of the Indians of California (1925) remains a classic work in the field.

His interest in cultural patterns and cultural evolution are related. He was intrigued with looking for common denominators of cultures, their common humanness. His discussions of culture in his textbook, Anthropology, emphasize its dynamic quality; "what culture is," he wrote, "can be better understood from knowledge of what forms it takes and how it works than by a definition." [8] Its first characteristic is "openness, its receptivity."[9] In the study of cultural patterns emerges both unity and diversity, each necessary for the vitality of a specific culture. Theodora Kroeber summarized his belief in cultural evolution as follows:

> that biological and human evolution are parts of a

     single process; that motion (process) is or can be
     toward realization, toward becoming more human; that
     all aspects of culture including ethics and values are
     engaged in an evolution ever more significant, and
     that all these aspects can be studied and scientifi-
     cally analysed.[10]

Many scholars have already commented on Le Guin's interest in the
details of culture, the interweaving of environment and society, and
on how frequently her fiction focuses on an individual and/or society
at the moment of change. Even the most casual reader of Le Guin is
reminded of the history of the Hainish world where some eighty to
one hundred planets were "seeded" with a humanoid species by the
Hainish race, left to develop, and many of them later reunited, first
as the League of All Worlds, and later as the Ekumen. Analogous to
her father's interest in process and change is her use of the individual journey as the protagonist's key action.

    By pointing out these parallels, I am certainly not suggesting
that Le Guin merely followed in her parents' footsteps. Her mother's
Ishi books, for example, were written after Le Guin had left home.
Furthermore, there are many other sources for her attitudes which she
herself has named--Dunsany, Tolkien, Herbert Read, Paul Goodman,
Islandia, Norse myths, Taoism. But the milieu, the importance of
art, the ambiguities of truth and storytelling, the historical and
anthropological perspectives were clearly shaping factors of Le Guin's
imagination and creativity. Having grown up myself with a father who
was an "old style" historian (educated when history was considered
one of the humanities), I know the extent to which parental perspectives permeate a household. "Historical perspective" is like the cat
sleeping under the rocking chair--if you stir up much conversation,
it makes its presence known. In a 1977 interview, Le Guin discussed
the general influence of both parents.

     They were neat people, and there were a lot of hang-
     ups I was spared. For instance, nobody assumed from
     the fact that I was a girl that I had to go in any
     particular direction. That was a pretty unusual atti-
     tude then. One of them was an anthropologist, the
     other had an M.A. in psychology. I think most of the
     influence they have had is temperamental, inherited--
     like a willingness to get outside of your own culture,
     and also a sensitivity to how culture affects person-
     ality, which is what my father was concerned with. My
     father felt very strongly that you can never actually
     get outside your own culture. All you can do is try.
     I think that feeling sometimes comes out in my writing.
     My father studied real cultures and I make them up--
     in a way, it's the same thing.[11]

The most consistent thread in her life that concerns us here is

the writing. Le Guin has commented on several occasions that she did
not decide to become a writer because she has always been a writer.
Her writing has been intertwined with those biographical events which
are now in the public record. Her early reading included Dunsany,
Austin Tappan Wright, and science fiction. The experience of discovering Dunsany at the age of twelve is the opening of her only
autobiographical essay and source of its title, "A Citizen of Mondath" (1973); she tries to analyze the significance of the event:

> I don't entirely understand why Dunsany came to me as a
> revelation, why that moment was so decisive. I read a
> lot, and a lot of my reading was myth, legend, fairy-
> tale; first-rate versions, too, such as Padraic Colum,
> Asbjornsson, etc. I had also heard my father tell
> Indian legends aloud, just as he had heard them from
> informants, only translated into a rather slow, im-
> pressive English; and they were impressive and mys-
> terious stories. What I hadn't realised, I guess, is
> that people are still making up myths. One made up
> stories oneself, of course; but here was a grown-up
> doing it, for grown-ups, without a single apology to
> common sense, without an explanation, just dropping us
> straight into the Inner Lands. . . . Whatever the
> reason, the moment was decisive. I had discovered my
> native country![12]

This essay also describes her first completed short story, "written
at age nine. It is about a man persecuted by evil elves. People
think he is mad, but the evil elves finally slither in through the
keyhole, and get him."[13] She remembered in a 1979 interview that she
was writing "scurilous poems" about Ernest O. Lawrence. Because her
father was amused by them, she wrote more but is unclear now why she
hated Lawrence.[14]

Her childhood writing included not only the story about the elves
but also, at the age of ten or eleven, her first science fiction
story. "It involved time travel and the origin of life on Earth, and
was very breezy in style."[15] Because she and her brothers had been
reading science fiction, she submitted the story to Amazing Stories
who rejected it. "I don't remember being very downcast," she wrote,
"rather flattered by a real rejection slip. I never submitted anything else to anybody until I was twenty-one, but I think that was
less cowardice than wisdom."[16] At age twenty-one, Ursula Kroeber was
attending Radcliffe College, from which she was graduated in 1951.
Awarded membership in Phi Beta Kappa, her honors thesis submitted
9 April was titled, "The Metaphor of the Rose as an Illustration of
the 'Carpe Diem' theme in French and Italian Poetry of the Renaissance." At Radcliffe, she took a creative writing class. "It was
taught by a man who wrote for The Saturday Evening Post," she reports,
"under a feminine pen name. I decided I was allergic to creative
writing at that point."[17] In an interview in 1979 she could not re-

call either name of the teacher.

She earned her M.A. from her father's alma mater, Columbia University, in 1952, submitting a thesis on "Aspects of Death in Ronsard's Poetry." Beginning doctoral work at Columbia, she was soon awarded a Fulbright Scholarship to France (1952-1953) to study the poetry of Jean Lemaire de Belges.

During her twenties she was writing poetry, short stories, and novels. "I was trying to appeal to the short story market of Ladies Home Journal, Saturday Evening Post and the like," she records[18] and for twelve years (about 1950-1962) her material was rejected. In a 1979 interview, she commented that she wrote "A Week in the Country" in her early twenties and upon its completion, although she has revised it many times since, she felt she had finished her apprenticeship. This short story and four of her five novels written during this period were about Orsinia:

> One of the novels was set in contemporary San Francisco, but the others were set in an invented though nonfantastic Central European country, as were the best short stories I had done. They were not science fiction, they were not fantasy, yet they were not realistic. Alfred Knopf said (in 1951) that he would have published the first of them, ten years ago, but he'd lose too much money on it now. Viking and other publishers merely remarked that "this material seems remote."[19]

During this period, Le Guin was also becoming a wife, teacher, and mother. Her Fulbright to France introduced her to Charles A. Le Guin and they were married in Paris, 22 December 1953. On their return to the United States, she taught in the French Department at Mercer University (Macon, Georgia) and was a department secretary at Emory University (Atlanta, Georgia) where her husband completed his Ph.D. degree in French history in 1956. The decision not to continue her own doctorate was based on at least two factors. In a 1974 interview, she explained that "she feared that even with a Ph.D., as a woman she would be relegated to teaching freshman French classes."[20] In a 1975 interview, coupling the decision to marry and to give up doctoral studies, she said:

> The point is one that any fair minded feminist would understand. The two of us needed one income. I'd always intended to teach in order to support myself while writing. And I married. If Charles had been the writer, I would have been the teacher.[21]

Charles Le Guin accepted a teaching position at the University of Idaho (Moscow) and the couple lived there three years. During this time (1956-1959), she taught in the French Department, published a

book review and a poem, and had a daughter--Elisabeth (1957). In a
1971 interview, she recounted that "The first thing I published was
poetry . . . my father got bored with my not publishing and offered
to send my poems around for me."[22]

The following few years are just as full and show the inter-
twining of her literary and family lives. In 1959, the family moved
to Portland where Charles joined the history faculty of Portland State
University, a position he currently holds, and the second child was
born, Caroline. In October 1960, Ursula's father died, an experience
she has linked with her coming of age. In 1961, her first short story
("An die Musik") was published and she wrote a long poem describing
her coming of age experience. In 1962, she made her first professional sale ("April in Paris") to Cele Goldsmith Lalli at Fantastic.
In 1964, her son Theodore was born. She has lived in Portland since
1959 with the exception of two years in London (1968-69 and 1975-76)
while her husband was on sabbatical leave.

2. Publishing career.
    The 1962 professional sale of "April in Paris" is often cited as
the beginning of Le Guin's writing career and with good reason.
Behind that sale is her decision to reach out for an audience. She
explains in "Mondath":

>   I had been writing all my life, and it was becoming a
>   case of publish or perish. You cannot keep filling up
>   the attic with mss. Art, like sex, cannot be carried
>   on indefinitely solo; after all they have the same
>   mutual enemy, sterility. I had had a number of poems
>   published, and one short story, in little magazines;
>   but this wasn't enough, considering that I had written
>   five novels in the last ten years. I had either to
>   take off, or give up.[23]

But because her Orsinian material had been repeatedly rejected, she
also had to be practical; she "was reduced to fitting a category."
Attracted by the new work in science fiction, especially that of
Cordwainer Smith, she decided to write SF in order to get published.
The first of these early published stories which she sees as more
than "trivial"[24] is "Semley's Necklace," the seventh published (1964).

    In 1965 she became a charter member of the Science Fiction Writers
of America, organized by Damon Knight. In 1966 she published her
first two novels, Rocannon's World and Planet of Exile, then a third
the following year, City of Illusions. That same year Herman Schein,
publisher of Parnassus Press, invited her to write a book for young
adults:

>   He gave me complete freedom as to subject and approach.
>   Nobody until then had ever asked me to write anything;

I had just done so, relentlessly. To be asked to do
it was a great boon. The exhilaration carried me over
my apprehensions about writing "for young people,"
something I had never seriously tried.[25]

The result, A Wizard of Earthsea, was published in 1968; she describes
it as her "first fully achieved book."[26] It appeared on Best Book
lists by April and May 1969 and won the Boston Globe-Horn Book Award
in 1969. Also in 1969 she published "Nine Lives," her most frequently
anthologized story. It was published in Playboy under the name U.K.
Le Guin, the only known incident when she was discriminated against
as a woman. Her best known novel, The Left Hand of Darkness was published in 1969, and in 1970 she was given both the Hugo and Nebula
awards for it. In that same year, she published her first critical
essay on science fiction ("Prophets and Mirrors: Science Fiction as
a Way of Seeing"), began publishing poetry after a nine-year hiatus,
and published a shortened version of the second volume of the Earthsea
trilogy, The Tombs of Atuan in Worlds of Fantasy.

In 1971 she published The Lathe of Heaven and was a teacher in
the Clarion Writers' Workshop at the University of Washington. In
1972, Tombs was awarded the Newbery Silver Medal Award, and she published "The Word for World is Forest" and the third volume of the
trilogy, The Farthest Shore. She again taught at Clarion. In 1973,
Shore won the National Book Award and "Word" won a Hugo. She published two of her major fantasy essays, From Elfland to Poughkeepsie
and "Dreams Must Explain Themselves." She also published "The Ones
Who Walk Away from Omelas" which won a Hugo in 1974. In 1974, she
became a contributing editor for Science-Fiction Studies and published
"Why Are Americans Afraid of Dragons?". She published The Dispossessed
and "The Day Before the Revolution." She delivered a lecture at the
Library of Congress, which was later published as an essay, "The
Child and the Shadow" (1975). In 1975, she won both the Hugo and
Nebula for The Dispossessed and a Nebula for "The Day Before." She
was the Guest of Honor at the 33rd World Science Fiction Convention
in Australia.

I have named only the most outstanding activities and publications of the intense 1966-1974 period in which she published seven
science novels, three fantasy novels, sixteen short stories, nine
poems, five book reviews, and sixteen essays. There is, of course,
a real consistency here. Her earliest publications reflect these
same interests: a book review in 1958, a poem in 1959, an Orsinian
short story in 1961, and a fantasy-sf short story in 1962. There are
the same areas in which she has continued to publish since 1974.

The post-1974 period has been less intense; she has published
less fiction and more nonfiction. She published one novella and
three novels, two young person's books, two short story collections
and two poetry collections, and edited three short story anthologies.
She published sixteen book reviews which began appearing in Times

Introduction

Literary Supplement, the New Republic, and The Washington Post, twenty-four essays/introductions, one movie review, and sixteen head-notes for The Wind's Twelve Quarters.

The writing of this period is more diverse in terms of audience, style, and setting. If a reader knew Le Guin only by these writings, she would appear more clearly experimental and more mainstream than the earlier fiction demonstrates. But this would be partly mis-leading. The works of recent years grow out of previous novels and even out of her apprenticeship writing. Orsinian Tales and Malafrena are from her oldest imaginary country. The Wind's Twelve Quarters collects stories from 1962 to 1974; Wild Angels collects poems from 1970 to 1975. The Eye of the Heron is an exploration of concepts of colonization (treated in "The Word for World is Forest") and the relationship between individual and society (fully treated in The Dispossessed). Her essays suggest that she has been occupied with a reassessment of her own work (five introductions to previously pub-lished novels) and with setting down her literary principles and standards. They reflect the confidence of a mature writer.

In the post-1974 period, 1975 was a significant year. Prior to the World Con, she taught a science fiction writing workshop in Australia, students from which are still paying her tribute. She published a retrospective collection of her short stories, The Wind's Twelve Quarters. Many readers became aware of her poetry for the first time in 1975 when she published Wild Angels and six of her translations of one of her favorite poets, Rainer Maria Rilke. Her polemical, "American SF and The Other" made clear her sharp criticism of American science fiction. In 1976, readers were again surprised with Orsinian Tales, for many their introduction to Le Guin's first invented country, Orsinia. She edited the eleventh collection of Nebula stories, published a book for adolescents, Very Far Away from Anywhere Else and a dystopian short story, "The Diary of The Rose." Several major essays appeared in 1976, demonstrating her high and well conceived literary standards: "Is Gender Necessary?", "Intro-duction" to The Left Hand of Darkness, "Science Fiction and Mrs. Brown," "Myth and Archetype in Science Fiction." Orsinian Tales was nominated for a National Book Award in 1977, but she withdrew "Diary" from the Nebula nominations because of her dismay over SFWA's treat-ment of Stanislaw Lem. Besides new introductions to Rocannon's World and "The Word for World is Forest," she published a clear statement on why she disagreed with SFWA's revoking Lem's honorary membership which they had given him in 1973.

In 1978, the novel Eye of The Heron appeared. Bucknell gave her an Honorary Doctor of Literature, and she received a special citation from the Association for the Psychophysiological Study of Sleep. The Jubal Trio gave the premier performance of Joseph Schwantner's com-position, "Wild Angels of the Open Hills," inspired by Le Guin's poetry. She published three introductions--one to Tiptree's collec-tion of short stories and two on her own novels, Planet of Exile and

Introduction

<u>City of Illusions</u>.

In 1979, <u>A Wizard of Earthsea</u> received the Lewis Caroll Shelf Award and she published three strikingly different works: <u>Leese Webster</u>, a book for children; <u>Malafrena</u>, an Orsinian novel; and the Tillai poems, which place Hindu mythology in contemporary settings. Her publications appeared in magazines of the literary establishment-- <u>The New Yorker</u> and <u>Kenyon Review</u>. Susan Wood's edited collection of her essays was published and she was an invited participant in the University of Chicago's symposium on narrative with such contemporary scholars as Robert Scholes, Jacques Derrida, and Paul Ricoeur.

In 1980, she published the full version of <u>The Beginning Place</u> and edited, with Virginia Kidd, two anthologies of short stories, <u>Interfaces</u> and <u>Edges</u>. She was appointed to the advisory board of <u>Dreamworks: An Interdisciplinary Journal</u> and worked with six other Portland artists to produce a theatrical version of "The Ones Who Walk Away from Omelas." Her Chicago speech was published in <u>Critical Inquiry</u> ("It Was A Dark and Stormy Night, Or Why Are We Huddling About the Campfire?"), and an essay responding to the Mt. St. Helens eruption (visible from the upstairs windows of her home) appeared in <u>Parabola</u>. Early in 1981, Harper and Row published her second collection of poetry, <u>Hard Words</u>.

Any overall assessment of her work cannot be done at this time. As a contemporary author she is as predictable and original as her spider, Leese Webster. Like the spider predictably spinning webs, Le Guin spins tales that have marks of her style and texture. But just as soon as readers, scholars, or bibliographers catalog and categorize her fiction, she, like Leese, escapes "outside," sees things in a different light, and creates something new. The boldest experimental works are "The New Atlantis," the Shiva poems, and <u>The Beginning Place</u>. Even cataloging her work by the imaginary country she uses will not hold all of her work. She has moved from a blend of fantasy and science fiction, to a clear separation of them, to a melding of fantasy and realism. There is always in her work to date, however, an invented place.

In a 1978 interview Le Guin spoke of those things that attract her about world invention:

> science fiction allows a fiction writer to make up
> cultures, to <u>invent</u>--not only a new world, but a new
> <u>culture</u>. Well, what is a culture besides buildings
> and pots and so on? Of course it's ideas, and ways
> of thought, and legends. It's all the things that go
> on inside the heads of the people. . . . Of course,
> where the myths and legends come from is from your <u>own</u>
> head, the whole thing's coming out of your own head;
> but it's a sort of combination process of using your
> intellect to make a coherent-looking body of culture,

that you can refer to.[27]

Her pleasure is analogously expressed in her fiction. In "Winter's King," the young king from Gethen asks his tutor about the purpose of the Ekumen and is answered thus:

> To weave some harmony among them, at least. Life loves
> to know itself, out to its furthest limits; to embrace
> complexity is its delight. Our difference is our
> beauty. All these worlds and the various forms and
> ways of the minds and lives and bodies on them--to-
> gether they would make a splendid harmony."
>   "No harmony endures," said the young king.
>   "None has ever been achieved," said the Plenipoten-
> tiary. "The pleasure is in trying."[28]

3. Non-fiction essays

Le Guin's wholescale world invention places her fiction in the category of the fantastic; and although she avoids theoretical discussions, her numerous book reviews, introductions, editorials, essays, and interviews reveal her thinking about the genres and the nature of art. In the bibliography, Section D, are listed numerous essays on her fiction but outside of some reviews of The Language of the Night, no discussion of her nonfiction. Therefore, this section will piece together her aesthetic ideas and show that the theory is woven out of the same cloth as her fiction.

We can examine the theory through her two main essay topics: the nature of art and the nature of the fantastic. She explains the nature of art by means of two ideas: (1) the similarity between art and myth; (2) the link between art and nature.

3.1 Art and Myth

Le Guin has argued in detail that art and myth are similar. First, both rely on mental operations other than reason. "Myth," she explains:

> is an expression of one of the several ways the human
> being, body/psyche, perceives, understands, and re-
> lates to the world. Like science, it is a product of
> a basic human mode of apprehension. To pretend that
> it can be replaced by abstract or quantitative cogni-
> tion is to assert the human being is, potentially or
> ideally, a creature of pure reason, a disembodied
> Mind.[29]

Le Guin's models are the Easterners who "have never worshipped reason, but have equally respected reason and mystical perception, and common sense, and habit, intuition, dream, revery, imagination, emotion, and all the other operations of the human mind in its full complexity."[30]

Specifically, myth and art bridge the conscious and the unconscious. They use the language, that is, the symbols and archetypes, from the unconscious to illustrate "certain aspects of psychological reality."[31] They listen to this language and connect it to one's perception of reality, thus creating a new perception of reality.

In order to hear the language of the unconscious, of course one must make the journey inward. The journey is absolutely essential for the artist; and it is a feat that must be accomplished alone-- "you have to know yourself," Le Guin tells young writers, "before you can say anything anywhere near the truth."[32] Addressing a more general audience, she describes what the author (and by implication the reader) confronts:

> So it would seem that true myth arises only in the process of connecting the conscious and the unconscious realms. I won't find a living archetype in my bookcase or my television set. I will find it only in myself: in that core of individuality lying in the heart of the common darkness. Only the individual can get up and go to the window of his house, and draw back the curtains, and look out into the dark.[33]

The individual dreams, dragons, and darknesses are the only way to connect with the collective unconsciousness, at which point the author and reader have connected with human kind--a journey inward leads outward, or as she expresses it in The Dispossessed, "to go is to return." It denies, she asserts, that alienation is the ultimate human condition.

Every one of her novels and most short stories call for this integration of the self. Her protagonists in science fiction experience alien cultures and alien humans that cause them to reexamine their assumptions and evaluations of their own selves and of reality. Genly Ai, for all his exposure to and training in the Ekumen of eighty worlds, is amazingly myopic and self-assured on Gethen among the androgynes. Her protagonist in fantasy directly confronts the unconscious, that is, the shadow and the land of death. In both fictions, the guide into self-examination is the Other, the shadowy alien.

Art is one of the primary forms of integration, not only of the conscious and the unconscious, but of all the multiple aspects of the self. In 1974, an interviewer commented that he liked the concept of "Dragon Lord" in Earthsea as someone who does not rule dragons but can converse with them. Le Guin replied:

> Now I know what I was talking about, because I've read

some Jung since then. Freud says that you're supposed to master your unconsciousness--you're supposed
to make yourself lord over it. And Jung says you're
supposed to get in communication with it, and you are
neither lord nor servant of your unconscious. You get
in communication, and the really, integrated, differ-
entiated person is the guy who can feed back and forth
between conscious and unsconcious.[34]

Her fiction examines both problems of integration--those who have not
integrated because they primarily look externally for truth (Ai, Ged,
Shevek, Davidson) and those who primarily look internally (Kaph,
Arha). Art translates dream language into real-world language.

3.2 Art and Nature
Not only does art integrate the conscious and the unconscious of
the self, it connects that self with "the entirety of the universe."
Her argument explaining the relationship between art and nature can
be pieced together into the following logical form:

1. Art is a natural activity.
2. It is a natural activity because it is a manifestation of
    the tendency toward order.
3. The manifestation of the tendency toward order is also ex-
    emplified in science.
4. Art and science, therefore, perform the same function: they
    seek out and describe this order.
5. Thus, any statements about the essence of art also become
    statements about the function of art.

In 1971 she defined art as "the rearrangement of experience in an
orderly fashion, tending to produce aesthetic satisfaction."[35] She
demonstrated the order of the universe by examining the tendency
toward order in physics and biology, in the galaxies and the paramecium. Her view is quite complex.

First, it includes the diversity of the universe, as her definition of the "biocosmos" illustrates: "a superjungle of interwoven
competing interdependent conflicting murderous maternal inexhaustible
lives and deaths."[36] Second, it is based on modern, speculative
science which is "anti-absolute; it perceives, discerns, describes,
but it does not give out the Final Word, and it does not seek the
Big Answer."[37] "Praise then creation unfinished," one of her characters says. Third, it emphasizes the significance of Things in the
external world. The contemporary novel, then, must acknowledge not
only human interrelations but relations with the material world:

The novel's been Confucian, one might say, and it's
time that it went Taoist. A human has relationships
with things, things he handles and uses; with machines;

with animals; with landscapes; with ideas; with the
earth as a whole, and with the entirety of things.[38]

In this Taoist picture of the universe, of constant creation and
process, man's role is limited but necessary. Man is not the measure
of all things, but he is the measure of things on this planet because
he, of all living creatures, "has organized more complex material
more effectively."[39] Man is the consciousness of the things he knows:
"If we stop looking, the world goes blind. If we cease to speak and
listen, the world goes deaf and dumb. If we stop thinking, there is
no thought."[40]

As a result of this perspective, Le Guin argues adamantly for the
importance of characterization, quoting Virginia Woolf's definition
of the novel as being an expression of character and recording that
her novels begin with images of persons:

> A book does not come to me as an idea, or a plot, or
> an event, or a society, or a message; it comes to me
> as a person. A person seen, seen at a certain dis-
> tance, usually in a landscape. The place is there,
> the person is there. I didn't invent him, I didn't
> make her up: he or she is there. And my business
> is to get there too.[41]

What, then, is the function of art? The function is identical to
its essence--it integrates and orders. Art is

> one manifestation--a terrifically complex and there-
> fore fragile manifestation--of a basic natural ten-
> dency towards order. . . . Its processes, like those
> of the atom and the Paramecium, obey the laws of
> Creation. And if these "laws" are simply the way in
> which mind perceives the world, as I think they are,
> that makes no difference. Mind is, after all, part
> of the world. The laws of physics, or of harmony in
> music, or of the growth of an embryo, or of the devel-
> opment of the novel have no existence in themselves,
> on stone tablets as it were, handed down to us from
> above, some supra-natural agency. They exist only as
> embodied in individual things, and as perceived and
> generalised by the human mind. No external, absolute
> assurance of their existence is possible, or neces-
> sary.[42]

Art, she argues, can reflect this order in two different ways:
by its aesthetics and by its ethics. Art is to please and to instruct. Its instructions should not be to uphold a particular ideology but to uphold humankind; to explore, describe, remind its
readers what it means to be human, to have an integrated conscious
and unconscious, to function as a member of a human community, to

exercise moral action, to view the universe in light of scientific revelations. Her most strongly stated essays have been written on this issue. In "The Stalin in the Soul," she argues that censorship of the marketplace is damaging American fiction, its writers and its readers. If artists succumb to the censorship that encourages their writing "Vulg the Visigoth or Deep Armpit," then they have let Stalin into their souls. Artists, like scientists, must ask the significant questions--not what or how, but why: "When it asks why, it rises from mere emotional response to real statement, and to intelligent ethical choice. It becomes, not a passive reflection, but an act."[43]

In "Why Are Americans Afraid of Dragons?" she argues that we are basically afraid of the imagination and the freedom it offers.

She has, however, been critical of her own art for being too moralistic:

> I have found, somewhat to my displeasure, that I am an
> extremely moral writer. I am always grinding axes and
> making points. I wish I wasn't so moralistic, because
> my interest is aesthetic. What I want to do is make
> something beautiful like a good pot or a good piece of
> music, and the ideas and moralism keep getting in the
> way. There's a definite battle on.[44]

And certainly critics have chided her for just that, particularly in "The Word for World is Forest," The Dispossessed, and The Farthest Shore. She has not, in other words, always achieved that balance of aesthetics and idea that she feels is ideal.

Her fiction illustrates, in several ways, the connection between art and nature that she has discussed in her essays. First, the recognition of creation unfinished is reflected in the open-endedness of her novels, particularly Planet of Exile, City of Illusions, The Left Hand of Darkness, The Dispossessed, and Orsinian Tales. Second, her world invention is an anthropological activity in that she invents a world, a culture which is a product of that natural environment, and a protagonist who is a product of that culture and world.

Third, each of the three imaginary countries in which most of her fiction occurs is a metaphor for complex interconnections. The science fiction stories take place on the "known worlds," that is, those settled by the Hainish so that all human life is connected by ancient Hainish parentage. Reaching to another world is not only a metaphor for contact with the other, but is also quite literally, contact with the self. Her fantasy trilogy is set in Earthsea, hundreds of islands which rose out of the sea when the word of creation was spoken; the balance between sea and land suggests the principle of balance and harmony that operates among all things in Earthsea. Orsinia is an imaginary middle European country whose unifying element is European history, the history of mankind. All men are brothers in having to deal with authoritarian governments, with personal pain, death, and suffering.

Fourth, she uses numerous metaphors to suggest connections. The art or function of arching in order to connect appears as bridges, webs, weavings, tree roots and branches, roads (especially up and over mountains), space flight trajectory, arches, maps, journeys out from and back to home, male-female bondings. They are metaphorically related to methods and devices of communication, to myths, and to other art objects such as music, jewels, and mobiles.

3.3 The Fantastic
For Le Guin, two of the genres of the fantastic exemplify the two aspects of art I have been discussing: fantasy is primarily concerned with myth, science fiction is concerned with man's relationship to nature.

Fantasy focuses on the relationship between the conscious and the unconscious. Human desires, intuitions, fears, uncomfortable feelings, and words become forces, characters and causes of plot turnings. In her best defense of fantasy, "The Child and the Shadow," she wrote:

> The great fantasies, myths, and tales are indeed like dreams: they speak _from_ the unconscious _to_ the unconscious, in the _language_ of the unconscious--symbol and archetype. Though they use words, they work the way music does: they short-circuit verbal reasoning, and go straight to the thoughts that lie too deep to utter. They cannot be translated fully into the language of reason, but only a Logical Positivist, who also finds Beethoven's Ninth Symphony meaningless, would claim that they are therefore meaningless. They are profoundly meaningful, and useful--practical--in terms of ethics; of insight; of growth.[45]

Science fiction, on the other hand, focuses on man's coping with, finding his place in, the universe as described by modern science. Science fiction, she has said, "is a new integrative effort, a way of enabling the contemporary, scientific, individualistic consciousness to achieve the collective creative power of myth, to cope with thunder and suffering by aesthetic, integrative means."[46] She has often used the metaphor of the thought experiment to explain how science fiction works, or how she writes science fiction:

> This kind of world-making is a thought-experiment, performed with the caution and in the controlled, receptive spirit of experiment. Scientist and science-fictioneer invent worlds in order to reflect and so to clarify, perhaps to glorify, the "real world," the objective Creation. The more closely their work resembles and so illuminates the solidity, complexity, amazing-

ness, and coherence of the original, the happier they
are.[47]

Le Guin is not particularly interested in participating in the
quarrel over the definitions of science fiction and fantasy; she
prefers to emphasize the nature of the fantastic as a whole. Le Guin
uses the term "fantasy" to identify the category which contains the
genres of fantasy and science fiction; but to avoid confusion, I am
using the term "the fantastic." She has chosen this form in which to
explore her vision of reality; all her works share its qualities.

First, the reality presented in the fantastic can function as a
metaphor for the reality recognized by the late twentieth century.
In her National Book Award speech, she explained and praised this
very quality, as follows:

> Sophisticated readers are accepting the fact that an
> improbable and unmanageable world is going to produce
> an improbable and hypothetical art. At this point,
> realism is perhaps the least adequate means of under-
> standing or portraying the incredible realities of our
> existence. . . . The fantasist, whether he uses the
> ancient archetypes of myth and legend or the younger
> ones of science and technology, may be talking as
> seriously as any sociologist—and a good deal more
> directly—about human life as it is lived, and as it
> might be lived, and as it ought to be lived. For
> after all, as great scientists have said and as all
> children know, it is above all by the imagination that
> we achieve perception, and compassion and hope.[48]

Her statement suggests two other qualities of the fantastic: it
demonstrates the importance of the imagination and the invented world
gives the reader a new experience.

The importance of the imagination is a frequent topic for Le Guin
and she discusses its ethical ramifications. Use of the imagination
brings to the author and reader both freedom and awesome responsibility; it is the quality of mind that will aid integration of conscious and unconscious, of man and Things. She defines it as follows:

> By "imagination," I personally mean the free play of
> the mind, both intellectual and sensory. By "play"
> I mean recreation, re-creation, the recombination of
> what is known into what is new. By "free" I mean
> that the action is done without an immediate object
> of profit—spontaneously.[49]

To make the invented world seem real, the fantastic genres depend heavily on vivid description, a quality Le Guin's writing is
always praised for. The individual; and the setting; and the culture,

ideas, history, myth; and the Things must all be made real. Especially, the language of these invented worlds must reflect an alternate world. Many of her essays discuss these high standards for the literature of fantasy.

The imaginative experiencing of the fantasy world may alter the reader's perception. When this happens, the writer and reader have been jolted out of old habits and prejudices, have grown and matured. It is a theory that can be verified by psychoanalytic theories. She argues strongly that this quality does not make the fantastic "escapist" literature in the derogatory sense of running away from what needs to be done. She paraphrases Tolkien's answer:

> Yes, he said, fantasy is escapist, and that is its
> glory. If a soldier is imprisoned by the enemy, don't
> we consider it his duty to escape? The money-lenders,
> the knownothings, the authoritarians have us all in
> prison; if we value the freedom of the mind and soul,
> if we're partisans of liberty, then it's our plain
> duty to escape, and to take as many people with us as
> we can.[50]

Le Guin has referred to this quality of the fantastic as "distancing."

The category of the fantastic, then, requires the use of both reason and nonreason (imagination, intuition); it reaches subjective truths which are more valuable than facts; it uses the imagination because metaphors and language must carry the entire meaning. This is why she writes in the fantastic genres. Both artist and reader are on the frontiers of town, so to speak.[51] So we have to come back to her basic idea about the nature of art--its essence is also its function, a concept she has illustrated with the metaphor of ouroborous. In discussing her fantasy trilogy, Le Guin points out that it is really about the process of creativity:

> Wizardry is artistry. The trilogy is, then, in this
> sense, about art, the creative experience, the crea-
> tive process. There is always this circularity in
> fantasy. The snake devours its tail. Dreams must
> explain themselves.[52]

To bring this discussion to a close, it is appropriate to mention Le Guin's most recent essay: "It was a Dark and Stormy Night; or Why Are We Huddling About the Campfire?" In a roundabout, witty, allusive and elusive answer she says, because we are human--because we wish to assert our existence (even after the storyteller is dead), because we wish to state what existence is, because we wish to bear witness to our existence and the existence of other things, because we wish to re-create and hold the moment. In this capstone essay, she uses the metaphor of the hoop snake:

> When a hoop snake wants to get somewhere--whether
> because the hoop snake is after something, or because
> something is after the hoop snake--it takes its tail
> (which may or may not have rattles on it) into its
> mouth, thus forming itself into a hoop, and rolls.
> Jehovah enjoined snakes to crawl on their belly in
> the sun, but Jehovah was an Easterner. Rolling along,
> bowling along, is a lot quicker and more satisfying than
> crawling. But, for the hoop snakes with rattles, there
> is a drawback. They are venomous snakes, and when they
> bite their own tail they die, in awful agony, of
> snakebite. All progress has these hitches. I don't
> know what the moral is.[53]

The story is almost a condensation of the experience of art. Humankind creates art; the impulse is ambiguous--either because they wish
to discover something or because something is trying to get out of
the unconscious and be discovered. So art is always an examination
of its own processes and the workings of the unconscious--a biting of
its own tail, so to speak. This examination leads to greater vision
and a changed view of reality. Biting into the unconscious brings
up news and fear of death, brings certain pain and suffering. But it
is worth the risk, Le Guin asserts. There is only death and nothing-
ness to be gained at the end of life, therefore rolling and bowling
through the narrative is definitely preferable.

4. Critical Reception

Just as Le Guin's own fictional patterns are still being woven,
so the critical material continues to be published. In contrast to
Le Guin's twenty-three years of published fiction, there have been
only ten or twelve years of critical attention; and the criticism
lags perceptibly behind her creative imagination. Outside of initial
book reviews, there has been very little published on her later
pieces, her poetry, and her nonfiction essays. Significantly, however, the reviewers and critics have been writing in the United
States, United Kingdom, and Australia; more recently, critical articles have appeared in France, Spain, and Italy. The international
attention will no doubt increase because translations of her fiction
have appeared in Argentina, Brazil, Finland, France, Germany, Israel,
Italy, the Netherlands, Norway, Spain, and Sweden.

To give an overall picture of the development of the criticism,
I will examine it chronologically, and limit it to the twelve novels.
I will point out the commentary, from the earliest reviews to the
first major essay(s) on each novel and then summarize what I see as
the major trend in the later essays.

Le Guin's apprentice novels, Rocannon's World, Planet of Exile,
and City of Illusions, received little critical attention when they
were first published in 1966 and 1967. But the earliest reviews

cited the qualities for which they are still valued--the mixture of fantasy and science fiction; the writing style; the interrelationship between environment, society, and individual; the Taoist philosophy; the well-drawn, detailed settings. The reviews indicated her instant international appeal for they appeared in the United States, United Kingdom, and Australia. Of course, the organs for serious literary criticism of science fiction were not yet available (Science-Fiction Studies, 1973; Foundation, 1972; and Extrapolation was a small news-letter, seven years old). The three novels were more widely reviewed when they reappeared in new editions, especially when issued a decade later in hardcover, each accompanied by her new introductory essay. One or more of the three novels is often used now in critical articles which trace the development of her artistry.

Le Guin's next two novels established her reputation in two countries and in two genres--in the long run, British critics have recognized the quality of her fantasy novel, A Wizard of Earthsea, and American critics have recognized the quality of her science fic-tion novel, The Left Hand of Darkness.

Wizard elicited the first critical essay on Le Guin's fiction, and the Earthsea trilogy which developed has been less controversial than Left Hand. Le Guin has called it her best work and the literary establishment, as already noted, gave it early recognition. Early reviews praised its knack of making the unreal seem real ("an imagi-nary garden absolutely hopping with real toads"),[54] its poetic style, and multiple meanings. They compared it favorably to Tolkien and preferred it to C.S. Lewis's theologized Narnia Tales. They often included discussions on the allegorical nature of fantasy, the value of fantasy, and the fallacy of classifying fantasy as children's literature. The first critical essay appeared in the April 1971 issue of The Horn Book Magazine: Eleanor Cameron's "High Fantasy: A Wizard of Earthsea" which is still a fine introduction to the con-cerns of the novel and, as it turns out, to the trilogy itself. This essay was followed in 1972 and 1973 by two essays in Britain and in 1974 by two significant assessments of Le Guin in the same month. In "On Ursula Le Guin's 'A Wizard of Earthsea,'" Douglas Barbour dis-cussed two aspects of the novel that have now become common interests of Le Guin scholars: the Taoist philosophy reflected in the concept of balance and in the ideal of unaction which Ged must learn; and her complex use of light/dark imagery. Robert Scholes's essay, "The Good Witch of the West," is the fullest treatment of the contrast between Le Guin and C.S. Lewis.

Left Hand was also praised early on for qualities most reviewers agreed upon and was, like Wizard, quickly compared to other well known books in the field. Its themes of the nature of human love and of human communication were praised as well as its detailed setting, invention of language, and anthropological quality. It was compared favorably to Frank Herbert's Dune. But the very quality Darko Suvin praised it for in his overview of the science fiction novel in 1969

after it had won the Nebula and Hugo Awards, was the quality that
critics have come to disagree about. He praised the novel's development through "binary oppositions,"[55] while others have argued that
the opposing pieces of the novel are not unified. The sexual nature
of the Gethenians is not fully drawn so that they come across only as
males and their biological nature is not fully integrated with the
nature of their culture. The structure of the novel, some asserted,
is flawed. This controversy is well illustrated in a series of
articles published in the Australian fanzine, SF Commentary; a favorable review by George Turner in 1970 was followed by an unfavorable
review by Stanislaw Lem which elicited responses from Turner, Aldiss,
and Le Guin herself.

Critical articles soon appeared. In 1973, David Allen discussed
the novel in a handbook for science fiction teachers and students.
And David Ketterer's essay, criticizing her dependence on myth, was
the first to comment that the novel was also about writing fiction.
Willis McNelly initiated the discussion of the novel in Jungian terms.

As with Wizard, 1974 was a significant year for Left Hand criticism, and it involved the same two scholars--Barbour and Scholes.
Barbour examined the five Hainish novels then in print, recounted
the Hainish history, and traced Le Guin's development and her use of
Taoism. Scholes argued specifically for its structural integrity.

The culmination of all this critical attention was Darko Suvin's
special issue of Science-Fiction Studies on Le Guin published in
November 1975. But while the critics were slowly discovering
Le Guin's fiction and trying to understand its complexities, Le Guin
blithely continued publishing.

Oddly enough, the next two novels, The Tombs of Atuan and The
Lathe of Heaven, have received critical attention with reservations
mainly because readers do not seem to know what to "do with them,"
a tribute to Le Guin's artistry. Instead of continuing with Ged as
protagonist, the second Earthsea volume offers a female protagonist.
Instead of developing another chapter in the Hainish history, Lathe
is a 1998 Portland story about a situation that seemed to some more
fantasy than science fiction. In 1981, however, it is clear that
Lathe begins a strain that is continued in the Shiva poems and The
Beginning Place, that tense combination of realism and fantasy/myth.

On the first round of reviews, Lathe and Tombs were generally
well received which is surprising in light of their later assessment
as being enigmatic novels. Early reviewers compared Lathe to Philip
K. Dick's fiction and its concern with the nature of reality. Many
welcomed it as a novel emphasizing social and ethical issues, not
gadgetry. Most found it inventive, credible, and ironic although a
few criticized inadequate characterization, especially of George Orr,
and expository discussions of dreaming. Douglas Barbour published
the first critical essay (1973) and focused on its Taoist philosophy.

Introduction

Tombs was praised for its theme of the responsibility of freedom and its use of mythic patterns, with Iphigenia and Ariadne/Theseus being identified very early. Most reviewers commented on the dark, haunting tone of the novel and praised its storytelling. A few found it pale in contrast to Wizard, even incomplete. Many praised her skill at building a believable world out of words. Critical attention did not begin until 1977 when T.A. Shippey discussed the entire trilogy.

The last Earthsea volume, The Farthest Shore, was again noted for its mythic pattern, particularly the Homeric journey, the initiation theme, and similarity to the last half of Beowulf. It was also praised for not endorsing a particular political or religious ideology and for building a believable world. It was occasionally judged less effective than the previous two and criticized for its uneven pace and abstractness. It elicited a number of articles which essentially reviewed the entire trilogy. In 1974, Peter Nicholls published a lucid review/article of Shore which led him to discuss her language, imagery, and metaphysics. He was one of the first to say that not only was Le Guin's work similar to Tolkien's, it was better.

"The Word for World is Forest" (1972) has an unusual critical history. It was not reviewed extensively as a separate piece until it appeared in book form in 1976, four years after its initial publication. At that time, reviewers were not responding to its first appearance nor on its "real" sequence in her publishing history. Furthermore, the critical essays started appearing before and simultaneously with the initial reviews. Its theme of colonization and exploitation was noted, as well as its emotional and intellectual effect. It was criticized for being too didactic and dated by its Viet Nam references. The first critical study was Ian Watson's 1975 essay which analyzed its use of the forest as metaphor for the mind but found the dependence on metaphor inadequate for a novel about politics and ecology. In 1976, it was analyzed in two dissertations, and Thomas J. Remington treated it as one of several stories on the theme of self and other.

The appearance of The Dispossessed in 1974 brought her considerable immediate attention. The New York Review of Books, The New York Times Book Review, Time, and The Yale Review all reviewed it. This attention was due to several factors: the quality of The Dispossessed, its unusual nature as an ambiguous utopia and as a utopia since much recent science fiction has been dystopian, and its coming after Left Hand and the Earthsea trilogy which had steadily increased her audience. The early reviews considered it carefully and as a result contained a greater mixture of positive and negative criticism. Many asserted that the novel had significance beyond the science fiction genre. The novel was praised for its characterization, especially of Shevek, and criticized for its characters being only representations of ideas. Many praised it for its combination of narrative and debate, several criticized it for its earnestness, its didacticism. Most liked the open endedness, and its complex discussion of the

Introduction

relationship between individual and society; some criticized the lack
of integration in character, plot, and social ideas. Within her own
work, it was most frequently compared to Left Hand and occasionally
Lathe. It led to reviews on utopian literature and anarchist thought,
and was compared to We, Brave New World, and the Victorian, historical
novel.

It drew critical attention more quickly than the previous novels,
but after all, by 1974 there were a number of people who were following her career and reading all her works. In 1975, there were five
major essays on The Dispossessed. In February, George Turner discussed it at length in SF Commentary, particularly focusing on its
structure. In Foundation, in November, Ian Watson considered its
artistry in many respects, including the scientific. That same month
saw the publication of the Science-Fiction Studies special edition
with Judah Bierman and Donald F. Theall looking at the novel extensively, and several other authors referring to it. In December,
Angus Taylor discussed her similarity to Dick, again in SF Commentary.

In May, 1980, Philip Zaleski reviewed Le Guin's most recent
books--Malafrena, The Beginning Place, and Leese Webster--pointing
out that all three focus on protagonists at "the moment between
childhood and adulthood when home becomes a prison" and their searches
lead them to self-discovery.[56] Immediate reception of the novels
was generally favorable and coupled with the recognition of their
similarity in theme to her previous work.

Malafrena was categorized as a historical novel, or a mainstream
novel and some expressed disappointment at her apparent withdrawal
from the science fiction/fantasy genres. Most recognized her theme
as being the search for freedom and the disappointment that follows
the gap between ideals and achievement. Some found the portrayal of
suffering realistic and relevant in light of the social unrest of the
1960s in America; others found it remote. Some praised the irony,
others found the plot slow and predictable and the characters unbelievable. Many noted the comparison to Tolstoy and also felt it
was not of the same high quality. They either liked the conclusion's
ambiguity or criticized the lack of a conclusion. So far, there have
been no critical articles on Malafrena.

The Beginning Place was favorably reviewed in both Time and The
New Yorker, but harshly criticized in the Washington Post. Several
reviewers commented on her new, tighter style and many praised the
novel's blend of realism and fantasy. The theme was most often
stated as being the nature of love and/or fear, and the world creation praised as a Le Guin trademark. A few spoke to the critique of
the adolescent's need to have and to outgrow fantasy. They disagreed
over the plot's pacing and the significance of the conclusion. Most
felt it avoided preaching. There has been no critical essay on the
novel thus far.

As one looks over all that has been written to date, certain consistencies become evident. Regularly praised are her lyrical style, humanistic ethic, ideal of integration, and ability to make imaginary worlds believable (a factor often attributed to her exposure to anthropology). Analyses have often focused on her images and metaphors, particularly the light and dark imagery, the significance of the shadow, the symbolic meaning of touching. Her Taoist philosophy has been explored, as has her affinity with the Romantic poets. The journey motif has been examined, especially as it affects the development of plots and characters. Her interest in the significance of history has appeared in more recent criticism. The complex theme of balance and integration has been analyzed from several points of view--ecological, political, and ethical.

Adverse criticism has usually focused on her elitism, especially of the intellectual, or her idealism which fails to provide relevant, complex solutions for modern society. Most consistent has been the charge that choices in her fiction are made on the basis of message, not aesthetics. This results in novels with more telling than showing, and it distances the reader from her characters. In specific novels, the focus has been on the failure of structure, especially in Left Hand where a certain group have argued that the Gethenian sexuality is never made a tight element of the plot. Ketterer also argued that its plot events were selected to serve the underlying myth of death and rebirth and do not have their own internal logic. Feminist critics have complained about her male protagonists and her bias toward marriage.

Grouping the essays reveals a variety of categories in which study has taken place and suggest the multiple levels of her work. Since 1970, she has attracted the feminist critics, particularly with the androgyny of Left Hand, and their responses have varied from extreme rejection to the defense that she has gone beyond current traditional feminist issues. Her work has attracted the Jungians and myth critics since 1971, which must be balanced against the knowledge that Le Guin did not read Jung's works until after the Earthsea trilogy was completed. Since 1971, she has attracted the Marxist critics as well as politically oriented critics of the Left. She has attracted teachers who have published pedagogical articles since 1972. The type of classroom has become increasingly varied, from elementary to college, from literature to geography. She has attracted the genre critics in science fiction and fantasy. Her work has also been analyzed by other science fiction writers who are also critics: Joanna Russ, Harlan Ellison, Vonda McIntyre, Ian Watson, Samuel Delany, Barry Malzberg.

Collections of critical material appeared early, beginning with Andy Porter in 1973, followed by Science-Fiction Studies in 1975, two essay collections in 1979 and two special journal issues in 1980. None is inclusive or definitive, but each marks a serious reading of her work. This serious, careful reading is also indicated by that

core of scholars who have done the major criticism--a group of about
a dozen people who have published several articles on Le Guin's fiction, that reflect an extensive knowledge on their part of all that
she has written, some of whom are working out a single interpretation
of her work.

The criticism, it seems to me, has become increasingly special-
ized, focusing in on single novels or on single symbols that run
throughout her work. The next wave will perhaps be more integrative,
like the work of James Bittner and Thomas J. Remington. Certainly,
the next essays that trace her development as an artist can be more
accurate than those of the 1970s. There will probably be more essays
which place her in the context of science fiction and compare her to
other authors as has already been done with Brunner, Dick, Herbert,
and Lem, as well as compare her to other novelists, especially the
nineteenth century novelists that she admires and regularly rereads.

The strongest articles have been those by critics who reach a
perspective from which the unity of Le Guin's ideas, of form and content can be recognized. Because of the variety of influences and the
sharpness of her intellect, any fixation on a single approach or a
single philosophy falsely limits the Le Guin perspective. As one
essayist commented of her work: "No truth is allowed to stand as the
entire truth; every insight is presented as partial, subject to revision and another perspective."[57]

Making a single interpretation of Le Guin's work is similar to
trying to make a single, all-embracing interpretation or story of the
paradoxical Shiva myth of which Le Guin is so fond. Because Shiva
"embodies all of life, in all its detail, at every minute."[58] no
single myth can embrace the plenum. Further, Shiva represents all
qualities--the erotic and the ascetic, the male and the female. Thus
a reader must approach Le Guin's work knowing she will offer no Final
Solution but that, as storyteller, she will offer the pleasure of
trying to weave some harmony out of the complexity.

Notes

(References in the text to titles which are in the bibliography and
can be found by means of the indexes have not been footnoted.)

1. Le Guin's own translation of the opening lines is: "The way
    that can be gone/ is not the Eternal Way./ The name that can
    be named/ is not the eternal Name." In City of Illusions (New
    York: Ace, 1967), pp. 138-39.
2. "Introduction," The Left Hand of Darkness (New York: Ace, 1976),
    p. [vi].
3. The 1961 version, completed in August 1960, is the best known
    account. In 1964, she published a young adult version; in
    1976, she published a new edition of the 1961 text adding
    photographs, drawings, and maps. In 1979, with Robert F.

Heizer, she edited the primary and secondary documents relating to Ishi. [1961--Berkeley: University of California;
1964--Ishi, Last of His Tribe (Berkeley: Parnassus); 1976--
Ishi In Two Worlds, deluxe, illus. ed. (Berkeley: University
of California); 1979--Ishi The Last Yahi: A Documentary History (Berkeley: University of California).]

4. The Inland Whale (Berkeley: University of California, 1974),
   p. 12.
5. Claude Levi-Strauss, "The Acquisitive Society," Times Literary
   Supplement, 26 November 1976.
6. In a review/interview, Junior Literary Guild [catalog], September 1972, p. 44.
7. "Science Fiction and the Future of Anarchy: Conversations with
   Ursula K. Le Guin," interviewer Charles Bigelow, J. McMahon,
   Oregon Times 4 (December 1974):28-29.
8. Anthropology, rev. ed. (New York: Harcourt, Brace, 1948),
   p. 252.
9. Ibid., p. 256.
10. Alfred Kroeber: A Personal Configuration (Berkeley: University
    of California, 1971), p. 241.
11. "Creating Realistic Utopias," interviewer Win McCormack and Anne
    Mendel, Seven Days 1 (11 April 1977):39.
12. "A Citizen of Mondath," Foundation 4 (July):30.
13. Ibid., p. 31.
14. Personal interview by Elizabeth Cogell, 25 and 27 October 1979.
    All subsequent references to "a 1979 interview" refer to this
    material. She speculated that perhaps Lawrence and her
    father's friend, Robert Oppenheimer, were already in disagree-
    ment and that she was aware of her father's sympathies.
15. "A Citizen of Mondath," p. 31.
16. Ibid., p. 33.
17. "Interview with Ursula K. Le Guin," interviewer Karen McPherson
    et al., 10 Point 5, no. 5 (Spring 1977), p. 14.
18. "Fiction Writer Le Guin: Portrait of the Artist . . . ," in-
    terviewer Alan Russell, Triton Times, 24 May 1977, p. 1.
19. "A Citizen of Mondath," p. 32.
20. "She Writes about Aliens--Men Included," interviewer Paula
    Brookmire, Milwaukee Journal, 21 July 1974, part 6, p. 3.
21. "Galaxy of Awards for Ursula Le Guin," interviewer Anthony Wolk
    and Susan Stanley Wolk, Willamette Week, 30 June 1975, p. 11.
22. "The Lionization of Ursula K. Le Guin," interviewer Susan
    Stanley Wolk, Review Magazine 17 (1971):149.
23. "A Citizen of Mondath," p. 32.
24. Ibid., p. 33.
25. "Dreams Must Explain Themselves," Dreams Must Explain Themselves
    (New York: Algol, 1975), p. 8.
26. "Ursula K. Le Guin: An Interview," interviewer Paul Walker,
    Luna Monthly, no. 63 (March 1976), p. [1].
27. "Interview: Ursula K. Le Guin," interviewer Dorothy Gilbert,
    California Quarterly, nos. 13/14 (Spring/Summer 1978), p. 43.
28. "Winter's King," in Orbit 5, ed. Damon Knight (New York:

Putnam's, 1969), p. 78.
29. "Myth and Archetype in Science Fiction," Parabola 1 (Fall 1976): 42.
30. "The Crab Nebula, the Paramecium, and Tolstoy," Riverside Quarterly 5 (February):95.
31. "Introduction," The Left Hand of Darkness, p. [v].
32. "Talking About Writing," in The Language of the Night, ed. Susan Wood (New York: Putnam, 1979), p. 200.
33. "Myth and Archetype," p. 46.
34. "Science Fiction and the Future of Anarchy," p. 27.
35. "The Crab Nebula," p. 89.
36. Ibid., p. 91.
37. Ibid.
38. Ibid., p. 96.
39. Ibid., p. 92.
40. "Science Fiction and Mrs. Brown," in Science Fiction At Large, ed. Peter Nicholls (London: Gollancz, 1976), p. 116.
41. Ibid., p. 110.
42. "The Crab Nebula," p. 95.
43. "The Stalin In The Soul," in The Future Now, ed. Robert Hoskins (Greenwich, Conn.: Fawcett, 1977), p. 19.
44. "Creating Realistic Utopias," p. 39.
45. "The Child and The Shadow," Quarterly Journal of the Library of Congress 32 (April 1975):141.
46. "Ursula K. Le Guin: An Interview," Luna Monthly, p. 3.
47. "Do-It-Yourself Cosmology," Parabola 2, no. 3, (1977):16.
48. "National Book Award Acceptance Speech," in The Language of the Night, pp. 57-58.
49. "Why Are Americans Afraid of Dragons?" Pacific North West Library Association Quarterly 38 (Winter 1974):41.
50. "Escape Routes," Galaxy 35 (December 1974):43.
51. "Introduction," in Edges, ed. Le Guin and Virginia Kidd (New York: Pocket, 1980).
52. "Dreams Must Explain Themselves," p. 11.
53. Critical Inquiry 7 (Autumn 1980):193-94.
54. Robert Nye, "Doings in Earthsea," New York Times Book Review, 18 February 1973, p. 8.
55. Darko Suvin, "The SF Novel in 1969," in Nebula Award Stories 5, ed. James Blish (London: Gollancz, 1970), p. 203.
56. Parabola 5 (May 1980):118.
57. N.B. Hayles, "Androgyny, Ambivalence, and Assimilation in The Left Hand of Darkness," in Ursula K. Le Guin, ed. James D. Olander and Martin Harry Greenberg (New York: Taplinger, 1979), p. 114.
58. Wendy Doniger O'Flaherty, Asceticism and Eroticism in The Mythology of Siva (London: Oxford, 1973), p. 315.

Part A: Fiction

A1 "An die Musik." <u>Western Humanities Review</u> 15 (Summer):247-58.

In <u>Orsinian Tales</u>, 1976. [See A58.]

A2 "April in Paris." <u>Fantastic</u> 11 (September):54-65.

<u>Strange Fantasy</u>, no. 10 (Fall 1969).
Ted White, ed. <u>The Best From Fantastic</u>. New York: Manor,
      1973 [paper].
In <u>The Wind's Twelve Quarters</u>, 1975. [See A41. Includes
      headnote; see C96.]
Peter Haining, ed. <u>The Black Magic Omnibus</u>. New York:
      Taplinger, 1976.
Robert Boyer and Kenneth Zahorski, eds. <u>The Fantastic
      Imagination II: An Anthology of High Fantasy</u>. New
      York: Avon, 1978 [paper].

A3 "The Masters." <u>Fantastic</u> 12 (February):85-99.

<u>Sword and Sorcery Annual</u>. Flushing, N.Y.: Ultimate Pub-
      lishing Co., 1975.
In <u>The Wind's Twelve Quarters</u>, 1975. [See A41. Includes
      headnote; see C97.]

A4 "Darkness Box." <u>Fantastic</u> 12 (November):60-67.

<u>Weird Mystery</u>, no. 2 (Winter 1970).
In <u>The Wind's Twelve Quarters</u>, 1975. [See A41. Includes
      headnote; see C98.]

Part A: Fiction

Robert Boyer and Kenneth Zahorski, eds. <u>Dark Imaginings:</u>
<u>A Collection of Gothic Fantasy</u>. New York: Delta, 1978
[paper].

1964

A5   "The Word of Unbinding." <u>Fantastic</u> 13 (January):67–73. [Volume number incorrectly listed on spine as 12.]

    <u>Strange Fantasy</u>, no. 13 (Fall 1970).
    Damon Knight, ed. <u>The Golden Road: Great Tales of Fantasy</u>
      <u>and the Supernatural</u>. New York: Simon & Schuster, 1973.
    In <u>The Wind's Twelve Quarters</u>, 1975. [See A41. Includes
      headnote; see C99.]
    <u>Literary Cavalcade</u> 29 (April 1977).
    Ellen Kushner, ed. <u>Basilisk</u>. New York: Ace, 1980 [paper].

A6   "The Rule of Names." <u>Fantastic</u> 13 (April):79–88.

    <u>The Most Thrilling Science Fiction Ever Told</u>, no. 13
      (Summer 1969).
    <u>Algol</u>, whole no. 21 (November 1973).
    In <u>Dreams Must Explain Themselves</u>, 1975. [See A40.]
    In <u>The Wind's Twelve Quarters</u>, 1975. [See A41.]
    <u>Puffin Post</u> 10, no. 2, 1976 [With headnote; see C119.]
    Robert Boyer and Kenneth Zahorski, eds. <u>The Fantastic</u>
      <u>Imagination: An Anthology of High Fantasy</u>. New York:
      Avon, 1977 [paper].
    Jane Mobley, ed. <u>Phantasmagoria: Tales of Fantasy and the</u>
      <u>Supernatural</u>. Garden City: Anchor, 1977 [paper].
    Egbert W. Nieman et al., eds. <u>Adventures for Readers</u>.
      Book Two. Heritage Edition. New York: Harcourt, 1979.
    Cary Wilkins, ed. <u>A Treasury of Fantasy: Heroic Adven-</u>
      <u>tures in Imaginary Lands</u>. New York: Avenel, 1981.

A7   "Selection." <u>Amazing</u> 38 (August):36–45.

    <u>Science Fiction Greats</u>, no. 17 (Spring 1970).

A8   "The Dowry of Angyar." <u>Amazing</u> 38 (September):46–63.

    As "Prologue: The Necklace." In <u>Rocannon's World</u>, 1966.
      [See A9.]
    "The Dowry of Angyar." <u>SF Greats</u>, no. 19 (Fall 1966).
    As "The Dowry of the Angyar." Ted White, ed. <u>The Best</u>
      <u>From Amazing Stories</u>. New York: Manor, 1973 [paper].
      [Le Guin objects to this ungrammatical title; Angyar is
      the name of a country, not its people; see <u>The Wind's</u>
      <u>Twelve Quarters</u>, p. viii.]
    As "Semley's Necklace." In <u>The Wind's Twelve Quarters</u>,

1975. [See A41. Includes headnote; see C95. Le Guin's
preferred title; see The Wind's Twelve Quarters, p.
viii.]

1966

A9 Rocannon's World. New York: Ace [paper]. [An Ace Double,
    bound with The Kar-Chee Reign by Avram Davidson.]

    New York: Ace, 1972 [paper].
    London: Universal-Tandem, 1972 [paper].
    New York: Garland, 1975.
    New York: Harper & Row, 1977. [With a new introduction by
       the author; see C152. Errors in previous editions have
       been corrected.]
    In Three Hainish Novels, 1978. [See A73.]
    *London: Gollancz, 1979. [Cited in Bookseller, 22 Septem-
       ber 1979, p. 1479.]

A10 "Prologue: The Necklace." [See A8.]

A11 Planet of Exile. New York: Ace [paper]. [An Ace Double,
    bound with Mankind Under the Leash by Thomas M. Disch.]

    New York: Ace, 1971 [paper].
    London: Universal-Tandem, 1972 [paper].
    New York: Garland, 1975.
    New York: Harper & Row, 1978. [With a new introduction by
       the author; see C165.]
    In Three Hainish Novels, 1978. [See A73.]
    London: Gollancz, 1979.

1967

A12 City of Illusions. New York: Ace [paper].

    London: Gollancz, 1971.
    St. Albans, Herts. (UK): Panther, 1973 [paper].
    New York: Garland, 1975.
    New York: Harper & Row, 1978. [With a new introduction by
       the author; see C168.]
    In Three Hainish Novels, 1978. [See A73.]

1968

A13 A Wizard of Earthsea. Berkeley: Parnassus Press.

    New York: Ace, 1970 [paper].

Harmondsworth: Puffin, 1971 [paper].
London: Gollancz, 1971.
London: Heinemann, 1973.
New York: Bantam, 1975 [paper].
In Earthsea, 1977. [See A66.]
As "The Open Sea." Harold Schechter and Jonna Gormely
  Semeiks, eds. Patterns in Popular Culture: A Source-
  book for Writers. New York: Harper & Row, 1980 [paper].
  [Reprints novel's last chapter. Also contains essay;
  see C137.]

1969

A14 The Left Hand of Darkness. New York: Ace [paper].

New York: Walker, 1969.
New York: Walker, 1969 [Science Fiction Book Club].
London: Macdonald, 1969.
St. Albans, Herts. (UK): Panther, 1973 [paper].
New York: Ace, 1976 [paper]. [With a new introduction by
  the author; see C132.]
Recorded on "The Ones Who Walk Away From Omelas" as read by
  the author, 1976 [record]. [See B65.]
Excerpt. James Gunn, ed. The Road to Science Fiction #3:
  From Heinlein to Here. New York: Mentor, 1979 [paper].
  [Reprints chapter one.]
New York: Harper & Row, 1980.

A15 "Winter's King." In Orbit 5. Edited by Damon Knight. New
  York: Putnam's, pp. 67–88.

In The Wind's Twelve Quarters, 1975. [See A41. Includes
  headnote; see C100. Revised version: feminine pronoun
  used for each Gethenian.]
Robert Silverberg and Martin H. Greenberg, eds. The Arbor
  House Treasury of Modern Science Fiction. New York:
  Arbor House, 1980.

A16 "Nine Lives." Playboy 16 (November):128–29, 132, 220–30.
  [Includes author's comment; see C8. Story contains several
  changes of which Le Guin did not approve; see The Wind's
  Twelve Quarters, p. 129.]

Donald A. Wollheim and Terry Carr, eds. World's Best
  Science Fiction 1970. New York: Ace, 1970 [paper].
  [First appearance of correct version.]
Harry Harrison and Brian Aldiss, eds. Best SF: 1969. New
  York: Putnam's, 1970.
James Blish, ed. Nebula Award Stories 5. London:
  Gollancz, 1970.

Part A: Fiction

Editors of Playboy Magazine, eds. The Dead Astronaut.
Chicago: Playboy Press, 1971 [paper].
Editors of Playboy Magazine, eds. The Best From Playboy,
no. 7. Chicago: Playboy Press, 1973. [Magazine for-
mat.]
John S. Lambert, ed. The New Prometheans: Readings for
the Future. New York: Harper & Row, 1973 [paper].
Robin Scott Wilson, ed. Those Who Can: A Science Fiction
Reader. New York: Mentor, 1973 [paper]. [With an
essay; see C52.]
Charles William Sullivan III, ed. As Tomorrow Becomes
Today. Englewood Cliffs: Prentice-Hall, 1974.
Harvey A. Katz, Patricia Warrick, Martin Harry Greenberg,
eds. Introductory Psychology Through Science Fiction.
Chicago: Rand-McNally, 1974 [paper].
Stephen V. Whaley and Stanley J. Cook, eds. Man Unwept:
Visions from the Inner Eye. New York: McGraw-Hill,
1974.
Norman Spinrad, ed. Modern Science Fiction. Garden City:
Anchor, 1974 [paper].
Leslie A. Fiedler, ed. In Dreams Awake. New York: Dell,
1975 [paper].
In The Wind's Twelve Quarters, 1975. [See A41. Includes
headnote; see C102.]
Gerry Goldberg, ed. A Strange Glory. Toronto: McClelland
& Stewart, 1975 [paper].
Lee Harding, ed. Beyond Tomorrow: An Anthology of Modern
Science Fiction. Melbourne (Australia): Wren, 1976.
Pamela Sargent, ed. Bio-Futures: Science Fiction Stories
About Biological Metamorphosis. New York: Vintage,
1976 [paper].
Donald L. Lawler, ed. Approaches to Science Fiction.
Boston: Houghton Mifflin, 1978 [paper].
Barbara McKenzie, ed. Fiction's Journey. New York:
Harcourt, 1978 [paper].
Patricia Warrick, Martin Greenberg, Joseph Olander, eds.
Science Fiction: Contemporary Mythology. The SFWA-
SFRA Anthology. New York: Harper & Row, 1978.

1970

A17   "The End." In Orbit 6. Edited by Damon Knight. New York:
Putnam's, pp. 146-57.

Damon Knight, ed. The Best From Orbit Volumes 1-10. New
York: Berkeley-Putnam, 1975.
As "Things." In The Wind's Twelve Quarters, 1975. [See
A41. Includes headnote; see C103. Le Guin's preferred
title; see The Wind's Twelve Quarters, p. viii.]

Part A: Fiction

A18 "The Good Trip." Fantastic 19 (August):6-11, 145.

      Michel Parry, ed. Dream Trips: Stories of Weird and Un-
          earthly Drugs. St. Albans, Herts. (UK): Panther, 1974
          [paper].
      In The Wind's Twelve Quarters, 1975. [See A41. Includes
          headnote; see C101.]

A19 "A Trip to the Head." In Quark 1. Edited by Samuel R. Delany
     and Marilyn Hacker. New York: Paperback Library, pp. 36-
     42 [paper].

      Robert Hoskins, ed. The Liberated Future. Greenwich,
          Conn.: Fawcett, 1974 [paper].
      In The Wind's Twelve Quarters, 1975. [See A41. Includes
          headnote; see C104.]

A20 "The Tombs of Atuan." Worlds of Fantasy 1 (Winter):4-76.
     [Issue dated 1970-1971. Shortened version.]

      The Tombs of Atuan. New York: Atheneum, 1971.
      London: Gollancz, 1972.
      Harmondsworth: Puffin, 1974 [paper].
      London: Heinemann, 1974.
      New York: Bantam, 1975 [paper].
      Norman Weiser, adaptation, 1976 [filmstrip]. [See B142.]
      In Earthsea, 1977. [See A66.]

1971

A21 "The Lathe of Heaven." Amazing 44, part one (March):6-61;
     Amazing 45, part two (May):6-65, 121-23.

      The Lathe of Heaven. New York: Scribner's, 1971.
      New York: Scribner's, 1971 [Science Fiction Book Club].
      Louisville: American Printing House for the Blind, 2 vols.,
          1972 [Braille].
      London: Gollancz, 1972.
      New York: Avon, 1973 [paper].
      St. Albans, Herts. (UK): Panther, 1974 [paper].
      David Loxton, producer, 1980 [television movie]. [See
          B146.]
      New York: Avon, 1980 [paper]. [Cover has photos from the
          TV production; see B146.]

A22 The Tombs of Atuan. [See A20.]

A23 The Lathe of Heaven. [See A21.]

A24 "Vaster Than Empires and More Slow." In New Dimensions I:

6

Fourteen Original Science Fiction Stories. Edited by
Robert Silverberg. Garden City: Doubleday, pp. 87-121.

Terry Carr, ed. The Best Science Fiction of the Year #1.
New York: Ballantine, 1972 [paper].
Robert Hoskins, ed. Wondermakers 2. Greenwich, Conn.:
Fawcett, 1974 [paper].
Pamela Sargent, ed. Women of Wonder: Science Fiction
Stories By Women About Women. New York: Random, 1975
[paper]. [Editor's introduction reprints excerpts of
Le Guin-Lem letter exchange; see C32 and D59.]
In The Wind's Twelve Quarters, 1975. [See A41. Includes
headnote; see C105. Revised version: deletions in
opening pages.]
Robert Silverberg, ed. Explorers of Space: Eight Stories
of Science Fiction. Nashville: Thomas Nelson, 1975.

1972

A25 "The Word for World is Forest." In Again, Dangerous Visions.
Edited by Harlan Ellison. Garden City: Doubleday, pp. 30-
108. [With an author's afterword (see C39) and an editor's
introduction (see D85).]

The Word for World is Forest. New York: Berkley-Putnam,
1976.
The Word for World is Forest. London: Gollancz, 1977.
[With a new introduction by author; see C160.]
"The Word for World is Forest." Isaac Asimov, ed. The
Hugo Winners Volume 3. Garden City: Doubleday, 1977.
The Word for World is Forest. Louisville: American
Printing House for the Blind, 1977 [Braille].
The Word for World is Forest. St. Albans, Herts. (UK):
Panther, 1980 [paper].

A26 The Farthest Shore. New York: Atheneum. [Junior Literary
Guild edition, issued two months later, appears to be a
reissue of the first edition with new boards.]

London: Gollancz, 1973. [Revised: deletions, primarily
in the chapter, "Orm Embar."]
Harmondsworth: Puffin, 1974 [paper].
London: Heinemann, 1975.
New York: Bantam, 1975 [paper].
In Earthsea, 1977. [See A66.]

1973

A27 "Cake and Ice Cream." Playgirl (February/March), pp. 36, 50-
55.

Part A: Fiction

A28 "The Dowry of the Angyar." [See A8.]

A29 "The Ones Who Walk Away From Omelas (Variations on a Theme by
     William James)." In New Dimensions III. Edited by Robert
     Silverberg. New York: Signet, pp. 1-7 [paper].

        Terry Carr, ed. The Best Science Fiction of the Year #3.
           New York: Ballantine, 1974 [paper].
        In The Wind's Twelve Quarters, 1975. [See A41. Includes
           headnote; see C109.]
        Recorded on "The Ones Who Walk Away From Omelas" as read by
           the author, 1976 [record]. [See B65.]
        Isaac Asimov, ed. The Hugo Winners Volume 3. Garden City:
           Doubleday, 1977.
        Robert Scholes, Carl Klaus, Michael Silverman, eds.
           Elements of Literature. New York: Oxford, 1978 [paper].
        X.J. Kennedy, ed. An Introduction to Fiction. 2d ed.
           Boston: Little, Brown, 1979 [paper].
        Robert Silverberg, ed. The Best of New Dimensions. New
           York: Pocket, 1979 [paper].
        Northrop Frye, Sheridan Baker, George Perkins, eds. The
           Practical Imagination: Stories, Poems, Plays. New
           York: Harper & Row, 1980.
        Beaty, Jerome, ed. The Norton Introduction to Fiction. 2d
           ed. New York: W.W. Norton, 1981.
        Bain, Carl E. et al., eds. The Norton Introduction to
           Literature. 3d ed. New York: W.W. Norton, 1981.

A30 "Field of Vision." Galaxy 34 (October):83-99.

        Editors of Galaxy Magazine, eds. The Best From Galaxy,
           Volume II. New York: Award, 1974 [paper].
        As "The Field of Vision." In The Wind's Twelve Quarters,
           1975. [See A41. Includes headnote; see C107. Le Guin's
           preferred title; see The Wind's Twelve Quarters, p.
           viii.]

A31 "Direction of the Road." In Orbit 12. Edited by Damon
     Knight. New York: Putnam's, pp. 31-38. [Includes
     author's comment; see C51.]

        In The Wind's Twelve Quarters, 1975. [See A41. Includes
           headnote; see C108.]
        Recorded on "The Ones Who Walk Away from Omelas" as read by
           the author, 1976 [record]. [See B65.]

A32 "Imaginary Countries." Harvard Advocate 106 (Winter):40-43.

        In Orsinian Tales, 1976. [See A58.]

8

Part A: Fiction

1974

A33 "Schrödinger's Cat." In Universe 5. Edited by Terry Carr. New York: Random, pp. 31-40.

A34 The Dispossessed: An Ambiguous Utopia. New York: Harper & Row.

   New York: Harper & Row, 1974 [Science Fiction Book Club].
   London: Gollancz, 1974.
   New York: Avon, 1975 [paper].
   St. Albans, Herts. (UK): Panther, 1975 [paper].

A35 "The Day Before the Revolution." Galaxy 35 (August):17-30. [Includes author's comment; see C69.]

   Pat Rotter, ed. Bitches and Sad Ladies: An Anthology of Fiction By and About Women. New York: Harper's Magazine Press, 1975.
   In The Wind's Twelve Quarters, 1975. [See A41. Includes headnote; see C110.]
   James Baen, ed. The Best From Galaxy, Volume III. New York: Award, 1975 [paper].
   James Gunn, ed. Nebula Award Stories 10. London: Gollancz, 1975.
   Pamela Sargent, ed. More Women of Wonder. New York: Vintage, 1976.
   James Baen, ed. Galaxy: The Best of My Years. New York: Ace, 1980 [paper].

A36 "The Stars Below." In Orbit 14. Edited by Damon Knight. New York: Harper & Row, pp. 92-112. [Includes speech excerpt (see C43) and comment (see C64).]

   In The Wind's Twelve Quarters, 1975. [See A41. Includes headnote; see C106.]
   Gardner Dozois, ed. Another World: A Science Fiction Anthology. Chicago: Follett, 1977.

A37 "Intracom." In StopWatch. Edited by George Hay. London: New English Library, pp. 81-97.

   Recorded on "Gwilan's Harp" and "Intracom": Read by the author, 1977 [record]. [See B74.]

A38 "The Author of the Acacia Seeds and Other Extracts from the Journal of the Association of Therolinguistics." In Fellowship of the Stars: Nine Science Fiction Stories. Edited by Terry Carr. New York: Simon & Schuster, pp. 213-22.

   Terry Carr, ed. The Best Science Fiction of the Year

9

<u>#4</u>. New York: Ballantine, 1975 [paper].

1975

A39 "The New Atlantis." In <u>The New Atlantis and Other Novellas of</u>
     <u>Science Fiction</u>. Edited by Robert Silverberg. New York:
     Hawthorn, pp. 57-86.

     Terry Carr, ed. <u>The Best Science Fiction of the Year #5</u>.
     New York: Ballantine, 1976 [paper].
     R.V. Cassill, ed. <u>The Norton Anthology of Short Fiction</u>.
     New York: W.W. Norton, 1978.
     R.V. Cassill, ed. <u>The Norton Anthology of Short Fiction</u>.
     Shorter Ed. New York: W.W. Norton, 1978.

A40 <u>Dreams Must Explain Themselves</u>. Compiled by Andrew Porter.
     New York: Algol Press [paper]. [See C92.]

A41 <u>The Wind's Twelve Quarters</u>. New York: Harper & Row. ["Fore-
     word"; "Semley's Necklace," 1964; "April in Paris," 1962;
     "The Masters," 1963; "Darkness Box," 1963; "The Word of Un-
     binding," 1964; "The Rule of Names," 1964; "Winter's King,"
     1969; "The Good Trip," 1970; "Nine Lives," 1969; "Things,"
     1970; "A Trip to the Head," 1970; "Vaster than Empires and
     More Slow," 1971; "The Stars Below," 1974; "The Field of
     Vision," 1973; "Direction of the Road," 1973; "The Ones
     Who Walk Away from Omelas," 1973; "The Day Before the
     Revolution," 1974; numerous headnotes--see C95-110.]

     New York: Harper & Row, 1975 [Science Fiction Book Club].
     London: Gollancz, 1976.
     New York: Bantam, 1976 [paper].
     London: Panther-Granada, 2 vols., 1978 [paper].

A42 "Semley's Necklace." [See A8.]

A43 "Things." [See A17.]

A44 "The Field of Vision." [See A30.]

A45 "Mazes." In <u>Epoch</u>. Edited by Robert Silverberg and Roger
     Elwood. New York: Berkley-Putnam, pp. 83-88. [Includes
     afterword; see C115.]

A46 "Desperadoes of the Galactic Union" [postcard]. London: Post
     Card Partnership.

     <u>Science Fiction Review</u> [fanzine] 4 (August 1975).

A47 "A Week in the Country." <u>Little Magazine</u> 9 (Winter):28-46.

Part A: Fiction

[Issue dated 1975-1976.]

In Orsinian Tales, 1976. [See A58.]

1976

A48 The Word for World is Forest. [See A25.]

A49 "Brothers and Sisters." Little Magazine 10 (Spring-Summer):
     91-125. [With essay by Karl Kroeber; see D338.]

     In Orsinian Tales, 1976. [See A58.]

A50 Very Far Away From Anywhere Else. New York: Atheneum.

     As A Very Long Way From Anywhere Else. London: Gollancz,
     1976.
     As Very Far Away from Anywhere Else. New York: Bantam,
     1978 [paper].
     As A Very Long Way from Anywhere Else. Harmondsworth:
     Peacock, 1978 [paper].
     As "A Very Long Way from Anywhere Else." Monica Dickens
     and Rosemary Sutcliff, eds. Is Anyone There? Harmonds-
     worth: Peacock, 1978. [Excerpt consisting of the third
     segment, pp. 19-33 of the Atheneum edition.]
     As A Very Long Way from Anywhere Else. London: Heinemann,
     1979.

A51 A Very Long Way From Anywhere Else. [See A50.]

A52 "The Diary of The Rose." In Future Power: A Science Fiction
     Anthology. Edited by Jack Dann and Gardner R. Dozois. New
     York: Random, pp. 3-31.

     Gardner Dozois, ed. Best Science Fiction Stories of the
        Year, Sixth Annual Collection. New York: Dutton, 1977.
     Kenneth B. Melvin, Stanley L. Brodsky, Raymond D. Fowler,
        Jr., eds. Psy-Fi One: An Anthology of Psychology In
     Science Fiction. New York: Random, 1977.

A53 "Solomon Leviathan's Nine Hundred and Thirty-First Trip Around
     the World." In The First Puffin's Pleasure. Edited by
     Kaye Webb and Treld Bicknell. Harmondsworth: Puffin,
     pp. 18-22.

A54 The Water Is Wide. Pendragon Press: Portland [single short
     story]. [According to Lloyd W. Currey (see D541) issued as
     50 copies hardbound and autographed; 200 copies bound in
     wrappers and autographed; 750 copies bound in wrappers.]

A55   "The Eye Altering." In <u>The Altered I: An Encounter with
Science Fiction by Ursula K. Le Guin and Others</u>. Edited
by Lee Harding. Carlton (Australia): Norstrilia Press,
pp. 108-17 [paper]. [Contains other Le Guin material; see
A56, C117, C118.]

     As "The Eye Altering (II)." Lee Harding, ed. <u>The Altered
I</u>. New York: Berkley Windhover, 1978 [paper]. [Re-
vised version.]

A56   "No Use to Talk to Me." In <u>The Altered I: An Encounter with
Science Fiction by Ursula K. Le Guin and Others</u>. Edited by
Lee Harding. Carlton (Australia): Norstrilia Press, pp.
90-91. [Also contains "The Eye Altering"; see A55.]

A57   "The Barrow." <u>Fantasy & Science Fiction</u> 51 (October):52-59.

     In <u>Orsinian Tales</u>, 1976. [See A58.]

A58   <u>Orsinian Tales</u>. New York: Harper & Row. ["The Fountains,"
1976; "The Barrow," 1976; "Ile Forest," 1976; "Conversations
at Night," 1976; "The Road East," 1976; "Brothers and Sisters," 1976; "A Week in the Country," 1975; "An die Musik,"
1961; "The House," 1976; "The Lady of Moge," 1976; "Imaginary Countries," 1973.]

     London: Gollancz, 1977.
     New York: Bantam, 1977 [paper].
     London: Panther-Granada, 1978 [paper].

A59   "The Fountains." In <u>Orsinian Tales</u>, pp. 1-5. [See A58.]

A60   "Ile Forest." In <u>Orsinian Tales</u>, pp. 19-35. [See A58.]

     <u>Women's Journal</u> (London) (January 1978).

A61   "Conversations at Night." In <u>Orsinian Tales</u>, pp. 37-70. [See
A58.]

A62   "The Road East." In <u>Orsinian Tales</u>, pp. 71-82. [See A58.]

A63   "The House." In <u>Orsinian Tales</u>, pp. 169-81. [See A58.]

A64   "The Lady of Moge." In <u>Orsinian Tales</u>, pp. 183-97. [See A58.]

A65   <u>Nebula Award Stories 11</u> [anthology]. London: Gollancz.
[Contains introduction by Le Guin; see C141.]

     New York: Harper & Row, 1977.
     London: Corgi, 1978 [paper].

New York: Bantam, 1978 [paper].

1977

A66 Earthsea. London: Gollancz [A Wizard of Earthsea, 1968; The
       Tombs of Atuan, 1971; The Farthest Shore, 1972].

    As The Earthsea Trilogy. Harmondsworth: Puffin, 1979
       [paper].

A67 "Three." Encore (Portland, Ore.) 1 (April/May):8-9. [Includes
       two short stories, "Courtroom Scene" and "Ghost Story," and
       one poem, "Everest." Accompanied by an illustration,
       "Dragon."]

A68 "Courtroom Scene." [See A67.]

A69 "Ghost Story." [See A67.]

A70 "Gwilan's Harp." Redbook 149 (May):229-30.

    The Australian Women's Weekly 45 (21 September 1977).
    Recorded on "Gwilan's Harp" and "Intracom": Read by the
       author, 1977 [record]. [See B74.]
    Folk Harp Journal 21 (June):1978.
    Literary Cavalcade 31 (October):1978.
    Roy Carlson, ed. Contemporary Northwest Writing. Cor-
       vallis: Oregon State University Press, 1979 [paper].
    As Gwilan's Harp. Northridge, Calif.: Lord John Press,
       1981. [According to Lloyd W. Currey, the press run in-
       cluded 50 copies bound in cloth and autographed, 300
       copies bound in decorated paper and autographed.]

1978

A71 "The Eye Altering (II)." [See A55.]

A72 "The First Report of the Shipwrecked Foreigner to the Kadanh
       of Derb." Antaeus 29 (Spring):144-49.

A73 Three Hainish Novels. Garden City: Doubleday [Science Fic-
       tion Book Club]. [Rocannon's World, 1966; Planet of Exile,
       1966; City of Illusions, 1967.]

A74 "The Eye of the Heron." In Millennial Women. Edited by
       Virginia Kidd. New York: Delacorte, pp. 124-302.

    Virginia Kidd, ed. The Eye of The Heron and Other Stories.
       London: Panther-Granada, 1980 [paper].

Part A: Fiction

A75   "SQ." In Cassandra Rising. Edited by Alice Laurance. Garden
      City: Doubleday, pp. 1-10.

      Donald A. Wollheim, ed. The 1979 Annual World's Best SF.
      New York: Daw, 1979.

A76   "A Very Long Way from Anywhere Else." [See A50.]

1979

A77   The Earthsea Trilogy. [See A66.]

A78   "The Pathways of Desire." In New Dimensions 9. Edited by
      Robert Silverberg. New York: Harper & Row, pp. 2-32.

A79   Leese Webster. New York: Atheneum. [Short story for
      children.]

A80   Malafrena. New York: Putnam's.

      London: Gollancz, 1980.
      New York: Berkley, 1980 [paper].

A81   "Last Word." Omni 2 (October):178.

A82   "Malheur Country." Kenyon Review, n.s. 1 (Winter):22-30.

A83   "Two Delays on the Northern Line." New Yorker (12 November),
      pp. 50-57.

A84   "The Crossing." Redbook 154 (December):165-89. [Condensed
      version.]

      As The Beginning Place. New York: Harper & Row, 1980.
      As Threshold. London: Gollancz, 1980.

1980

A85   The Beginning Place. [See A84.]

A86   With Virginia Kidd. Interfaces [anthology]. New York: Ace
      [paper]. [Contains introduction by the editors; see C186.]

      New York: Ace, 1980 [paper]. [First mass market edition.]

A87   "The Open Sea." [See A13.]

A88   Threshold. [See A84.]

Part A: Fiction

A89 With Virginia Kidd. <u>Edges: Thirteen Tales From The Border-
     lands of the Imagination</u> [anthology]. New York: Pocket
     [paper]. [Contains introduction by Le Guin; see C199.]

A90 "The White Donkey." <u>TriQuarterly 49</u> (Fall), pp. 259-61.

15

Part B: Miscellaneous Media

1959

B1 "Folksong from the Montayna Province" [poem]. Prairie Poet
    (Charleston, Ill.) (Fall), p. 75.

B2 "A Dedication" [poem]. Literary Calendar (Shreveport, La.)
    (December), p. 7.

1960

B3 "On Sappho's Theme" [poem]. Husk (Mt. Vernon, Ia.) 39 (March):
    87.

B4 "An Expert in Youngness" [poem]. Husk (Mt. Vernon, Ia.) 39
    (May):127.

B5 "The Year without an Easter" [poem]. Quicksilver (Ft. Worth,
    Tex.) 13 (Summer):14.

B6 "The Entrance of Mr. Audiot and Mr. Elen Into Heaven" [poem].
    Nimrod (Tulsa, Okla.) 5 (Fall):15-16.

B7 "The Team" [poem]. In Today The Stars: Avalon Anthology,
    1960 Compiled by Lilith Lorraine. Alpine, Tex.: Different
    Press, p. 36.

B8 "Napa Valley: Fort Valley" [poem]. New Athenaeum (Crescent
    City, Fla.) (Winter), p. 13.

1961

B9 "Notes from an Excursion" [poem]. Quicksilver (Ft. Worth,

17

Tex.) 14 (Spring):18-19.

B10 "A Scene from an Opera" [poem]. Minority of One 3 (August):9.

B11 "Botticelli" [poem]. Galley Sail Review (San Francisco) 3 (Fall):26.

1970

B12 "Warp and Weft" [poem]. In Alfred Kroeber: A Personal Con-figuration, by Theodora Kroeber. Berkeley: University of California Press, p. 216.

    As "Coming of Age." In Wild Angels, 1975. [See B27.]

B13 "Roots" [poem]. Kinesis (Milford, Penn.), no. 3 (December), p. 6.

B14 "The Wolves" [poem]. Kinesis (Milford, Penn.), no. 3 (Decem-ber), p. 6.

B15 "Discovery" [poem]. Kinesis (Milford, Penn.), no. 3 (Decem-ber), p. 6.

1971

*B16 "Therem's Quatrain." [A sample of Karhidish literature in-cluded in "Le Guin II."] Entropy Negative [fanzine], no. 3, p. 4. [Cited in Bittner; see D532.]

B17 "Rakaforta" [poem]. Mr. Cogito 1 (Fall):14.

B18 "Crab Nebula" [recipe]. In Cooking Out of This World. Edited by Anne McCaffrey. New York: Ballantine, pp. 104-5.

B19 "Fresh Gichymichy" [recipe]. In Cooking Out of This World. Edited by Anne McCaffrey. New York: Ballantine, pp. 105-6.

B20 "Primitive Chocolate Mousse (Also Known as Mousse au chocolat, Chocolate Moose, Brown Mouse, and Please Sir I want some More)" [recipe]. In Cooking Out of This World. Edited by Anne McCaffrey. New York: Ballantine, p. 107.

B21 Translation. "The Plain of Ice," by Ugo Malaguti [chapter two of Italian novel, Il Palazzo nel Cielo]. Edge, nos. 5/6 (Autumn/Winter), pp. 62-68, 73. [Includes Le Guin's note; see C55.]

Part B: Miscellaneous Media

B22   "Ursula Le Guin: Women of Science Fiction" [tape]. Charlotte
      Reed, interviewer. North Hollywood, Calif.: Center for
      Cassette Studies, no. 33459.

1974

B23   "Tao Poem" [poem]. Papers, Inc. (Framingham, Mass.), p. 18.

        As "Tao Song." In Wild Angels, 1975. [See B27.]
        As "Tao Song." Earth heart Almanac [calendar]. Lake
          Grove, Ore.: Oneword Graphics, 1978. [Poem appears for
          October.]

B24   "Für Elise" [poem]. Papers, Inc. (Framingham, Mass.), 2d
      ed., p. 5.

        In Wild Angels, 1975. [See B27.]

B25   "Mount St. Helens/Omphalos" [poem]. Quarter (Portland, Ore.),
      no. 2 (August), p. 3.

        In Wild Angels, 1975. [See B27.]

B26   Introduction. [Tape of speech given at Harry C. Kendall
      Planetarium's adaptation and performance of "Nightfall" by
      Isaac Asimov; see C78.]

1975

B27   Wild Angels [collection of poems]. Santa Barbara: Capra
      Press. [Two hundred copies hardbound and autographed; 2000
      copies bound in wrappers.] ["O wild angels of the open
      hills"; "Coming of Age," 1970; "There"; "Footnote"; "Hier
      Steh' Ich"; "Song"; "Archaeology of the Renaissance"; "From
      Whose Bourne"; "March 21"; "The Darkness"; "Dreampoem";
      "The Young"; "The Anger"; "Ars Lunga"; "The Molsen"; "The
      Withinner"; "Offering"; "Arboreal"; "Dreampoem II"; "A
      Lament for Rheged"; "The Rooftree"; "Some of the Philoso-
      phers"; "Snow"; "Flying West from Denver"; "Winter-Rose";
      "Mount St. Helens/Omphalos," 1974; "For Robinson Jeffers'
      Ghost"; "For Bob"; "Für Elise," 1974; "For Ted"; "Elegy:
      For Reese"; "Tao Song," 1974.]

        In The Capra Chapbook Anthology. Edited by Noel Young.
          Santa Barbara: Capra Press, 1979.

B28   "O wild angels of the open hills" [poem]. In Wild Angels, p. 7.
      [See B27.]

19

B29   "Coming of Age." [See B12.]

B30   "There" [poem]. In <u>Wild Angels</u>, pp. 17-18. [See B27.]

B31   "Footnote" [poem]. In <u>Wild Angels</u>, p. 19. [See B27.]

B32   "Hier Steh' Ich" [poem]. In <u>Wild Angels</u>, p. 20. [See B27.]

B33   "Song" [poem]. In <u>Wild Angels</u>, p. 21. [See B27.]

B34   "Archaeology of the Renaissance" [poem]. In <u>Wild Angels</u>,
       p. 22. [See B27.]

B35   "From Whose Bourne" [poem]. In <u>Wild Angels</u>, p. 23. [See
       B27.]

B36   "March 21" [poem]. In <u>Wild Angels</u>, p. 24. [See B27.]

B37   "The Darkness" [poem]. In <u>Wild Angels</u>, p. 25. [See B27.]

B38   "Dreampoem" [poem]. In <u>Wild Angels</u>, p. 26. [See B27.]

B39   "The Young" [poem]. In <u>Wild Angels</u>, p. 27. [See B27.]

B40   "The Anger" [poem]. In <u>Wild Angels</u>, p. 28. [See B27.]

B41   "Ars Lunga" [poem]. In <u>Wild Angels</u>, p. 29. [See B27.]

       Alice Fannin, Rebecca Lukens, Catherine Hoyser Mann, eds.
          <u>Woman: An Affirmation</u>. Lexington, Mass.: Heath, 1979
          [paper].

B42   "The Molsen" [poem]. In <u>Wild Angels</u>, p. 30. [See B27.]

B43   "The Withinner" [poem]. In <u>Wild Angels</u>, p. 31. [See B27.]

B44   "Offering" [poem]. In <u>Wild Angels</u>, p. 32. [See B27.]

B45   "Arboreal" [poem]. In <u>Wild Angels</u>, p. 33. [See B27.]

B46   "Dreampoem II" [poem]. In <u>Wild Angels</u>, p. 34. [See B27.]

B47   "A Lament for Rheged" [poem]. In <u>Wild Angels</u>, pp. 35-37.
       [See B27.]

B48   "The Rooftree" [poem]. In <u>Wild Angels</u>, p. 38. [See B27.]

       Steven Nemirow, Stephen Thomas, Barbara la Morticella, eds.
          <u>Confluence: A Portland Anthology</u>. Portland: Multnomah
          Art Center, 1979 [paper].

B49   "Some of the Philosophers" [poem]. In Wild Angels, p. 39.
      [See B27.]

B50   "Snow" [poem]. In Wild Angels, p. 40. [See B27.]

B51   "Flying West from Denver" [poem]. In Wild Angels, p. 41.
      [See B27.]

B52   "Winter-Rose" [poem]. In Wild Angels, p. 42. [See B27.]

B53   "For Robinson Jeffers' Ghost" [poem]. In Wild Angels, p. 44.
      [See B27.]

B54   "For Bob" [poem]. In Wild Angels, p. 45. [See B27.]

B55   "For Ted" [poem]. In Wild Angels, p. 47. [See B27.]

B56   "Elegy: For Reese" [poem]. In Wild Angels, pp. 48-49. [See
      B27.]

B57   Translation. "Ebauches et Fragments," by Rainer Maria Rilke,
      #689 [French poem]. Mr. Cogito 1 (Winter):8.

B58   Translation. "Les Fenêtres," by Rainer Maria Rilke, #587/III
      [French poem]. Mr. Cogito 1 (Winter):9.

B59   Translation. "Vergers," by Rainer Maria Rilke, #518/4 [French
      poem]. Mr. Cogito 1 (Winter):10.

B60   Translation. "Les Roses," by Rainer Maria Rilke, #576/VI
      [French poem]. Mr. Cogito 1 (Winter):11.

B61   Translation. "Les Roses," by Rainer Maria Rilke, #582/XXI
      [French poem]. Mr. Cogito 1 (Winter):12.

B62   Translation. "Les Roses," by Rainer Maria Rilke, #576/V
      [French poem]. Mr. Cogito 1 (Winter):13.

                              1976

*B63 Aussiecon Audio and Video Tapes. Melbourne, Victoria:
      Aussiecon. [Three items record Le Guin's participation at
      the 33rd World Science Fiction Convention (August 1975).
      Guest of Honor Speech (see C113); panel on "Discovering
      Worlds"; panel on "Myths and Legends in Science Fiction."
      Cited in Bittner; see D532.]

B64   Cartoon drawing. Citadel (Arlington, Tex.) [fanzine], p. 11.
      [All contributions were on the subject, "How Dinosaurs Did
      It." Le Guin's drawing is of a winged dinosaur with a

sling in its beak containing a baby dinosaur.]

B65 "The Ones Who Walk Away From Omelas" as read by the author
[record]. Alternate World Recordings, AWR 7476. ["The
Ones Who Walk Away From Omelas," 1973; "Direction of the
Road," 1973; "An Orgota Creation Myth," chapter seventeen
from The Left Hand of Darkness, 1969. Brief comments by
the author; see C138. Liner notes by Vonda McIntyre; see
D345.]

B66 Walking in Cornwall: A Poem for the Solstice [poem]. Portland: Pendragon Press. [Privately printed. Twelve pages;
includes drawings by Charles Le Guin. Five hundred fifty
copies printed; 200 for Le Guin, 350 for friends of Pendragon Press.]

In Hard Words, 1981. [See B104.]

1977

B67 "Travelling" [poem on postcard]. Binghamton, N.Y.: Bellevue
Press. [From a set edited by Jack Dann; printed by Stuart
McCarty II. Cited in Levin-Bittner as 1976; see D704.]

Australian Science Fiction Review, March 1978.

B68 "Ursula Le Guin in conversation with Barbara Firsir" [tape].
Special Collections, University of California, San Diego;
La Jolla, California.

B69 "Dragon" [drawing]. [See A67.]

B70 "Everest" [poem]. [See A67.]

In The Language of the Night, 1979. [See C175; excerpt.]
In Hard Words, 1981. [See B104.]

B71 "Equinox '75" [poem]. Speculative Poetry Review, no. 1, p. 24.

B72 "From Hsin Ch'i-chi, 1140-1207" [poem on postcard]. Binghamton, N.Y.: Bellevue Press. [Printed by Stuart
McCarty II.]

B73 "Invocation" [poem]. Speculative Poetry Review, no. 2, p. 4.

In Hard Words, 1981. [See B104.]

B74 "Gwilan's Harp" and "Intracom": Read by the author [record].
Caedmon, TC 1556. ["Gwilan's Harp," 1977; "Intracom," 1974.
Liner notes by author; see C158.]

B75 "The Song of the Dragon's Daughter" [poem]. <u>Algol</u> 15 (Winter): 47–49.

B76 "In San Spirito Square" [poem]. <u>Oregon East</u> (La Grande, Ore.) 8:55. [Issue dated 1977–1978.]

1978

B77 "California: For Lowry Pei" [poem]. <u>Australian Science Fiction Review</u> (March), p. 130.

B78 "October 6" [poem]. <u>10 Point 5</u>, no. 7 (Summer), p. 7.

B79 "Supermouse Comix: Supermouse Meets Pussa The Great!" [cartoon Christmas card]. Portland: Pendragon Press. [Privately printed.]

B80 "Tao Song." [See B23.]

1979

B81 "The Dancing at Tillai" [series of eleven poems]. <u>Kenyon Review</u>, n.s. 1 (Summer):70–79. [Contains "The Night," "Siva and Kama," "Epiphany," "Carmagnole of the Thirtieth of June," "School," "Middle," "Tale," "A Semi-Centenary Celebration," "Pasupati," "Drums," "The Dancing at Tillai."]

   In <u>Tillai And Tylissos</u>, 1980. [See B101.]
   In <u>Hard Words</u>, 1981. [See B104.]

B82 "The Night" [poem]. Included in "The Dancing at Tillai" series, p. 70. [See B81.]

   In <u>Hard Words</u>, 1981. [See B104.]

B83 "Siva and Kama" [poem]. Included in "The Dancing at Tillai" series, p. 71. [See B81.]

   In <u>Hard Words</u>, 1981. [See B104.]

B84 "Epiphany" [poem]. Included in "The Dancing at Tillai" series, p. 71. [See B81.]

   In <u>Hard Words</u>, 1981. [See B104.]

B85 "Carmagnole of the Thirtieth of June" [poem]. Included in "The Dancing at Tillai" series, pp. 72–73. [See B81.]

   In <u>Hard Words</u>, 1981. [See B104.]

B86 "School" [poem]. Included in "The Dancing at Tillai" series,
     p. 73. [See B81.]

   In Hard Words, 1981. [See B104.]

B87 "Middle" [poem]. Included in "The Dancing at Tillai" series,
     p. 74. [See B81.]

   In Hard Words, 1981. [See B104.]

B88 "Tale" [poem]. Included in "The Dancing at Tillai" series,
     p. 74. [See B81.]

   In Hard Words, 1981. [See B104.]

B89 "A Semi-Centenary Celebration" [poem]. Included in "The
     Dancing at Tillai" series, pp. 75-76. [See B81.]

   In Hard Words, 1981. [See B104.]

B90 "Pasupati" [poem]. Included in "The Dancing at Tillai" series,
     p. 77. [See B81.]

   In Hard Words, 1981. [See B104.]

B91 "Drums" [poem]. Included in "The Dancing at Tillai" series,
     p. 78. [See B81.]

   In Hard Words, 1981. [See B104.]

B92 "The Dancing at Tillai" [poem]. Included in "The Dancing at
     Tillai" series, pp. 78-79. [See B81.]

   In Hard Words, 1981. [See B104.]

B93 "Six Poems" [series of six poems]. Kenyon Review, n.s. 1
     (Fall):61-64. [Contains "The Mind Is Still," "Self,"
     "Amazed," "Wordhoard," "Simple Hill," "Vita Amicae."]

B94 "The Mind Is Still" [poem]. Included in "Six Poems" series,
     p. 61. [See B93.]

   In Hard Words, 1981. [See B104.]

B95 "Self" [poem]. Included in "Six Poems" series, p. 62. [See
     B93.]

   In Hard Words, 1981. [See B104.]

B96 "Amazed" [poem]. Included in "Six Poems" series, p. 62.
     [See B93.]

In <u>Hard Words</u>, 1981. [See B104.]

B97 "Wordhoard" [poem]. Included in "Six Poems" series, p. 63.
     [See B93.]

     In <u>Hard Words</u>, 1981. [See B104.]

B98 "Simple Hill" [poem]. Included in "Six Poems" series, p. 64.
     [See B93.]

     In <u>Hard Words</u>, 1981. [See B104.]

B99 "Vita Amicae" [poem]. Included in "Six Poems" series, p. 64.
     [See B93.]

     In <u>Hard Words</u>, 1981. [See B104.]

1980

B100 "Commentary" [two poems and discussion]. <u>Dreamworks: An
      Interdisciplinary Quarterly</u> 1 (Summer):156-57. [See C190.]

B101 <u>Tillai And Tylissos</u> [poetry collection]. St. Helena, Berkeley,
      and Portland: Red Bull Press. [Contains "The Dancing at
      Tillai," 1979 (see B81) and "The Dancing At Tylissos"--
      three poems by Theodora K. Quinn. Privately printed.]

B102 "To Siva The Unmaker" [poem on card]. Huntsville, Ark.:
      Science Fiction Poetry Association.

B103 In collaboration with: Eric Funk, Henk Pander, Judy Patton,
      Susan Sweeney, Peter West, Ric Young. <u>Omelas</u> [stage pro-
      duction]. Portland Civic Theatre and Storefront Theatre.
      Portland Civic Theatre, Portland, 3 October.

1981

B104 <u>Hard Words</u> [collection of poems]. New York: Harper & Row.
      [Contains five sections: I. WORDHOARD--"For Karl and
      Jean," "Wordhoard" (1979), "Danae 46," "The Man Who Shored
      Up Winchester Cathedral," "Invocation" (1977), "Transla-
      tion," "The Mind Is Still" (1979), "The Marrow," "Hard
      Words," "More Useful Truths," "The Writer to the Dancer";
      II. THE DANCING AT TILLAI--"The Night" (1979), "Siva and
      Kama" (1979), "Epiphany" (1979), "Carmagnole of the Thir-
      tieth of June" (1979), "School" (1979), "Middle" (1979),
      "Tale" (1979), "A Semi-Centenary Celebration" (1979),
      "Pasupati" (1979), "Drums" (1979), "The Dancing at Tillai"

(1979); III. LINE DRAWINGS--"At Three Rivers, April 80,"
"Slick Rock Creek, September," "Smith Creek," "Torrey Pines
Reserve," "Coast," "Ted with Kite," "Central Park South, 9
March 1979," "For Mishka," "Richard," "Morden Lecture,
1978," "Everest" (1977), "North," "Landscape, Figure,
Cavern," "The Journey," "Kish 29 IV 79: To the Owners,"
"Winter Downs"; IV. WALKING IN CORNWALL (1976)--"1. Chun,"
"2. Men-an-Tol, the Nine Maidens, Dingdong Mine, and
Lanyon Quoit," "3. Castle An Dinas and Chysauster Village";
V. SIMPLE HILL--"Simple Hill" (1979), "At a Quarter to
Fifty," "The Child on the Shore," "The Indian Rugs,"
"Cavaliers," We Are Dust," "The Well of Baln" ("1. Count
Baln," "2. Baln's Wife," "3. Baln's Daughter"), "Totem,"
"Amazed" (1979), "Self" (1979), "Tui," "Vita Amicae" (1979),
"Uma."]

B105 "For Karl and Jean" [poem]. In Hard Words, p. 3. [See B104.]

B106 "Danae 46" [poem]. In Hard Words, p. 5. [See B104.]

B107 "The Man Who Shored Up Winchester Cathedral" [poem]. Hard
      Words, p. 6. [See B104.]

B108 "Translation" [poem]. In Hard Words, p. 8. [See B104.]

B109 "The Marrow" [poem]. In Hard Words, p. 10. [See B104.]

B110 "Hard Words" [poem]. In Hard Words, p. 11. [See B104.]

B111 "More Useful Truths" [poem]. In Hard Words, p. 12. [See
      B104.]

B112 "The Writer to the Dancer" [poem]. In Hard Words, p. 13.
      [See B104.]

B113 "At Three Rivers, April 80" [poem]. In Hard Words, p. 33.
      [See B104.]

B114 "Slick Rock Creek, September" [poem]. In Hard Words, p. 34.
      [See B104.]

B115 "Smith Creek" [poem]. In Hard Words, p. 35. [See B104.]

B116 "Torrey Pines Reserve" [poem]. In Hard Words, p. 36. [See
      B104.]

B117 "Coast" [poem]. In Hard Words, p. 37. [See B104.]

B118 "Ted with Kite" [poem]. In Hard Words, p. 38. [See B104.]

B119 "Central Park South, 9 March 1979" [poem]. In Hard Words,

p. 39. [See B104.]

B120 "For Mishka" [poem]. In Hard Words, p. 40. [See B104.]

B121 "Richard" [poem]. In Hard Words, p. 41. [See B104.]

B122 "Morden Lecture, 1978" [poem]. In Hard Words, p. 42. [See B104.]

B123 "North" [poem]. In Hard Words, p. 45. [See B104.]

B124 "Landscape, Figure, Cavern" [poem]. In Hard Words, p. 46. [See B104.]

B125 "The Journey" [poem]. In Hard Words, p. 47. [See B104.]

B126 "Kish 29 IV 79: To the Owners" [poem]. In Hard Words, p. 48. [See B104.]

B127 "Winter Downs" [poem]. In Hard Words, p. 49. [See B104.]

B128 "At a Quarter to Fifty" [poem]. In Hard Words, p. 66. [See B104.]

B129 "The Child on the Shore" [poem]. In Hard Words, p. 67. [See B104.]

B130 "The Indian Rugs" [poem]. In Hard Words, p. 68. [See B104.]

B131 "Cavaliers" [poem]. In Hard Words, p. 69. [See B104.]

B132 "We Are Dust" [poem]. In Hard Words, p. 70. [See B104.]

B133 "The Well of Baln" [three-part poem consisting of "Count Baln," "Baln's Wife," and "Baln's Daughter"]. In Hard Words, pp. 71-73. [See B104.]

B134 "Totem" [poem]. In Hard Words, p. 74. [See B104.]

B135 "Tui" [poem]. In Hard Words, p. 77. [See B104.]

B136 "Uma" [poem]. In Hard Words, p. 79. [See B104.]

SECTION TWO: ADAPTATIONS OF AND CREATIVE
RESPONSES TO LE GUIN'S WORKS

1970

B137 KUEHLER, STEPHEN. "Earthsea" [poem]. Horn Book 46 (August): 419.

1972

B138   ANON. "Letter from Gethen." International Women's Day [book-
       let to commemorate IWD, 8 March], p. 26. [Letter purported
       to be from "Your sisters on Gethen" to "Our Sisters in
       Santa Cruz."]

1973

B139   Student drawings. "Notes on 'teaching' A Wizard of Earthsea."
       Edited by Geoff Fox. [See D137; contains five drawings and
       references to games, drama, music done by schoolchildren.]

B140   BARBOUR, DOUGLAS. "Song 96: For Ursula K. Le Guin and Joanna
       Russ." In Songbook. Vancouver: Talonbooks, n.p. [paper].

1975

B141   BUCKLEY, KATHY, and GERRAND, ROB. "Pegasus" [poem]. SF Com-
       mentary, nos. 44/45 (December), p. 11. [Poetic response
       to Le Guin's writer's workshop held in Australia, August
       1975.]

1976

B142   WEISER, NORMAN, adapt. The Tombs of Atuan. New York: Newbery
       Award Records, Inc. [A filmstrip and two cassettes; direct-
       ed by Leslie Corn; narrated by Andrew Jarkowsky; cast in-
       cludes Jane Anderson, William Griffis, Richard Pilcher, and
       Catherine Wolf. Teaching notes by Eleanor Kulleseid; see
       D339.]

1977

B143   SCHWANTNER, JOSEPH. "Wild Angels of the Open Hills" [music].
       [Premier performance 2 February 1978; by the Jubal Trio,
       New York. Favorably reviewed by Donal Henahan, the New
       York Times; see D474. For program notes, see D495.]

1978

B144   RIBBLER, EILEEN, and SPENCER, KATHLEEN, dirs. The New At-
       lantis. Wright State University, Dayton, Ohio. [Month and
       day not known. Probably a reading rather than a stage pro-
       duction. Program divides cast into two groups: Portlanders

and Atlantis voices.]

1979

B145   BARLOWE, WAYNE DOUGLAS, and SUMMERS, IAN. "Athshean" [draw-
       ing]. In Barlowe's Guide To Extraterrestrials. New York:
       Workman, pp. 16-17. [Full-page, color illustration of one
       of the natives from "The Word for World is Forest," accom-
       panied by a description of their physical characteristics,
       habitat, and culture.]

1980

B146   The Lathe of Heaven. Writers Roger Swaybill and Diane English.
       Executive Producer David Loxton. Directors David Loxton
       and Fred Barzyk. New York: Television Laboratory at
       WNET/13. PBS, 9 January. [Le Guin listed as Creative Con-
       sultant.]

B147   Omelas. [See B103.]

Part C: Nonfiction

C1 "The Metaphor of the Rose as an Illustration of the 'Carpe Diem' theme in French and Italian Poetry of the Renaissance." Senior thesis, Radcliffe College. [Title page reads: Thesis submitted in partial fulfillment of the requirements for the degree of A.B. with honour in the Department of Romance Languages and Literature, Harvard University, 9 April.]

C2 "Aspects of Death in Ronsard's Poetry." Master's thesis, Columbia University. [Title page reads: Submitted in partial fulfillment of the requirements for the degree of Master of Arts in the Faculty of Philosophy, Columbia University, April.]

C3 Review of Jean Lemaire de Belges: Le Temple d'honneur et de vertus, edited by Henri Hornik. Romanic Review 49 (October): 210-11.

C4 Letter to Damon Knight. SFWA Bulletin 2 (January):6. [Praises the Bulletin, complains of the exclusion of fantasy from the SFWA awards, laments the shrinking sf magazine market.]

Part C: Nonfiction

1967

C5   Letter to editor. Australian Science Fiction Review [fanzine],
      no. 12 (October), pp. 43-44. [Response to five reviews of
      her work; see D3-7.]

1968

C6   Letter to editor. Australian Science Fiction Review [fanzine],
      no. 17 (September), pp. 35-36. [Report on West Coast
      Nebula Awards Banquet, Summer.]

1969

*C7   Letter to editor. New Millennial Harbinger, no. 4 (January),
      p. 11. [Cited in Bittner; see D532.]

C8   Comment. Playboy 16 (November):3. [Editors quote one state-
      ment; issue includes "Nine Lives."]

1970

C9   Letter. Science Fiction Review [fanzine], no. 35 (February),
      pp. 48-49. [Objects to statement that praises her at ex-
      pense of Disch and Delany.]

C10   Contribution to panel on "Science Fiction and the Literary
      Scene." In Between Worlds. Proceedings of the Day Program
      and Nebula Awards Banquet, 14 March, Berkeley. Mimeo-
      graphed. Philadelphia: Terminus, Owslick, and Ft. Mudge
      Electric Street Railway Gazette, pp. 23, 25, 27, 28, 29,
      30, 31, 34.

C11   Review of Enchantress From The Stars, by Sylvia Louise Engdahl.
      New York Times Book Review, 3 May, pp. 22-23.

      Carolyn Riley, ed. Children's Literature Review. Vol. 2.
      Detroit: Gale Research Co., 1976. [Excerpt.]

C12   "Meet Ursula: She can shape you a universe." Clifford E.
      Landers, interviewer. Northwest Magazine (Sunday supple-
      ment to the Portland Oregonian) (26 July), pp. 8-10.

C13   "Prophets and Mirrors: Science Fiction as a Way of Seeing"
      [essay]. Living Light 7 (Fall):111-21.

*C14 Letter. Renaissance [fanzine] 2, no. 4:14. [Cited in Levin;
      see D573.]

Part C: Nonfiction

C15 Letter to Ted White. <u>Amazing</u> 44 (November):133. [Response to his reviews; see D25 and D43. Distinguishes between writing for adults and for teenagers.]

C16 Letter to Richard Geis. <u>Science Fiction Review</u> [fanzine], no. 41 (November), p. 51. [Criticizes comment that she does not write like a woman.]

C17 Letter to Jeffrey D. Smith. <u>Phantasmicom</u> [fanzine], no. 2 (Winter), p. 51. [Response to two reviews; see D37.]

C18 Letter to Alfred Kroeber. In <u>Alfred Kroeber: A Personal Configuration</u>, by Theodora Kroeber. Berkeley: University of California Press, p. 262.

1971

C19 Review of <u>Earth Times Two</u>, by Pamela Reynolds. <u>New York Times Book Review</u>, 21 February, p. 22.

C20 "Bems Scarce at Hibited Get-Together." Jacques Khouri, interviewer. <u>Vancouver Sun</u>, 10 April, p. 8. [Le Guin in Vancouver as convention guest of honor; see C31 for her speech.]

C21 "The View In" [essay]. <u>Scythrop</u> [Australian fanzine], no. 22 (April), pp. 1-3.

    *<u>Philosophical Gas</u> [fanzine], no. 25 (Spring), pp. 10, 13-14. [Cited in Levin; see D573.]
    Cy Chauvin, ed. <u>A Multitude of Visions</u>. Baltimore, Md.: T-K Graphics, 1975 [paper].

C22 Letter. <u>SF Commentary</u> [Australian fanzine], no. 20 (April), pp. 43-44. [Response to issue no. 17 which contained a Philip K. Dick letter with the editor's comment.]

*C23 "Le Guin I." Mike Bailey, interviewer. <u>Entropy Negative</u> [fanzine], no. 3, pp. 17-22. [Cited in Levin; see D573.]

*C24 "Le Guin II." Daniel Say, questionnaire. <u>Entropy Negative</u> [fanzine], no. 3, pp. 23-26. [Cited in Levin; see D573.]

C25 "Ursula K. Le Guin" [interview]. <u>Colloquy</u> 4 (May):7.

C26 Letter. <u>SF Commentary</u> [Australian fanzine], no. 23 (September), pp. 5-6. [Response to issues no. 19 and 20.]

*C27 Letter. <u>Entropy Negative</u> [fanzine], no. 4 (October), p. 39. [Cited in Levin; see D573.]

C28 "The Lionization of Ursula K. Le Guin." Susan Stanley Wolk,
     interviewer. Review Magazine (Portland State University),
     pp. 17, 145-54.

                              1972

C29 Response to "Speculative Fiction: Out of the Ghetto," by
     Harlan Ellison. 1972 Writer's Yearbook, no. 43, p. 33.
     [Issue includes Ellison's article and brief responses by
     six authors.]

C30 "Ursula Le Guin: What's Wrong with our New Left is We're
     Trying to Work Through the Existing Power Structure."
     Daniel Yost, interviewer. Northwest Magazine (Sunday sup-
     plement to the Portland Oregonian) 13 February, p. 8.

C31 "The Crab Nebula, the Paramecium, and Tolstoy." Riverside
     Quarterly 5 (February):89-96. [Guest of honor speech,
     Vancouver science fiction convention, February 1971. See
     interview, C20.]

C32 Letter. SF Commentary [Australian fanzine], no. 26 (April),
     pp. 90-93. [Response to review/article by Stanislaw Lem,
     "Lost Opportunities"; see D59.]

     Pamela Sargent, ed. Women of Wonder. New York: Vintage,
        1975.

*C33 Letter. Philosophical Gas [fanzine], no. 13 (June), pp. 12-
     13. [Cited in Levin; see D573.]

C34 "Invasion of Creature from Feminist World." Mary Knoblauch,
     interviewer. Chicago Today (2 July), p. 55.

C35 "The Book Bin: How To Write Science Fiction." Larry Rumley,
     interviewer. Seattle Times, 6 August, p. D4.

*C36 "Thea and I." Entropy Negative, no. 5, pp. 37-38. [Cited in
     Levin; see D573.]

C37 "'Teen Passions' Motivate Author Here." Helen L. Mershon,
     interviewer. Oregon Journal, 8 September, sect. 2, p. 1.

C38 "Fifteen Vultures, The Strop, and the Old Lady" [essay]. In
     Clarion II: An Anthology of Speculative Fiction and Criti-
     cism. Edited by Robin Scott Wilson. New York: New Amer-
     ican Library, pp. 48-50 [paper].

     In The Language of The Night, 1979. [See C175; excerpt.]

C39 Afterword to "The Word for World is Forest." In Again,
     Dangerous Visions I. Edited by Harlan Ellison. New York:
     Doubleday, p. 126.

                              34

C40 Untitled essay. In <u>Ursula K. Le Guin</u>. New York: Atheneum.
    [A promotional pamphlet with photo and autobiographical
    essay.]

                              1973

C41 "Pink Mists in Oregon." Denis Bethell, interviewer. <u>Times</u>
    <u>Educational Supplement</u>, 11 February.

C42 "The Book Bites Back Is Topic At Library By Ursula K. Le Guin."
    <u>Lake Oswego Review</u> (12 April). [Quotations from her pre-
    sentation and her answers to audience's questions, 5 April.]

C43 "National Book Award Acceptance Speech." <u>Locus</u>, no. 140 (28
    April), p. 3. [Accompanied by letter; see C46. Originally
    given at Lincoln Center, New York, 12 April. Speech re-
    leased without copyright.]

      <u>Fantasiae</u> 1 (May 1973).
      As "In Defense of Fantasy." <u>Horn Book</u> 49 (June 1973).
        [Excerpt.]
      <u>Top of the News</u> 29 (June 1973). [Excerpt within article;
        see D157.]
      <u>Writer</u> (July 1973). [Excerpt.]
      <u>SFWA Bulletin</u> 9, whole nos. 47-48 (Summer 1973).
      <u>Signal 12</u> (September 1973). [Excerpt.]
      <u>Algol</u> [fanzine], no. 21 (November 1973).
      Damon Knight, ed. <u>Orbit 14</u>. New York: Harper & Row,
        1974. [Excerpt. Book includes "The Stars Below."]
      <u>Philosophical Gas</u> [fanzine], no. 26 (Summer 1974).
      In <u>Dreams Must Explain Themselves</u>, 1975. [See C92.]
      As "In Defense of Fantasy." Paul Heins, ed. <u>Crosscurrents</u>
        <u>of Criticism: Horn Book Essays 1968-1977</u>. Boston:
        Horn Book, 1977. [Excerpt.]
      In <u>The Language of The Night</u>, 1979. [See C175.]

C44 "Author Broke into Print by Writing Out of This World"
    [interview]. Portland <u>Oregonian</u>, 16 April, sect. 2, p. 8.

C45 "McLuhan, Youth and Literature: Part I" [letter]. <u>Horn Book</u>
    49 (April):99. [Response to an article by Eleanor Cameron,
    "McLuhan, Youth, and Literature," <u>Horn Book</u> 48 (October
    1972).]

C46 Letter. <u>Locus</u>, no. 140 (28 April), p. 3. [Accompanies her
    NBA Speech which she regards as her chance to speak for the
    science fiction community.]

C47 "On Norman Spinrad's <u>The Iron Dream</u>" [review]. <u>Science-</u>
    <u>Fiction Studies</u> 1 (Spring):41-44.

Part C: Nonfiction

R.D. Mullen and Darko Suvin, eds. <u>Science-Fiction Studies,</u>
<u>Selected Articles on Science Fiction 1973-1975.</u> Boston:
Gregg Press, 1976.

C48 "In Defense of Fantasy." [See C43.]

C49 <u>From Elfland to Poughkeepsie</u> [essay]. Portland: Pendragon
Press. [According to Lloyd W. Currey (see D541) issued as
26 copies hardbound and autographed by author, McIntyre,
and photographer; 100 copies bound in wrappers and autographed; 650 copies bound in wrappers. Includes introduction by Vonda McIntyre; see D148.]

Damon Knight, ed. <u>Orbit 15.</u> New York: Harper & Row,
1974. [Two-paragraph excerpt.]
In <u>The Language of The Night</u>, 1979. [See C175.]

C50 "A Citizen of Mondath: The Development of a Science Fiction
Writer: IV." <u>Foundation</u> 4 (July):20-24. [A significant
autobiographical essay.]
In <u>The Language of The Night</u>, 1979. [See C175.]

C51 Comment in "Arcs and Secants." In <u>Orbit 12.</u> Edited by Damon
Knight. New York: Putnam's, pp. 248-49. [Book includes
"Direction of The Road."]

C52 "On Theme" [essay]. In <u>Those Who Can: A Science Fiction</u>
<u>Reader.</u> Edited by Robin Scott Wilson. New York: New
American Library, pp. 203-9. [Accompanies "Nine Lives,"
1969.]

C53 "Dreams Must Explain Themselves" [essay]. <u>Algol</u> [fanzine],
no. 21 (November), pp. 7-10, 12, 14. [Significant essay on
genesis of the Earthsea trilogy. Issue contains other
Le Guin material; see A6, C43, C54, D130, and D147.]

In <u>Dreams Must Explain Themselves</u>, 1975. [See C92.]
<u>Signal 19</u> (UK), January 1976.
In <u>The Language of The Night</u>, 1979. [See C175.]

C54 "From an Interview: Jonathan Ward." Jonathan Ward, interviewer. <u>Algol</u> [fanzine], no. 21 (November), p. 24. [Inter-
view taped in New York after the National Book Awards, 12
April.]

As "Ursula K. Le Guin." <u>Algol</u> [fanzine] 12 (Summer 1975).
[Fuller text of the interview.]
As "Interview With Ursula K. Le Guin." In <u>Dreams Must Ex-</u>
<u>plain Themselves</u>, 1975. [See C92.]

C55 Comment. <u>Edge</u> 5/6 (Autumn/Winter):112. [Accompanies her
translation of Italian novel; see B21.]

Part C: Nonfiction

C56   "Surveying the Battlefield" [essay]. Science-Fiction Studies
      1 (Fall):88-90. [Response to Blish-Rottensteiner exchange
      on Marxism in same issue.]

       R.D. Mullen and Dark Suvin, eds. Science-Fiction Studies:
         Selected Articles on Science Fiction 1973-1975. Boston:
         Gregg Press, 1976.

C57   Letter. BCSFA Newsletter [fanzine], no. 6 (December), p. 3.

C58   "The Ursula Major Construct; Or, A Far Greater Horror Loomed"
      [essay]. In Clarion III. Edited by Robin Scott Wilson.
      New York: New American Library, pp. 32-37.

1974

C59   Letter. SF Echo [fanzine], no. 19 (January), pp. 123-24.
      [Response to a review (see D127) and an article.]

*C60   Letter. BCSFA Newsletter [fanzine], no. 8 (February), p. 4.
      [Cited in Levin; see D573.]

C61   "European SF: Rottensteiner's Anthology, the Strugatskys, and
      Lem." Science-Fiction Studies 1 (Spring):181-85. [Review
      of View From Another Shore, edited by Franz Rottensteiner;
      Hard to Be a God, by Arkady and Boris Strugatsky; The In-
      vincible, by Stanislaw Lem.]

C62   "The Staring Eye" [essay]. Vector 67-68 [British fanzine]
      (Spring), pp. 5-7. [One of three articles on Tolkien under
      the general title, "Three Views of Tolkien," pp. 5-15.]

       In The Language of The Night, 1979. [See C175.]

C63   "No, Virginia, There is not a Santa Claus." Foundation 6
      (May):109-12. [Review of Red Shift, by Alan Garner.]

C64   Comment in "Arcs & Secants." In Orbit 14. Edited by Damon
      Knight. New York: Putnam's, p. 209. [Book includes "The
      Stars Below."]

C65   "Science Fiction Writer Ursula Le Guin: 'It's all pigeon-
      holes.'" Richard Ramella, interviewer. Berkeley Paper
      (August).

C66   "Science Fiction Tomorrow." Christian Science Monitor, 8 July,
      p. 13. [One of a series of articles by various authors
      under the general title, "Exploring the future."]

C67   "She Writes about Aliens--Men Included." Paula Brookmire, interviewer. Milwaukee Journal, 21 July, part 6, p. 3.

Biography News 1 (October 1974).
Barbara Nykoruk, ed. Authors In The News. Vol. 1.
    Detroit: Gale Research Co., 1976.

*C68 Letter to editor. Son of Machiavelli, no. 13 (July). [Cited in Bittner; see D532.]

C69 Comment. Galaxy 35 (August):2. [Single statement in table of contents on "The Day Before the Revolution."]

C70 "Ursula Le Guin." Roger Scafford, interviewer. Prism (Oregon State University) (Fall), pp. 11-13.

C71 "SSF Interviews Ursula K. Le Guin." James Cowan, interviewer. UWM Union SSF (University of Wisconsin-Milwaukee) 3 (Fall): 31-40. [Conducted at 1974 SFRA Annual Conference.]

C72 Letter. SF Echo [fanzine], no. 21 (November), pp. 132-33.

C73 "Why Are Americans Afraid of Dragons?" [essay]. Pacific Northwest Library Association Quarterly 38 (Winter):14-18. [Originally a speech at the PNLA Conference, Portland, 21-24 August.]

As "The Fear of Dragons." Edward Blishen, ed. The Thorny Paradise: Writers on Writing for Children. Harmondsworth: Kestrel Books, 1975.
In The Language of The Night, 1979. [See C175.]
Literary Cavalcade 33 (February 1981).

*C74 Letter. Gonzo, no. 18 (December), p. 4. [Cited in Levin; see D573. Probably a fanzine.]

C75 "Vertex Interviews Ursula K. Le Guin." Gene Van Toyer, interviewer. Vertex 2 (December):34-39, 92, 96-97.

C76 "Science Fiction and the Future of Anarchy: Conversations with Ursula K. Le Guin." Charles Bigelow, J. McMahon, interviewer. Portland Oregon Times 4 (December):24-29.

C77 "Escape Routes" [essay]. Galaxy 35 (December):40-44. [Subsequent issues include reply by Lester del Rey (see D233) and Le Guin's answer (see C88).]

Antaeus, nos. 25/26 (Spring/Summer 1977). [Also reprints del Rey's reply.]
In The Language of The Night, 1979. [See C175.]

C78 Program notes on Asimov's "Nightfall." Program for planetarium

show, "Nightfall." Portland, Ore.: Harry C. Kendall
Planetarium, Oregon Museum of Science and Industry.
[Le Guin's notes are excerpted from her introduction given
at the planetarium show. See B26.]

1975

C79 Letter. Women and Men (WAM!) [fanzine], no. 4 (February 1),
    p. 4. [Response to previous issue.]

C80 Letter to Richard Geis, editor. Science Fiction Review
    [fanzine] 4, whole no. 12 (February):29-30. [Response to
    Geis's review of The Dispossessed in the previous issue;
    see D178.]

C81 "SF in a Political-Science Textbook." Science-Fiction Studies
    2 (March):93-94. [Review of Political Science Fiction: An
    Introductory Reader, edited by Martin Harry Greenberg and
    Patricia S. Warrick.]

C82 "The Child and the Shadow" [essay]. Quarterly Journal of The
    Library of Congress 32 (April):139-48. [Originally a lec-
    ture, Library of Congress, 11 November 1974.]

    John Donovan, "American Dispatch." Signal 18 (UK)
        (September 1975). [Excerpt.]
    In The Language of The Night, 1979. [See C175.]

C83 "Ursula Le Guin interview: Tricks, Anthropology Create New
    Worlds." Barry Barth, interviewer. Portland Scribe 4
    (17-25 May):8-9.

    As "Ursula Le Guin: An Interview." Women and Men (WAM!)
        [fanzine] 2 (October 1980).

C84 "Galaxy of Awards for Ursula Le Guin." Anthony Wolk and Susan
    Stanley Wolk, interviewers. Willamette Week, 30 June,
    p. 11.

C85 "Ursula K. Le Guin." [See C54.]

C86 "Ketterer on The Left Hand of Darkness." Science-Fiction
    Studies 2 (July):137-39. [Originally a paper given in a
    forum on David Ketterer's New Worlds for Old, Science Fic-
    tion Research Association conference, Milwaukee, Wisc.,
    June. For the complete forum, see D262 and D326.]

C87 "Envoy From Planet Gethen & Other Strange Worlds." Robert
    Feldman, interviewer. Australian Women's Weekly, 16 July,
    p. 7.

C88   Letter to James Baen, editor. <u>Galaxy</u> 36 (August):157.
        [Answer to Lester del Rey's reply to her earlier essay;
        see D233 and C77.]

C89   "At the Sci-Fi Summit." Helen Frizell, interviewer. <u>Sydney</u>
        <u>Morning Herald</u> (Australia), 21 August, p. 7.

C90   "Ursula K. Le Guin" [interview]. <u>Get Out</u> [fanzine], no. 18
        (September), p. 7.

C91   Letter. <u>The Witch and the Chameleon</u> [fanzine], no. 4 (Septem-
        ber), pp. 25-26. [Response to feminist concerns in two
        previous issues.]

C92   <u>Dreams Must Explain Themselves</u>. [Compiled by Andrew Porter.]
        New York: Algol Press [paper]. ["Dreams Must Explain
        Themselves," 1973; "The Rule of Names," 1964; "National
        Book Award Acceptance Speech," 1973; "Interview with Ursula
        K. Le Guin," 1975.] [See D153.]

C93   "Interview With Ursula K. Le Guin." [See C54.]

C94   "Foreword." In <u>The Wind's Twelve Quarters</u>, pp. vii-viii.
        [See A41.]

C95   Headnote. "Semley's Necklace." In <u>The Wind's Twelve Quarters</u>,
        p. 1. [See A41.]

C96   Headnote. "April in Paris." In <u>The Wind's Twelve Quarters</u>,
        p. 25. [See A41.]

C97   Headnote. "The Masters." In <u>The Wind's Twelve Quarters</u>,
        p. 40. [See A41.]

C98   Headnote. "Darkness Box." In <u>The Wind's Twelve Quarters</u>,
        p. 60. [See A41.]

C99   Headnote. "The Word of Unbinding." In <u>The Wind's Twelve</u>
        <u>Quarters</u>, p. 71. [See A41.]

C100   Headnote. "Winter's King." In <u>The Wind's Twelve Quarters</u>,
        p. 93. [See A41.]

C101   Headnote. "The Good Trip." In <u>The Wind's Twelve Quarters</u>,
        p. 118. [See A41.]

C102   Headnote. "Nine Lives." In <u>The Wind's Twelve Quarters</u>, pp.
        129-30. [See A41.]

C103   Headnote. "Things." In <u>The Wind's Twelve Quarters</u>, p. 161.
        [See A41.]

Part C: Nonfiction

C104 Headnote. "A Trip to the Head." In The Wind's Twelve
      Quarters, p. 173. [See A41.]

C105 Headnote. "Vaster Than Empires and More Slow." In The Wind's
      Twelve Quarters, p. 181. [See A41.]

C106 Headnote. "The Stars Below." In The Wind's Twelve Quarters,
      pp. 218-19. [See A41.]

C107 Headnote. "The Field of Vision." In The Wind's Twelve
      Quarters, p. 242. [See A41.]

C108 Headnote. "Direction of the Road." In The Wind's Twelve
      Quarters, p. 267. [See A41.]

C109 Headnote. "The Ones Who Walk Away From Omelas." In The Wind's
      Twelve Quarters, p. 275. [See A41.]

C110 Headnote. "The Day Before the Revolution." In The Wind's
      Twelve Quarters, p. 285. [See A41.]

C111 "American SF and The Other" [essay]. Science-Fiction Studies
      2 (November):208-10. [Originally a speech at Bellingham,
      Wash., 1974. This is the special Le Guin issue; see D279.
      Following issue contains a response to Le Guin's essay (see
      D324) and Le Guin's answer (see C122).]

      R.D. Mullen and Darko Suvin, eds. Science-Fiction Studies:
        Selected Articles on Science Fiction 1973-1975. Boston:
        Gregg Press, 1976.
      As "Science Fiction Chauvinism." Ariel: The Book of
        Fantasy. Vol. 2. Kansas City: Morning Star Press;
        Distributed by Ballantine Press, New York, 1977.
      In The Language of The Night, 1979. [See C175.]

C112 Symposium contribution. In "Women in Science Fiction: A
      Symposium." Edited by Jeffrey D. Smith. Khatru [fanzine],
      nos. 3-4 (November), pp. 5, 10, 16, 77, 90, 111. [Symposium
      of eleven authors, conducted by letters from 9 October 1974,
      to 8 May 1975.]

C113 "The Stone Ax and the Muskoxen" [essay]. Vector 71 2 (Decem-
      ber):5-13. [Originally a guest of honor speech at the 33rd
      World Science Fiction Convention, Melbourne, Australia,
      August 1975. Following issue contains several letter re-
      sponses.]

      Convention Journal 1. Cherry Hill, N.J.: Worldcon, 1976.
        [Official convention book of Suncon, 35th World Science
        Fiction Convention.]
      In The Language of The Night, 1979. [See C175.]

Part C: Nonfiction

C114 "The Fear of Dragons." [See C73.]

C115 Afterword. "Mazes." In _Epoch_. Edited by Roger Elwood and
      Robert Silverberg. New York: Berkley, p. 88.

1976

C116 "Future Tense." Phillip Oakes, interviewer. _Sunday Times_
      (UK), 29 February.

C117 Introduction to _The Altered I: An Encounter with Science Fic-_
      tion by Ursula K. Le Guin and Others. Edited by Lee
      Harding. Carlton, Victoria (Australia): Norstrilia Press,
      pp. 4-10.

         Lee Harding, ed. _The Altered I_. New York: Berkley Wind-
            hover, 1978.
         In _The Language of The Night_, 1979. [See C175.]

C118 "The Transglobal Workshop." In _The Altered I: An Encounter_
      with Science Fiction by Ursula K. Le Guin and Others.
      Edited by Lee Harding. Carlton, Victoria (Australia):
      Norstrilia Press, pp. 107-30. [Consists of Le Guin's
      introduction, Le Guin's story, "The Eye Altering," edited
      transcript of thirteen writers criticizing the story, and
      Le Guin's written response to their criticisms.]

         Lee Harding, ed. _The Altered I_. New York: Berkley Wind-
            hover, 1978.

C119 "A note about names. . . ." [Headnote to "The Rule of Names,"
      1964]. _Puffin Post_ 10, no. 2:5.

C120 "Ursula K. Le Guin: An Interview." Paul Walker, interviewer.
      Luna Monthly, no. 63 (March), pp. 1-7.

         Speaking of Science Fiction: The Paul Walker Interviews.
            Oradell, N.J.: Luna Publications, 1978.

C121 "A Response to the Le Guin Issue (SFS #7)." _Science-Fiction_
      Studies 3 (March):43-46. [See D279.]

         R.D. Mullen and Darko Suvin, eds. _Science-Fiction Studies:_
            Selected Articles on Science Fiction 1976-1977. Boston:
            Gregg Press, 1978.

C122 "In Response to Mr. Eisenstein" [note]. _Science-Fiction_
      Studies 3 (March):98. [See C111.]

C123 "New England Gothic." _Times Literary Supplement_, 26 March,

Part C: Nonfiction

p. 335. [Review of Lovecraft, by L. Sprague de Camp.]

C124 Review of The Cyberiad and The Futurological Congress, by
Stanislaw Lem. Vector 7³/4 3 (March):5-6.

C125 "Ursula Le Guin: The Soft Science Factor" [interview].
Street Life (London) 1 (April 17-30):14-16.

C126 Letter to Denys Howard. Women and Men (WAM!) [fanzine], no. 6
(May), pp. 3-4. [Response to Howard's letter in SF Review
(see D243) on homosexuality in The Dispossessed; followed
by Howard's reply (see D333).]

C127 "Is Gender Necessary?" [essay]. In Aurora: Beyond Equality.
Edited by Vonda N. McIntyre and Susan Janice Anderson.
Greenwich, Conn.: Fawcett, pp. 130-39 [paper].

In The Language of The Night, 1979. [See C175.]

C128 "All about Anne." Times Literary Supplement, 4 June, pp. 676-
77. [Review of The Wheel of Things: A Biography of L.M.
Montgomery, by Mollie Gillen.]

C129 Questionnaire responses. "The Writer and SF," by Barbara A.
Bannon. Publishers Weekly 209 (14 June):47, 48. [See D305.]

C130 "You Wouldn't Like Oregon." Foundation 10 (June):80-82.
[Review of Mrs. Frisby and the Rats of NIMH and Z for
Zachariah, by Robert C. O'Brien.]

C131 "Out of the Ice Age." Times Literary Supplement, 30 July,
p. 950. [Review of The Stochastic Man, by Robert
Silverberg; The Status Civilization, by Robert Sheckley;
The Space Machine, by Christopher Priest; Eye Among the
Blind, by Robert Holdstock.]

C132 Introduction to The Left Hand of Darkness. New York: Ace,
pp. xi-xvi.

In The Language of The Night, 1979. [See C175.]
In The Left Hand of Darkness. New York: Harper & Row,
1980.

C133 Letter. Maya 11 (July), pp. 12-13. [Response to an editorial
in Maya 9.]

C134 "Announcing the First Annual O'Melas Fill-In Contest."
O'Melas [fanzine] 1 (July):15. [Her response to "The
Greatest Stories Never Told Department."]

C135 "The Space Crone" [essay]. The CoEvolution Quarterly 10

(Summer):108–11.

As "On Menopause: The Space Crone." <u>Medical Self–Care</u> 2
    (Spring):1977.

C136 "Science Fiction and Mrs. Brown" [essay]. In <u>Science Fiction
    At Large</u>. Edited by Peter Nicholls. London: Gollancz,
    pp. 13–33. [Originally a lecture at the Institute of Con-
    temporary Arts in London, January 1975. See Parrinder's
    critical response, D593.]

    In <u>The Language of The Night</u>, 1979. [See C175.]

C137 "Myth and Archetype in Science Fiction" [essay]. <u>Parabola</u> 1
    (Fall):42–47.

    In <u>The Language of The Night</u>, 1979. [See C175.]
    Harold Schechter and Jonna Gormely Semeiks, eds. <u>Patterns
      in Popular Culture: A Sourcebook for Writers</u>. New York:
      Harper & Row, 1980. [Book also includes excerpt from <u>A
      Wizard of Earthsea</u>, 1968.]

C138 Comment [record jacket]. <u>"The Ones Who Walk Away From Omelas"
    as read by the author.</u> [One–sentence comment on each of
    the three stories; see B65.]

C139 "Science Fiction as Prophesy: Philip K. Dick" [essay]. <u>New
    Republic</u> 30 October:33–34. [Issue includes D359.]

    As "The Modest One." In <u>The Language of The Night</u>, 1979.
    [See C175. Le Guin's preferred title.]

C140 "Fantasy, Like Poetry, Speaks The Language of the Night"
    [essay]. <u>This World</u> (Sunday supplement to the <u>San Fran-
    cisco Examiner and Chronicle</u>), 21 November, p. 41.

    As "The Language of the Night." In <u>The Language of The
    Night</u>, 1979. [See C175; excerpt. Le Guin's preferred
    title.]

C141 Introduction to <u>Nebula Award Stories 11</u>, pp. 9–12. [See A65.]

                            1977

*C142 Review of <u>Watership Down</u>, by Richard Adams. <u>Hedgehog</u>, no. 1,
    pp. 22–23. [Cited in Levin; see D573. Probably a fanzine.]

    Damon Knight, ed. <u>Orbit 20</u>. New York: Harper & Row,
      1978. [Excerpt.]

Part C: Nonfiction

C143 Review of Close Encounters of the Third Kind and Star Wars.
Parabola 3 no. 1:92–94.

As "Noise and Meaning in SF Films." Future 1 (August 1978).

C144 "Open letter to the SFWA Bulletin and/or Forum and to Locus."
Locus 10 (March):5, 12. [Explains why she withdrew "The
Diary of a Rose" from the Nebula balloting. Letter did not
appear in the Bulletin.]

C145 "A Review." Science-Fiction Studies 4 (March):64. Review of
The Best from the Rest of the World, edited by Donald A.
Wollheim.

C146 "Concerning the 'Lem Affair'" [note]. Science-Fiction Studies
4 (March):100.

SFWA Bulletin 12, whole no. 62 (March 1977).

C147 "Creating Realistic Utopias: 'the obvious trouble with anarchism is neighbors.'" Win McCormack and Anne Mendel,
interviewers. Seven Days 1 (11 April):38–40. [Issue also
includes review; see D384.]

C148 Review of The Dark Tower and Other Stories, by C.S. Lewis.
New Republic (16 April), pp. 29–30.

C149 "'Real women' in Fantasies." Susan Stanley Wolk, interviewer.
Oregon Journal, 28 April, p. 21. [Interview/article with
Le Guin and Vonda McIntyre.]

C150 "On Menopause: The Space Crone." [See C135.]

C151 "Interview with Ursula K. Le Guin." Karen McPherson, Peter
Jensen, Alison Halderman, David Zelter, Karen Kramer,
interviewers. 10 Point 5 (Eugene, Ore.), no. 5 (Spring),
pp. 10–15. [Contains material not in previous interviews.]

C152 "Introduction to the 1977 Edition." In Rocannon's World. New
York: Harper & Row, pp. v–ix.

In The Language of The Night, 1979. [See C175.]

C153 "Fiction Writer Le Guin: Portrait of the Artist. . . ." Alan
Russell, interviewer. Triton Times (University of California, San Diego), 27 May, pp. 1–2.

C154 Letter to George Turner. SF Commentary, no. 52 (June), p. 21.

C155 "Do-It-Yourself Cosmology" [essay]. Parabola 2, no. 3:14–17.

45

Part C: Nonfiction

In <u>The Language of The Night</u>, 1979. [See C175.]

C156 "A New Book by the Strugatskys." <u>Science-Fiction Studies</u> 4
(July):157-59. Review of <u>Roadside Picnic and Tale of the
Troika</u>, by Arkady and Boris Strugatsky.

C157 "The not-so-science fiction of Ursula Le Guin." M.G.
Horowitz, interviewer. <u>Downtowner</u> (29 August), pp. 10-11.

C158 Liner notes. On "<u>Gwilan's Harp</u>" and "<u>Intracom</u>": <u>Read
by the author.</u> [See B74. Humorous essay on the experience
of making a record.]

C159 "Science Fiction Chauvinism." [See C111.]

C160 "Author's Introduction." In <u>The Word for World is Forest</u>.
London: Gollancz, pp. 5-10.

In <u>The Language of The Night</u>, 1979. [See C175.]

C161 "In Defense of Fantasy." [See C43.]

C162 "The Stalin In The Soul" [essay]. In <u>The Future Now: Saving
Tomorrow</u>. Edited by Robert Hoskins. Greenwich, Conn.:
Fawcett, pp. 11-21. [Originally a lecture given at Clarion
West Workshop, University of Washington, July 1973.]

In <u>The Language of The Night</u>, 1979. [See C175.]

C163 "Books Remembered" [essay]. <u>Calendar</u> 36 (November-June):n.p.
[Issue dated 1977-1978.]

In <u>The Language of The Night</u>, 1979. [See C175; excerpt.]

1978

C164 Introduction to <u>Star Songs of an Old Primate</u>, by James Tiptree,
Jr. New York: Ballantine, pp. vii-xii [paper].

In <u>The Language of The Night</u>, 1979. [See C175.]

C165 "Introduction to the 1978 Edition." In <u>Planet of Exile</u>. New
York: Harper & Row, pp. vii-xiii.

In <u>The Language of The Night</u>, 1979. [See C175.]

C166 "To Philip K. Dick" [letter]. <u>Science Fiction Review</u> 7
(February):79. [Response to Dick letter in same issue
clarifying that Lem's Polish publisher has not paid her for
<u>A Wizard of Earthsea</u>.]

Part C: Nonfiction

C167   "An Interview With Ursula K. Le Guin." Mark P. Haselkorn, interviewer. <u>Science Fiction Review</u> 7 (May):72-74.

C168   Introduction to <u>City of Illusions</u>. New York: Harper & Row, pp. v-viii.

      In <u>The Language of The Night</u>, 1979. [See C175.]

C169   "Interview: Ursula K. Le Guin." Dorothy Gilbert, interviewer. <u>California Quarterly</u>, nos. 13/14 (Spring/Summer), pp. 38-55.

C170   "Noise and Meaning in SF Films." [See C143.]

C171   Symposium presentation in "The Creative Spirit and Children's Literature: A Symposium," edited by Mae Durham Roger. <u>Wilson Library Bulletin</u> 53 (October):166-69. [Transcription of talks given at the annual symposium on children's literature, University of California-Berkeley, 11-15 July, 1977.]

C172   Letter. <u>Wilson Library Bulletin</u> 53 (November):219. [Corrects editor's comment in previous issue (see C171) that Le Guin would no longer write for children.]

C173   Symposium contribution in "SF in 2001: A Symposium," edited by Alan Sandercock. <u>Auto Dilirium</u> [Australian fanzine], pp. 16-17. [Symposium conducted by mail in 1971; eight authors were sent two questions each.]

1979

C174   "Le Guin Word Tapestries Defy Labels." Melody Ward, interviewer. <u>Oregon Daily Emerald</u> (Eugene), 31 January, p. 1. [Issue also contains article; see D511.]

C175   <u>The Language of The Night: Essays on Fantasy and Science Fiction by Ursula K. Le Guin</u>. Edited by Susan Wood. New York: Putnam's. Contains "A Citizen of Mondath," 1973; "Why Are Americans Afraid of Dragons?" 1974; "Dreams Must Explain Themselves," 1973; "National Book Award Acceptance Speech," 1973; "The Child and the Shadow," 1975; "Myth and Archetype in Science Fiction," 1976; "From Elfland to Poughkeepsie," 1973; "American SF and The Other," 1975; "Science Fiction and Mrs. Brown," 1976; "Do-It-Yourself Cosmology," 1977; "Introduction to the 1977 Edition of <u>Rocannon's World</u>," 1977; "Introduction to the 1978 Edition of <u>Planet of Exile</u>," 1978; "Introduction to the 1978 Edition of <u>City of Illusions</u>," 1978; "Introduction to <u>The Word for World is Forest</u>," 1977; "Introduction to <u>The Left Hand of Darkness</u>," 1976; "Is Gender Necessary?" 1976; "The

Staring Eye," 1974; "The Modest One," 1976; "Introduction to Star Songs of an Old Primate," 1978; "Introduction to The Altered I," 1976: "Talking About Writing," 1976; "Escape Routes," 1974; "The Stalin in the Soul," 1973; "The Stone Ax and the Muskoxen," 1976. Book also contains introductions by Susan Wood [see D646] and bibliographic checklist by Jeff Levin [see D573].

New York: Perigee, 1980 [paper].

C176 "The Language of the Night." [See C140.]

C177 "The Modest One." [See C139.]

C178 "Talking About Writing." In The Language of The Night, pp. 195-200. [See C175. Originally a speech given in January 1976 at Reading, England; and in February 1977 at Southern Oregon College, Ashland.]

C179 "Sci fi High Priestess Le Guin says Fantasy Fans on Increase." Mary Beth Allen, interviewer. Seaside Signal (Seaside, Ore.), 28 June, sect. 3, p. 1.

C180 Panel contribution. In "The Significance of SF as a Genre." Selected Proceedings of the 1978 Science Fiction Research Association National Conference. Cedar Falls, Ia.: University of Northern Iowa, pp. 246; 263-64. [Transcription of opening "Informal Comments" and subsequent discussion. Originally given at Waterloo, Iowa, 16-18 June, 1978. See also C181.]

C181 "Lagniappe: An Informal Dialogue with Ursula K. Le Guin." In Selected Proceedings of the 1978 Science Fiction Research Association National Conference. Cedar Falls, Ia.: University of Northern Iowa, pp. 269-81. [Transcription of dialogue between Le Guin and conference participants, Waterloo, Iowa, 16-18 June, 1978. See also C180.]

C182 "Re: Colonised Planet 5 Shikasta by Doris Lessing." New Republic (13 October), pp. 32-34. [Review of Shikasta, by Doris Lessing.]

C183 Abstract for Lecture, "'Twas a Dark and Stormy Night, or, Why Are We Huddled About the Campfire?" Program for symposium on "Narrative: The Illusion of Sequence," 26-28 October. Chicago: University of Chicago, p. [8]. [See C191.]

1980

C184 "'The Lathe of Heaven'" [essay]. TV Guide (5-11 January), pp. 17-18.

Part C: Nonfiction

C185 "The Lathe of Heaven" [essay]. Horizon 23 (January):32–36.

C186 With Virginia Kidd. Introduction to Interfaces, pp. v–x. [See A86.]

C187 "Some Answers to Some Questions I Get Asked a Lot." In Ursula K. Le Guin. New York: Atheneum. [A promotional pamphlet with photo and autobiographical essay.]

C188 "Where Giants Roam." Washington Post Book World, 23 March, pp. 1, 5. [Review of Freddy's Book and Vlemn, The Box-Painter, by John Gardner.]

C189 Review of The Marriages Between Zones Three, Four, and Five, by Doris Lessing. New Republic (29 March), pp. 34–35.

C190 "Commentary" [discussion and two poems]. Dreamworks: An Interdisciplinary Quarterly 1 (Summer):156–57. [See B100.]

C191 "It Was a Dark and Stormy Night; or, Why Are We Huddling about the Campfire?" [essay]. Critical Inquiry 7 (Autumn):191–99. [Originally given as a lecture at the symposium on "Narrative: The Illusion of Sequence," University of Chicago, 28 October 1979. See also editor's comments (D712) and Le Guin's abstract (C183).]

C192 "Fables Within Fables." Washington Post Book World, 10 August, p. 4. [Review of Kalila and Dimma: Selected Fables of Bidpai, retold by Ramsay Wood.]

C193 "Women: Paths through the Dark Wood." Washington Post Book World, 24 August, pp. 5, 11. [Review of Unfinished Business: Pressure Points in the Lives of Women, by Maggie Scarf.]

C194 "Interviews on the Eighties" [interview]. Oregon Foresight: Newsletter of the Institute for Policy Studies (Portland State University), 4 (August):103. [Institute interviews three individuals on problems in the 1980s for Oregon: Le Guin represents the arts; Monford Orloff, business; Keith Johnson, organized labor.]

C195 Review of Italian Folktales, by Italo Calvino. New Republic (27 September), pp. 33–34.

C196 Letter to editor. SF Commentary, nos. 60/61 (October), p. 2. [Response to past issues; expresses her disappointment with recent science fiction. Followed by editor's reply. See C197 for Le Guin's answer.]

C197 Letter to editor. SF Commentary, nos. 60/61 (October), pp. 2–

3. [Answer to editor's letter.]

C198 Letter to editor. SF Commentary, nos. 60/61 (October), p. 3.
[Favorable response to the anthology, Transmutations.]

C199 Introduction to Edges, pp. 9-12. [See A89.]

C200 "Ursula Le Guin: An Interview." [See C83.]

C201 "A Very Warm Mountain" [essay]. Parabola 5 (November):46-51.

1981

C202 "On Writing Science Fiction" [essay]. Writer 94 (February):
11-14.

C203 Letter to editor. Science Fiction Review 10 (Summer):32.
[Response to Philip K. Dick, correcting his misunderstand-
ing of her comments on Valis; see D749.]

C204 Letter to editor. Science Fiction Review 10 (Summer):32.
[Corrects Geis's statement that she no longer reads science
fiction; she now reads selectively; see D752.]

C205 "The Fanciful And the Fabulous." Washington Post Book World,
27 September, p. 11. [Review of Peake's Progress: Selected
Writings and Drawings of Mervyn Peake, edited by Maeve
Gilmore.]

Part D: Critical and Bio-Bibliographical Studies

1966

D1   CAWTHORN, JAMES. "I Love You, Semantics." <u>New Worlds</u> 49 (August):147.
         Review of <u>Rocannon's World</u>. Admires the deft combination of "starships and swords," as well as the characters and animals which "rank with the best of Norton and Brackett."

D2   MERRIL, JUDITH. "Books." <u>Fantasy and Science Fiction</u> 31 (December):33.
         Review of <u>Rocannon's World</u>. Cites the successful blend of fantasy and science fiction elements and the "charm and delicacy of the writing."

1967

*D3   BANGSUND, JOHN. Review of <u>Rocannon's World</u>. <u>Australian Science Fiction Review</u>, no. 7, p. 12. [Cited in <u>Australian Science Fiction Review</u>, no. 11, index.]

*D4   _____. Review of <u>Planet of Exile</u>. <u>Australian Science Fiction Review</u>, no. 7, p. 12. [Cited in <u>Australian Science Fiction Review</u>, no. 11, index.]

D5   _____. Review of <u>City of Illusions</u>. <u>Australian Science Fiction Review</u>, no. 10 (June), pp. 65-66.
         Delighted with her third novel, although finds second half faulty in plot development and characterization of aliens. The Taoist base reminds him of Philip K. Dick's <u>Man in the High Castle</u>, but he prefers Le Guin. Her forte is "writing about people and nature and their interrelation." [See C5 for Le Guin's response.]

*D6   DAHLSKOG, STEN. Review of <u>Rocannon's World</u>. <u>Australian</u>

Science Fiction Review, no. 8, p. 17. [Cited in Australian Science Fiction Review, no. 11, index.]

*D7 _____. Review of Planet of Exile. Australian Science Fiction Review, no. 8, p. 16. [Cited in Australian Science Fiction Review, no. 11, index.]

D8 de CAMP, L. SPRAGUE. "More Multiple Scroll." Amra [fanzine] 2, no. 44:11-12.
    Review of Rocannon's World and Planet of Exile. Suggests comparing them to Norton's witch-world series; praises her as an "excellent stylist."

D9 MILLER, P. SCHUYLER. "The Reference Library." Analog 80 (November):166.
    Review of Rocannon's World. Categorizes it as a Planet Stories type of tale. Compliments it, especially for not being "just an action yarn transplanted to another planet."

1969

D10 ANON. Review of A Wizard of Earthsea. Bulletin of the Center for Children's Books 22 (May):144-45.
    Finds the pace uneven; dramatic sections are intermixed with heavy, slowly developing passages.

D11 ANON. Review of The Left Hand of Darkness. Publishers Weekly 195 (27 January):99.
    Only the journey across the ice is exciting; remainder is "confusing" intergalatic politics.

D12 BOOK EVALUATION COMMITTEE. "Notable Children's Books of 1968." Booklist 65 (1 April):900-2.
    A Wizard of Earthsea is included in an annotated list of sixty-two books, selected by this committee of the Children's Services Division of the American Library Association.

D13 CLUTE, JOHN. "Slum Clearance." New Worlds, no. 194 (September/October), pp. 29-30.
    Review of The Left Hand of Darkness. Notes the anthropological thoroughness, especially in working out the implications of the Gethenians' sexuality. Claims the setting is a little too drab and the telling a little too restrained. Strong "in the application of real tools of analysis to a fictional world."

D14 DELAP, RICHARD. Review of The Left Hand of Darkness. Granfalloon [fanzine] 2 (October):14-15.
    Elements sometimes temporarily confuse the reader but, like the chapters containing stories and legends, become

clear in retrospect. Common emotional thread is "a sort
of anti-romantic romance" that will alter the reader's concept of love. Estraven is a convincing mixture of male and
female. Values the "vividly imagined" climate, the
Gethenian language, and Le Guin's style.

D15 GERHARDT, LILLIAN N.; SINGER, MARILYN R.; STAVN, DIANE G.;
and BAUMHOLTZ, JOYCE A. "Best Books of the Spring."
Library Journal 94 (15 May):2072-73.
    Includes A Wizard of Earthsea in an annotated list of
twenty-six books chosen from those reviewed since January;
selected by the editors of School Library Journal Book Review.

D16 GERHARDT, LILLIAN N.; SINGER, MARILYN R.; and STAVN, DIANE G.
"Best Books of the Year." Library Journal 94 (15 December):
4580-84.
    Includes A Wizard of Earthsea in its annotated list of
forty-six children's books.

D17 GILLILAND, ALEXIS. Review of The Left Hand of Darkness. WSFA
Journal [fanzine], no. 70 (December/February), p. 23.
    Believes the novel should be nominated for the 1970 Hugo
Award. Characters, plot action, and environment are totally
integrated. The hermaphroditic nature of the Gethenians
does not dominate the novel as it might have. Trip across
the ice explores the nature of love. Wishes for more information on the Gethenian governments.

D18 HARMON, ELVA. Review of A Wizard of Earthsea. Library Journal
94 (15 May):2104.
    Praises style of this "richly allegorical tale [of] the
nature and source of Evil."

*D19 MEBANE, BANKS. "The Novels of Ursula K. Le Guin." Double:
Bill [fanzine], no. 21 (Fall), pp. 24-26. [Cited in
Bittner, "A Survey of Le Guin Criticism," fn. 5; see D533.]

D20 MILLER, P. SCHUYLER. "The Reference Library." Analog 83
(August):167-68.
    Review of The Left Hand of Darkness. Admires the rich
detail concerning the planet and the customs and legends of
its people. Finds it more complex than Frank Herbert's
Dune novels. Although it is difficult to identify with
either Ai or Estraven, new insights will come from additional readings.

D21 PANSHIN, ALEXEI. "Books." Fantasy and Science Fiction 37
(November):50-51.
    Review of The Left Hand of Darkness. Story fails be-
cause, in spite of tremendous detail, the characters are

"held at arm's length, and her action is summarized rather
than shown." Gethenians do not come across as hermaphro-
dites but as males. This is not a novel, only "the theory
for one."

D22　ROTHERT, YVONNE. "Talented Women Enchant Youth." Sunday
　　　Oregonian, 5 October.
　　　　Discusses fiction for young readers published by Port-
　　　land women, including A Wizard of Earthsea.

D23　TETERIS, DENISE. Review of The Left Hand of Darkness. Science
　　　Fiction News (August), pp. 9-10.
　　　　Recognizes that novel's detail indicates Le Guin's
　　　knowledge of anthropology. Disagrees with cover blurb by
　　　Ted White that it contains a love story as compelling as
　　　Theodore Sturgeon's. Book deserves reading.

D24　VIGUERS, RUTH H. Review of A Wizard of Earthsea. Horn Book
　　　Magazine 45 (February):59-60.
　　　　Applauds Le Guin's style and total originality, along
　　　with her rootedness in "great literature of many kinds."

D25　WHITE, TED. "The Future in Books." Amazing 43 (July):124,
　　　128.
　　　　Review of The Left Hand of Darkness. Traces Le Guin's
　　　development in her published fiction, beginning with "The
　　　Dowry of Angyar" which "probably said all that will ever
　　　have to be said about the time-line displacement" of space
　　　travel. Praises three early novels and notes common setting,
　　　continued in The Left Hand of Darkness which he heralds as
　　　"one of the year's best." Praises her ability to draw cul-
　　　tures and show their interrelationship with ecology. Notes
　　　the solid politics, science, and psychology. Compares its
　　　depth and impact to Dune, the quality of its love story to
　　　Theodore Sturgeon's fiction. [For Le Guin's response, see
　　　C15.]

D26　WILLIAMS, RAGNHILD C. "Exciting New Books for Children,
　　　Teens." Catholic Voice (16 July), p. 15.
　　　　Review of A Wizard of Earthsea. Applauds the story's
　　　plausibility; blends fantasy and realism. Its themes will
　　　appeal to young boys. Ranks it as the best science fiction
　　　story of the year.

D27　WOODRUFF, CINDY. Review of A Wizard of Earthsea. Luna
　　　Monthly, no. 3 (August), p. 28.
　　　　Praises pace of story and the completeness and consis-
　　　tency of the imaginary world. Recommends it for adults and
　　　older children.

1970

D28   ANON. "All-purpose Human Being." <u>Times Literary Supplement</u>,
          8 January, p. 39.
              Review of <u>The Left Hand of Darkness</u>. After a difficult
          beginning, novel gives most detail on topography. This is
          typical American science fiction in being a story "in full
          romantic vein, with overtures of the picturesque."

D29   ANON. "Hugo Held Here." <u>Northwest Review of Sex, Politics,</u>
          <u>and Science Fiction</u> (September), p. 1.
              Announces Le Guin's winning the Hugo for <u>The Left Hand</u>
          <u>of Darkness</u>. Reports she received the news while on vaca-
          tion in a cabin with no phone or mail. She took the call
          at a neighbor's, "with a puppy chewing my ankle."

D30   BUCKLEY, KATHRYN. Review of <u>The Left Hand of Darkness</u>.
          <u>Vision of Tomorrow</u> [UK fanzine] 1 (June):31. [Authorship
          uncertain; see D32.]
              Because novel is better than the average science fiction
          novel, it should be held up to more rigorous criticism.
          Novel has four flaws: (1) inadequate exploration of effects
          of Gethenian ambisexuality on individual actions and moti-
          vations; (2) confusion over author's evaluation of ambi-
          sexuality reflected in author's equivocal use of "equal,"
          which sometimes means "identical to" and other times means
          "as good as"; (3) inadequate differentiation between Ai and
          Estraven, both of whom seem female; (4) use of Oriental and
          Western philosophies without choosing one set of values.

D31   BUDRYS, A[LGIS] J. "<u>Galaxy</u> Bookshelf." <u>Galaxy</u> 29 (February):
          144-45.
              Review of <u>The Left Hand of Darkness</u>. Objects to
          numerous endorsement blurbs on the Ace cover. Novel needs
          no introduction; offers a "fresh context" in which to ex-
          amine human love and strife. Every reader will learn from
          it.

D32   BULMER, PAMELA. Review of <u>The Left Hand of Darkness</u>.
          <u>Speculation</u> [UK fanzine] 3 (September/October):16-17.
          [Authorship uncertain. Note states: "A full review of
          this novel by Pam Bulmer recently appeared in <u>Vision of</u>
          <u>Tomorrow</u>; this section did not appear in the magazine at
          the time." However, the only 1970 review in <u>Vision</u> is
          under the name of Kathryn Buckley; see D30. Both reviews
          contain the same opening and closing paragraphs for this
          section.]
              Asserts that the analysis of Le Guin's flaws illustrates
          why good science fiction is difficult and rare. First, a
          good story must have dramatic pacing; this novel does not
          because there is "insufficient anticipation and tightening

and relaxation of tension." Second, the structure of the
story must have the "logic of the extrapolated . . . world";
this novel does not. The alien features are not an inte-
gral part of Gethenian culture.

D33 DeCLES, JON. "Sci-Fi Award to Berkeley Woman." Berkeley
     Daily Gazette, 18 March.
         Describes the West Coast Annual Nebula Awards Banquet
     of SFWA. Focuses on Le Guin because she was born in
     Berkeley, is the first woman to win a Nebula for a novel,
     and because her novel received so many votes.

D34 del REY, LESTER. "Among the Grimoires." Worlds of Fantasy 1
     (Winter):186. [Issue dated 1970/1971. Also contains "The
     Tombs of Atuan."]
         Review of A Wizard of Earthsea. Suspects it may be for
     "younger readers" since it is not as well developed as The
     Left Hand of Darkness. Hopes there will be a sequel.

D35 KROEBER, THEODORA. Alfred Kroeber: A Personal Configuration."
     Berkeley: University of California Press, 292 pp.
         This biography of Le Guin's father, written by her
     mother, depicts the milieu in which Le Guin grew up and
     offers insights into the nature of both parents.

D36 PANSHIN, ALEXEI. "A Basic Science Fiction Collection."
     Library Journal 95 (15 June):2223-29.
         Includes The Left Hand of Darkness in an annotated bib-
     liography of "basic science fiction since Jules Verne";
     selection by SFWA committee: James Blish, L. Sprague
     de Camp, Damon Knight, Andre Norton, Joanna Russ, Robert
     Silverberg, Jack Williamson, Alexei Panshin.

*D37 Phantasmicom, no. 1. Two reviews of Le Guin's work. [Cited
     in Le Guin's letter in no. 2; see C17.]

D38 RUSS, JOANNA. "The Image of Women in Science Fiction." Red
     Clay Reader 7. Charlotte, N.C.:Southern Review, pp. 35-
     40. Reprinted as "The Image of Women in Science Fiction"
     in Images of Women in Fiction: Feminist Perspectives.
     Edited by Susan Koppelman Cornillon. Bowling Green, Oh.:
     Bowling Green University Popular Press, 1972, pp. 79-94.
     Reprinted in Vertex 1 (February):1974.
         Severely criticizes science fiction for not speculating
     about "gender roles." Even the few authors who attempt
     some exploration have not advanced women beyond serving
     minor stereotyped functions in society. Essay closes with
     criticism of The Left Hand of Darkness. The novel does not
     depict family structure or child-rearing; the two central
     characters are male in gender, "thus the great love scene
     in the book is between two men." [See D273.]

*D39 STABLEFORD, BRIAN M. Review of The Left Hand of Darkness.
Speculation, no. 25 (January), pp. 20-21. [Cited in
Speculation, no. 27.]

D40 SUVIN, DARKO. "The SF Novel in 1969." In Nebula Award
Stories 5. Edited by James Blish. London: Gollancz, pp.
193-205. [Also includes "Nine Lives."]
    Examines the nominees for the Nebula, including The Left
Hand of Darkness, in the context of his science fiction
definition--"the literature of cognitive estrangement."
He groups Le Guin, Spinrad, Brunner, and Disch together as
the "new Left" who "question the Individualist ideology"
and show their concern for "collective humanism." He calls
Le Guin's novel "the most memorable of the year," praising
its blend of personal and political concerns and insights,
its development through "binary oppositions," and its style.

D41 TURNER, GEORGE. "Ursula Le Guin Giving a Lesson on How To Do
It." SF Commentary, no. 17 (November), pp. 37-38.
    Review of The Left Hand of Darkness. Finds plot and
style far better than in Rocannon's World. Functions on
three levels: envoy trying to bring a planet into an
intergalactic federation; Terran male trying to understand
"ambi-sexual race"; and two persons "of utterly opposed
psychological orientation" trying to understand each other.
The Gethenians "are probably the first true aliens presented in s.f." Novel's structure is slightly flawed but
its solution is absolutely valid.

D42 _____. "Allegory of disruption." Age (Melbourne), 26 December, p. 11.
    Review of The Left Hand of Darkness. Theme is the
"difficulty of meaningful communication." Outstanding
feature is the totally realized aliens. Protagonists
placed in plot where they must "communicate or die."
Praises her style and detail.

D43 WHITE, TED. Review of A Wizard of Earthsea. Amazing 43
(March):127-29.
    Rejects publishers/librarians' label, "juvenile," be-
cause it misleads readers. Finds same fine craft and close
attention to world-building detail as in her other novels.
Compares it to Tolkien's Lord of the Rings. Praises the
tough-minded handling of the theme of learning. Admires
her poetic style. [See C15 for Le Guin's response.]

D44 WOODRUFF, CINDY. Review of The Left Hand of Darkness. Luna
Monthly [fanzine], no. 11 (April), p. 32.
    Clear analysis of Ai's and Estraven's relationship and
the obstacles in it. Praises novel as a "sensitive study
of alienation in one of the most intimate, and most often

crudely exploited, of human relationships--sex."

1971

D45 ACKERMAN, DIANE. "Radioisotopes, Robot Brawls, White Light,
     and Green Flippers." Book World (Chicago Tribune), 19
     December, p. 6.
          Review of The Lathe of Heaven. Generally critical.
     Opening style is ponderous. Finds author more interested
     in the Augmentor than in Orr's mind and faults her for not
     casting "a pearl of a man" "before a swine of a machine."

D46 ANON. Review of The Lathe of Heaven. Kirkus Reviews 39 (1
     October):1095. Reprinted in Kirkus Reviews 39 (15 October):
     1137.
          Recommends it; Le Guin is a "literate, original, and
     threateningly plausible writer."

D47 ANON. Review of The Lathe of Heaven. Publishers Weekly 200
     (4 October):53.
          Excellent storytelling sustains reader through events
     that strain credibility.

D48 ANON. Review of The Tombs of Atuan. Kirkus Reviews 39 (1
     August):816.
          Notes that the exotic world of the tombs, so absorbing
     in the first section, becomes backgrounded when Ged enters.
     Admires the absence of a "tidy ending" and the story's
     organic allegory.

D49 CAMERON, ELEANOR. "High Fantasy: A Wizard of Earthsea."
     Horn Book Magazine 47 (April):129-38. Reprinted in Cross-
     currents of Criticism: Horn Book Essays 1968-1977. Edited
     by Paul Heins. Boston: Horn Book, 1977, pp. 333-41. Re-
     vised and reprinted in Children's Literature Review.
     Edited by Gerard J. Senick. Vol. 3. Detroit: Gale Re-
     search Co., 1978, pp. 124-25.
          Singles out the novel as "a rare book that not only
     moves with vividness and power, but embodies the philosoph-
     ical point of view of its creator," thus a fine example of
     high fantasy. Contains information about Le Guin's unpub-
     lished fiction and quotations from Le Guin about fantasy
     that have not been published elsewhere. Emphasizes the
     anthropological attitude in the novel, "not as a science
     but aesthetically as a mood of the writer" which includes
     delight in detail, differing cultures, and human kinship.
     Her analysis of the novel includes a statement of its theme
     ("the misuse of the power magic bestows") and its "deep
     subject" ("the necessity for the individual's return to
     self, the necessity for seeing one's self, one's acts, and

the motives for those acts in a clear, searching light").
She puzzles out Le Guin's central use of "names and
shadows" turning to Frazer and Jung for support. Praises
the novel as a great fantasy which "continually returns us
to the world about us . . . to ourselves . . . to the very
core of human responsibility."

D50   FISHER, MARGERY. Review of A Wizard of Earthsea. Growing
Point (October), p. 1806.
Praises the exploratory nature of the book. The voyage
has multiple meanings--"it could be of Man looking for a
place in the world, a hero pursued by a villain, a man escaping himself, a lad moving towards maturity." Finds the
setting convincingly developed. Legends come alive, not
only in narrative line, but also in style: the prose is
"sometimes colloquial and homely, sometimes plangent and
poetic," but always aesthetically and experientially suited.

D51   GARDNER, MARILYN. "Good Halfway Houses." Christian Science
Monitor, 11 November, p. B5.
Review of The Tombs of Atuan. Novel about the issue of
bondage and freedom which is "dark," "eerie," "exotic," and
well told.

D52   HALE, L. Review of The Left Hand of Darkness. Kliatt Paperback Book Guide 5 (September):62.
Recommends novel for its richness. Not only does it
describe strange customs, unusual physical setting, detailed society; but there is "depth of characterization"
and complex aspects of life involving sexual makeup, religion, and psychology.

D53   _____. Review of A Wizard of Earthsea. Kliatt Paperback
Book Guide 5 (February):sect. 2, p. 11.
A book for all readers, especially charming "in the
skill with which the unknown world of Earthsea is made
real."

D54   HALTERMAN, DAVID A. Review of The Left Hand of Darkness.
WSFA Journal, no. 78 (August/October), pp. 33-34.
Novel successfully deals with the two best science fiction themes: developing a credible secondary universe and
presenting "an alien sexual order." Provides good detail
and characterization.

D55   HAVILAND, VIRGINIA. "A Magical Tour." Children's Book World
(Washington Post), 7 November, p. 4.
Review of The Tombs of Atuan. Recommends this terse,
economic novel of the awesome and the strange.

D56   HAYNES, ELIZABETH. Review of The Tombs of Atuan. Library

Journal 96 (15 September):2930-31.
Calls novel "memorable," describing its prose, suspense,
and twin exploration of the maze of the tombs and Arha's
mind.

D57 HEINS, PAUL. Review of The Tombs of Atuan. Horn Book Magazine 47 (October):490.
Successful, multileveled novel with swift narrative
pace and good storytelling. Compares Tenar's escape from
sacrificial death to Iphigenia's. Impressed with novel's
mythic qualities—characters, tone, and subject; it "reflects universal patterns that were once embodied in Stone-
henge and in the Cretan labyrinth."

D58 JONES, OLIVE. "Innocence and Wizardry." Books and Bookmen
17 (December):8, 11.
Review of A Wizard of Earthsea. Likes the dramatic
narrative; but the fascinating qualities are the strange
names, the importance of words, and the kind of magic used.

D59 LEM, STANISLAW. "Part II: The Left Hand of Darkness" [in his
'Lost Opportunities']. SF Commentary, no. 24 (November),
pp. 22-24. Excerpts reprinted in Women of Wonder. Edited
by Pamela Sargent. New York: Vintage, 1975, pp. xxxii-iv.
Criticizes the novel's plot for emphasizing the issue of
the Gethenians' joining the Ekumen rather than emphasizing
the nature of the Gethenians. His central argument rests
on the assumption that "Mankind invented culture as religion and mythos in order to turn the cruel indifference of
blind statistics into a meaningful transcendence." The
Karhiders face more severe statistics than Terrans—they do
not know what sexual identity they will have nor to whom
they will be attracted in kemmer. Accompanying these un-
certainties, are the questions of the nature of love, and
of past sexual alliances, especially when one becomes a
different sex in the next kemmer phase. He thanks the
author for leading him to such thoughts as well as to the
conclusion that our sexual nature is not the worst in the
universe. He praises Le Guin's style and anthropological
understanding. He criticizes what he views as a traditional
science fiction happy ending and concludes, "What sort of
curse lies over sf so that even the most brilliant ideas
are doomed to wither in it, and disappear so quickly?"
[Essay translated from German by F. Rottensteiner and revised by B. Gillespie for publication. See responses by
Le Guin (C32), George Turner (D68), and Brian Aldiss
(D121).]

D60 [LEWIS, NAOMI.] "The Making of a Mage." Times Literary
Supplement, 2 April, p. 383. [Author identified by Bittner,
"A Survey of Le Guin Criticism," fn. 8; see D533.]

Review of <u>A Wizard of Earthsea</u>. Selects it as the outstanding book for young readers this year. Although it
parallels or borrows from <u>The Sword In The Stone</u>, Browning,
and Edwin Muir's "The Combat," it is a new "quest-story, an
original allegory." Cites three examples to show that
"every piece of mage-advice seems immediate and topical,"
in contrast to C.S. Lewis's obvious theologizing. Many
memorable and humorous passages, yet the novel, like the
boat Ged patches and binds up, has a "kind of wholeness."

*D61 <u>Listener</u> 86 (11 November):661. [Cited in <u>Book Review Index</u>,
1971.]
Review of <u>A Wizard of Earthsea</u>.

D62 LIVINGSTON, DENNIS. "Science Fiction Survey." <u>Futures</u> 3
(December):415-16.
Review of <u>The Left Hand of Darkness</u>. Places novel in
category of "social science fiction," which does not predict but envisions alternative human societies. Praises
the detail of the setting. Notes its complexity--an adventure story and a "psychological struggle" to accept what is
alien.

D63 LOVIN, ROGER. "The 1969, West-Coast Nebula Awards Banquet,
Revisited." <u>SFWA Bulletin</u> 7, whole no. 29 (July):3-4.
Informal description of banquet and awards.

*D64 PIERCE, J. [J.] Review of <u>Planet of Exile</u>. <u>Renaissance</u>
[fanzine] 3 (Summer):17. [Cited in <u>Science Fiction Book
Review Index, 1923-73</u>. Edited by H.W. Hall. Detroit:
Gale Research Co., 1975.]

D65 PRESCOTT, PETER S. "Dream Fiction." <u>Newsweek</u> (29 November):
106.
Review of <u>The Lathe of Heaven</u>. In context of dismissing
current science fiction, he finds this novel a rare accomplishment. Science fiction has been outrun by science,
"has turned to sex, sentimental religion and inept experiments with style," and its writers "lust" after respecta-
bility. In contrast, Le Guin's novel is inventive, speculative, ironic, and relevant.

D66 STURGEON, THEODORE. "Science Fiction: Memento Mori--Et Seq."
<u>National Review</u> (12 January), pp. 39, 41.
Review of <u>City of Illusions</u> and <u>A Wizard of Earthsea</u>.
Praises her competent writing. Is not surprised by fine
writing by a woman but is surprised at liking a swords-and-
sorcery book. <u>Wizard</u> is a delightful version of the ancient
journey story, believable and moral. <u>City</u> is more clearly
science fiction with believable settings and characters.
Wishes for more expanded treatment of the characters.

D67 TILNEY, HENRY. "Science Fiction." Observer (London), 4
     April, p. 36. Reprinted in Observer Review (5 March 1972).
          Review of The Lathe of Heaven. Fine description of the
     novel, including the comment that Haber's dream "mangles
     the world into a simulacrum of all the vulnerability,
     despair and terror of his unconscious." Praises characters,
     setting, and style, although there are "brief stretches of
     callow gnomicism."

D68 TURNER, GEORGE. Letter to the editor. SF Commentary, no. 25
     (December), pp. 8-10, 43.
          Response to criticism of The Left Hand of Darkness by
     Stanislaw Lem; see D59. Argues Lem has confused plot with
     theme. Novel's theme is "the need for meaningful communi-
     cation." Secondary to that is the plot and of least im-
     portance is "the fable . . . the purely external matter"
     of joining the Ekumen. This perspective shows the novel's
     subject is mankind and validates the novel's ending.
     Acknowledges that, like Lem, he would have liked more de-
     tail on the Gethenians' psycho-biological nature; but re-
     jects Lem's other arguments on this issue. Accuses Lem of
     thinking in the sexual mores of current culture.

D69 WALKER, PAUL. Review of City of Illusions. Luna Monthly, no.
     30 (November), p. 32.
          Although criticizing the unimaginative plot, he praises
     the detailed alien landscape. In surveying her work to
     date, he identifies her as being in the nineteenth-century
     novel tradition, that is, indifferent to plot and charac-
     terization and giving full attention to setting which co-
     stars as hero. Classifies her as "non-professional" (not
     writing to sell books) and praises her literary quality.
     He predicts she will abandon plot altogether, will write
     longer books, for audiences outside science fiction.

D70 YATES, J.V., ed. "Le Guin, Ursula K." In Authors and Writers
     Who's Who. 6th ed. Darien, Conn.: Hafner, p. 485.
          Condensed, biographical information and list of pub-
     lications which includes five novels.

                              1972

D71 ALDERSON, BRIAN. "The Power of Magic and the Supernatural."
     Times (London), 4 May.
          Review of The Tombs of Atuan. Contrasts atmosphere to
     that of the first volume and commends author for doing well
     in both. Drama heightened by Le Guin's use of the "classi-
     cal Unities" in the central episode.

D72 ANDREWS, SHERYL B. Review of The Farthest Shore. Horn Book

<u>Magazine</u> 48 (December):599-600.
Places novel in the tradition of Lord Dunsany's <u>At The
Edge of The World</u> and Lovecraft's <u>The Dream-Quest of Unknown Kadath</u>. Praises style and the ability to make Earthsea real. Criticizes the imbalance between theme and
vehicle--plot and characters are not strong enough to carry
the myth she created.

D73 ANON. "Magic and Myth." <u>Manas</u> 25 (1 November):5, 8.
Review of <u>A Wizard of Earthsea</u>. Objects to categorizing
it as escape literature. Dunsany stories are escape fantasy where morality is suspended. But this is fantasy
which develops the "mythopoeic faculty" and says things
which cannot be said in the realistic mode. Primarily the
novel shows that what one learns about the self are the
"crucial encounters." Supports with memorable quotes.
Novel echoes ancient myths of "the trials of discipleship
and the conditions of victory."

D74 ANON. "Myths of anti-climax." <u>Times Literary Supplement</u>, 23
June, p. 705.
Review of <u>The Lathe of Heaven</u>. Begins by asserting
science fiction has abandoned the outward galactic journey
for an inward psychic journey. Le Guin's novel is a disappointing example because it holds no surprises and is too
"toned-down." Reviewer finds Le Guin's brand of science
fiction ("'mature,' humble, realist") contradicts what
science fiction ought to do.

D75 ANON. "Newbery Honor Books." <u>Top of the News</u> 28 (April):
243-44.
Includes <u>The Tombs of Atuan</u> in an annotated list of five
books. Photograph.

D76 ANON. Review of <u>The Farthest Shore</u>. <u>Junior Literary Guild</u>
[catalog] (September), p. 44.
Assesses readership and subject matter for classroom
use. Includes statements by Le Guin which have not
appeared elsewhere. Commenting on her father's work, she
concludes that "science and writing were normal human activities, like dancing or whistling." She argues that a
fantasist is like a physicist and that both are deeply connected to reality.

D77 ANON. Review of <u>The Farthest Shore</u>. <u>Kirkus Reviews</u> 40 (1
July):728.
Although the narrative does not have the "concrete tensions" of the previous volumes, it shares their quality of
themes embedded in plot. Primary theme is the "'unmeasured
desire for life' and its mis-applications." Reader gains
sense of wholeness of all three volumes.

D78 ANON. Review of The Tombs of Atuan. Bulletin of the Center
     for Children's Books 25 (April):126.
         Although admiring the concept and writing style, criti-
     cizes the action for being slow; suggests book may have
     been expanded too much from the shorter version published
     in Worlds of Fantasy.

D79 BLISH, JAMES. "Books." Fantasy and Science Fiction 43
     (July):62-63.
         Review of The Lathe of Heaven. Reviews six books
     treating ESP, a topic Blish dislikes. Appropriately,
     Le Guin's novel about "historical breakage" does not share
     the historical background of her other novels. She is
     clearly writing a moral allegory but the believable charac-
     ters and the elicited emotion also make it a strong novel.
     Identifies the central concept as the interconnectedness of
     individual and history, "that every 'I' is in large
     part . . . an accretion of what has happened to it, good
     and bad alike; to undo history is to undo man."

D80 BLISHEN, EDWARD. "Plausible Worlds." Times Educational
     Supplement, 9 August.
         Review of The Tombs of Atuan. Acclaims novel as a
     worthy sequel to A Wizard of Earthsea. Recognizes that
     because the country's religion is actually controlled by
     the political tyrants, the Tombs are a "dead, evil core."
     In spite of the plot, novel is not Gothic but is filled
     "with a sense of brimming light" partly due to her exacting
     detail.

D81 BOOK EVALUATION COMMITTEE. "Notable Children's Books of
     1971." American Libraries 3 (April):419-21. Reprinted in
     Booklist 68 (1 April):668-70.
         Lists The Tombs of Atuan among forty-seven books
     selected by the Book Evaluation Committee of the Children's
     Services Division of the American Library Association.

D82 BOOTH, MARTIN. "It Stands Out Spell and Wand." Teacher
     (London), 9 June.
         Review of A Wizard of Earthsea. Dismisses Tolkien
     imitators and praises Le Guin for avoiding their flaws.
     Novel is inventive yet its imaginary world is made believ-
     able and children can identify with its story. Unquestion-
     ably suited for children and adults.

D83 C., M. Review of The Tombs of Atuan. Junior Bookshelf 36
     (August):251.
         Classifies Le Guin with Peter Dickinson as one who has
     made an original contribution in art. Labels this a dis-
     turbing, haunting book.

D84 del REY, LESTER. "Reading Room." Worlds of If 21 (April):
     121-22.
          Review of The Lathe of Heaven. Praises The Left Hand of
     Darkness, "Nine Lives," and the Earthsea novels, but finds
     this one of lesser quality, particularly in the second
     half. Novel appears not to have been planned out in ad-
     vance and becomes an "'anything goes' science fantasy."
     The significance of Lelache and the aliens is not clear.

D85 ELLISON, HARLAN, ed. Introduction to "The Word for World is
     Forest." In Again, Dangerous Visions. Garden City, N.Y.:
     Doubleday, pp. 26-29.
          An informal essay detailing his admiration for Le Guin's
     personal "grace and style." Includes a brief biographical
     sketch, quotations from two of her letters written while in
     England (1968-1969), and an account of her kindness to
     Ellison the weekend of the 1969 Nebula Awards.

D86 FISHER, MARGERY. "Things Counter, Original, Spare, Strange."
     Growing Point (June), pp. 1972-73.
          Review of The Tombs of Atuan. Recognizes main point of
     novel is change. Favors it as allegory without dogmatism,
     inviting the reader to imaginatively plunge into it.

D87 FRIEND, BEVERLY. "Virgin Territory: Women and Sex in Science
     Fiction." Extrapolation 14 (December):49-58.
          Begins with Asimov's three categories of science fiction:
     gadget, adventure, and social. Shows lack of extrapolation
     about women and sex in the first two. Stereotyping of
     women results in equally limiting stereotyping of men.
     Discusses the few authors who have broken the stereotypes
     in social science fiction: Roger Zelazny, "A Rose for
     Ecclesiastes"; John Wyndham, "Consider Her Ways"; Philip
     Jose Farmer, "My Sister's Brother"; Theodore Sturgeon,
     Venus Plus X; and Le Guin's The Left Hand of Darkness.
     Le Guin focuses, not on the Gethenian bisexuality but on
     Genly Ai's reactions: "he is not the destructive irrational
     representative of male narrowness." [For update, see D404.]

D88 GERHARDT, LILLIAN N.; BREGMAN, ALICE M.; and POLLACK, PAMELA
     D. "Best Books for Spring 1972." Library Journal 97 (15
     May):1884-87.
          Includes The Lathe of Heaven in an annotated list of
     forty-eight recommended books.

D89 _____. "Best Books of the Year." Library Journal 97 (15
     December):4055-58.
          Includes The Farthest Shore in an annotated list of 43
     books chosen from the over 2000 children's books reviewed
     in 1972.

D90 HAMILTON, DAPHNE ANN. Review of The Tombs of Atuan. Luna
  Monthly, nos. 38/39 (July/August), p. 21.
    Storytelling reflects oppressiveness of Arha's life;
  reader must be wary of being initially disappointed. Novel
  is "fantastically effective" but has more limited appeal
  than A Wizard of Earthsea.

D91 HANNABUSS, C.S. Review of The Tombs of Atuan. Children's
  Book Review (UK) 2 (June):78.
    Praises the spellbinding quality of Le Guin's story-
  telling and calls attention to the interplay of light and
  dark symbolism. Identifies the setting as a more ritual-
  istic time, thus its publication is timely, with current
  interest in Tutankhamun.

D92 HAY, GEORGE. Review of The Lathe of Heaven and The Tombs of
  Atuan. Foundation 2 (June):54-55.
    Compares Le Guin to Philip K. Dick in her concern about
  the nature of reality in The Lathe of Heaven. Notes her
  debt to Isak Dinesen and calls Le Guin a "classicist," and
  the book, "oracular." Recommends The Tombs of Atuan, yet
  describes it as a "slight work."

D93 HAYNES, ELIZABETH. Review of The Farthest Shore. Library
  Journal 97 (15 October):3461-62.
    Judges it "slightly less effective" than previous two.
  Story centers on Arren rather than on Ged.

D94 JAGO, WENDY. "'A Wizard of Earthsea' and the Charge of
  Escapism." Children's Literature in Education 8 (July):
  21-29.
    Uses the novel to illustrate her argument that children's
  literature is not escapist but instead shares with the
  adult novel a concern with the "developmental stages and
  crises" of the individual and deals with major "human im-
  pulses and myths." Through extensive quotes, she shows
  that the novel is about the "enactment of morality in
  choice" and that naming and recognition function as the
  central symbol. Thus Wizard is "significant because it is
  concerned with the individual as a potent agent in a complex world of pressures and choices."

D95 KELLMAN, AMY. "Books for Children." Grade Teacher 89 (May):
  58.
    Review of The Tombs of Atuan. Summarizes the plot and
  notes that "the main drama is internal."

D96 LESLIE, CECIL. "Baby Girl Becomes High Priestess of the Dark
  Powers." Eastern Daily Press (Norwich, Norfolk), 7 July.
    Review of The Tombs of Atuan. Notes that this novel
  and A Wizard of Earthsea are both about training. Praises

the novel's emotional effect and subtle meanings.

D97 [LEWIS, NAOMI.] "Earthsea Revisited." Times Literary
     Supplement, 28 April, p. 484. Excerpt reprinted in
     "Holiday Books for Children." Observer (London), 30 July.
     [First article is unsigned, but second is signed.]
          Review of The Tombs of Atuan. Demonstrates it has the
     same qualities as A Wizard of Earthsea--detailed, credible
     setting ("as unerring as that of the youthful Brontes'
     imaginary countries"); emphasis on human characters; plot
     changes caused by character action and development. Tenar
     moves from belief and ritual to freedom and responsibility;
     novel moves to a fulfilling but not "commonplace" solution.

D98 LEWIS, NAOMI. "Children's Books." Observer (London), 5
     March, p. 31.
          Review of A Wizard of Earthsea. Believes it is a book
     that will be read fifty years from now because its magic
     is so convincing and its lessons about naming are so rele-
     vant.

D99 LIVINGSTON, DENNIS. "Science Fiction Survey." Futures 4
     (June):195.
          Review of The Lathe of Heaven. Exemplifies science
     fiction that examines social policy issues. Plot allows
     her to examine the ethical problem of the scientist and
     his power, as well as the unwanted consequences of directed
     social change.

D100 LUPOFF, DICK. "Lupoff's Book Week." Algol 18 (May):12.
          Review of The Lathe of Heaven. Urging that Le Guin "has
     never written anything badly," he places this in the
     "utterly superb" category. Not only is it an investigation
     of the nature of reality, like Philip K. Dick's work, it
     also incorporates the Faust myth, incorporates hard science
     into fiction, and is a moving love story. His plot summary
     notes the difference between what a pulp hack and what
     Le Guin has done with the power of dreaming, that is, Haber
     desires to solve the world's problems rather than fulfill
     fantasy dreams of women and wealth. Praises style: "book
     is spare, suspenseful, thought-provoking, touching and ex-
     citing in turn." Claims it is the best he has read in
     years.

D101 MILLER, P. SCHUYLER. "The Reference Library." Analog 89
     (June):167-68.
          Review of The Lathe of Heaven.

D102 MINES, SAMUEL. Review of Planet of Exile. Luna Monthly, no.
     40 (September), p. 30.
          Brief, negative review which identifies novel as "sword

and dagger stuff," not science fiction. Although a good
book, it is not of the same quality as her previous novels.
Points out that it is based on an old adage, "the world is
what you think it is" and reminds him of Peter Ibbetson,
a Victorian novel/play by du Maurier.

D103   _____. "New SF: ESP, ZPG, etc. (No More BEM's)." Book
        World (Washington Post), 6 August, p. 9.
            Review of Planet of Exile. Notes she writes well, but
        finds the novel commonplace and not speculative.

D104   PATTEN, BRIAN. "Tripping on S-f." Books and Bookmen 17
        (June):73.
            Review of The Lathe of Heaven. Haber's discussions of
        dreaming sound too much like articles from the Sunday
        supplements.

*D105   PIERCE, J. [J.] Review of The Lathe of Heaven. Renaissance
        [fanzine] 4 (Spring):14-15. [Cited in Science Fiction Book
        Review Index, 1923-73. Edited by H.W. Hall. Detroit:
        Gale Research Co., 1975.]

D106   SANSUM, JEAN. "Seeking A Fascination Beyond Fields We Know."
        Vancouver Sun, 17 November, p. 33A.
            Review of The Farthest Shore. Recommends this novel and
        Andre Norton's Breed To Come to adults and children.
        Le Guin's novel praised for its believable world, laws of
        magic, and fallible human characters.

D107   SEARLES, BAIRD. "What If?" Village Voice, 3 February.
            Review of The Tombs of Atuan. Praises the volume and
        hopes for an additional Earthsea book. Its unique elements
        include using the viewpoint "of the guardian of the sought
        object instead of the seeker" and its retelling of the
        Ariadne/Theseus story.

D108   SHOEMAKER, MICHAEL T. Review of The Lathe of Heaven. Son of
        the WSFA Journal [fanzine], no. 75 (December), p. 9.
            Deserves the Hugo Award. Compares her interest in the
        nature of reality to Philip K. Dick and to Charles
        Harness's "The New Reality." Criticizes plot for piling up
        too many complications.

D109   SMITH, JENNIFER FARLEY. "Despair Pervades Prize Books."
        Christian Science Monitor, 2 May, p. 4.
            Review of The Tombs of Atuan. With one exception, finds
        the Newbery Medal books too desolate for children. Includes
        Le Guin's novel in her criticism.

D110   STORR, CATHERINE. "The Spice of Life." New Statesman 83 (2
        June):758-59.

Review of The Tombs of Atuan. Cites current new books
to illustrate the variety among children's books. Lists
this novel as one of several fantasies.

D111 STRAWN, LINDA. "Dreams After A Life." Calendar (Los Angeles
      Times), 9 January, p. 44.
           Review of The Lathe of Heaven. An exciting, well con-
      ceived, complex story. Brilliantly written, it "judges the
      values by which men live without judging the men."

D112 STURGEON, THEODORE. "Science Fiction: Of Mars and Reality."
      National Review (4 February), pp. 106-7.
           Review of The Lathe of Heaven. Forces the reader to
      examine own concepts of the nature of reality. Her knowl-
      edge of dream research is evident, and her criticism of the
      patient/psychiatrist relationship is sharp.

D113 _____. "If . . . ?" New York Times Book Review, 14 May,
      p. 33.
           Review of The Lathe of Heaven. Contrasts George Orr to
      Peter Ibbetson but compares results of dreams to "The
      Monkey's Paw." Noting Le Guin's reading on dream research,
      he praises novel as a "rare and powerful synthesis of
      poetry and science, reason and emotion."

D114 SUTHERLAND, ZENA. "Tell Me, Where is Fantasy Bred?" Saturday
      Review (25 March), p. 109.
           Responding to an inquiry about the absence of good fan-
      tasy, she defines fantasy and assets there is good fantasy
      being published. The Tombs of Atuan is one of several
      books cited.

D115 THOMPSON, DALE. Review of The Lathe of Heaven. Library
      Journal 97 (15 February):791.
           Notes the extrapolative plot and praises its development
      and suspensefulness.

D116 TOWNSEND, JOHN ROWE. "Four Myths and Only One Hit." Guardian
      (London), 17 May.
           Review of The Tombs of Atuan. First two Earthsea vol-
      umes are as fine as any fantasy, including J.R.R. Tolkien's.
      Acknowledges Le Guin's background in anthropology and
      modern psychology, but singles out the "breath of life" as
      the novel's essential quality. Commends the power not only
      of the story but also of the style. Le Guin's detail
      creates a world that exists beyond the novel's limits.
      [Title refers to Le Guin's novel being the only good one
      among the five he reviewed.]

D117 WHITE, TED. "Fantasy Books." Fantastic 21 (February):112-13.
           Review of The Tombs of Atuan. Disappointing after A

Wizard of Earthsea; he faults its brevity and incomplete
story. It lacks complexity and reads like a long introduction followed by two anticlimatic, closing chapters. Story
is incomplete on three levels: the political/religious
intrigue ought to be developed and made relevant to the
plot; Tenar's maturation process, just beginning at the end
of the book, ought to be the book's main body; Tenar's rejection of her life as priestess is not convincing. Reviewer hopes for a sequel which will develop Tenar or re-
establish Ged as a major figure. Finds the prose excellent.

D118 YORKS, SAM. "Science Fiction Really Is. . . ." Portland
Review Magazine 19 (December):10-14.
    Discusses Samuel Delany's Nova and Le Guin's The Left
Hand of Darkness.

1973

D119 ALDERSON, BRIAN. "Hero and Place." Times (London), 10 May.
    Review of The Farthest Shore. Although noting an uneven
pace and the development of nonessential events, he praises
the novel and the now completed trilogy. He finds scenes
memorable and regrets the story ending. "She exercises a
complete control over the Romanticism of her themes and the
rich, hieratic rhythms of her prose."

D120 ALDISS, BRIAN [W.]. Billion Year Spree: The History of
Science Fiction. London: Weidenfeld & Nicolson, pp. 305-
6.
    Mentions several of her works; praises her prose style,
quoting four paragraphs from the beginning of The Left Hand
of Darkness.

D121 _____. Letter to the editor. SF Commentary, no. 33 (March),
pp. 22-24.
    Response to criticism of The Left Hand of Darkness by
Stanislaw Lem [see D59] and to Le Guin's reply [see C32].
Admires the candor of Le Guin's response, but accepts Lem's
general criticism that "the bisexuality in the novel is
centrally interesting, yet never centrally examined."

D122 ALLEN, L. DAVID. "The Left Hand of Darkness." In Science
Fiction: An Introduction. Lincoln, Nebr.: Cliff Notes,
pp. 101-11. Reprinted as Science Fiction: Reader's Guide.
Lincoln, Nebr.: Centennial Press, 1974, pp. 184-97. [See
D160.]
    Praises it as one of the best science fiction novels,
listing its three accomplishments as: good handling of the
first contact theme, excellent adventure story, and convincing detail of the alien world and people. After

describing the storyline, he discusses its four main elements: the environment, ambisexuality, "exploration of
governments," and religion and legends. For each element,
he indicates its effect on human motivation and on the
Gethenian culture. The discussion of governments is well
detailed, especially the comparison of Tibe's and Estraven's
attitudes toward nation and humanity. Desires more detail
on the religions but admits it is not essential.

D123 ANDERSON, KRISTINE. Review of The Farthest Shore. Luna
      Monthly, no. 45 (February), p. 23.
          Asserts the plot "takes the form of an Odyssey" and has
      several layers of meaning, including allegorical. Praises
      not the excitement but the wonder; the "complexity of her
      universes and the characters that move in them is analogous
      to the complexity of our own."

D124 ANON. "Ursula K. Le Guin Wins National Book Award." Library
      Journal 98 (15 May):1622.
          News item which includes judges' statement.

D125 ANON. Review of From Elfland to Poughkeepsie. Fantasiae 1
      (August):9, 12. [Probably by Ian Slater.]
          Identifies it as a "hardheaded discussion of the literary
      nature of fantasy." Has high praise. Notes error in order
      of bound pages.

D126 ANON. Review of The Farthest Shore. Bulletin of the Center
      for Children's Books 26 (March):109.
          More "ornate" than the second volume, its writing has a
      "majestic intricacy."

D127 AYRES, DON. Review of The Lathe of Heaven. S.F. Echo, no.
      18 (October), pp. 153-56. [See C59.]
          Commends it as an outstanding novel. Questions the
      necessity of the quotations at the beginning of each chap-
      ter and Orr's lack of emotion.

D128 BAKER, JOHN. "Academe Dominates a Low-Key NBA." Publishers
      Weekly (30 April), p. 33.
          Recounts the noncontroversial tone of the awards cere-
      mony and authors' press conference. Found Le Guin "reti-
      cent"; cites her concern over reduced Federal aid to public
      libraries which is forcing children's sections to be closed.

D129 BARBOUR, DOUGLAS. Letter to the editor. Riverside Quarterly
      6 (August):93-94.
          Response to Ketterer's essay; see D143. He disagrees
      with its conclusion, asserting that Le Guin uses mythic
      patterns, not myths; and thus her work is not "overly con-
      scious." Rejects the idea that the novel is "badly put

together." The plot is enhanced by interpolated myths and reports. Ketterer's reading suggests "prejudiced expectations of plot-construction."

D130 _____. "The Lathe of Heaven: Taoist Dream." Algol, no. 21 (November), pp. 22-24.
 Novel is the most Taoist of all of her novels. In addition to the chapter epigraphs, internal allusions show Taoist influence--the character descriptions, images, and moral center of the novel. Orr is "an unconscious Taoist sage" and Haber is a utilitarian; the moral center of the novel is their disagreement about how Orr's power to change the world through dreams should be used. He quotes from the novel and from the Lao Tzu and the Chuang Tzu to support his assertions. Not only does the novel present the Taoist philosophy, it also demonstrates "brilliant characterization and great wit," as well as "fine stylistic control." [See letter in response, D194; and Barbour's reply, D167.]

D131 BLISHEN, EDWARD. "A World of Wizardry." Guardian (London), 29 March, p. 17. Reprinted in Guardian Weekly (London), 7 April, p. 26.
 Review of The Farthest Shore. All three novels contain memorable single scenes and rich detail that bring Earthsea (place and customs) to life. Singles out Le Guin's style, "She can turn a story on the sixpence of some utterly unexpected phrase." Children will be swept up by the story, adults will also be taken with the modern relevance of the central danger in the novel: "knowledge and greed together tempting man to a rebellion against mortality itself, and so to the destruction of the Balance."

D132 CARTER, LIN. Imaginary Worlds: The Art of Fantasy. New York: Ballantine, pp. 164-65 [paper].
 Describes each of the three Earthsea volumes and praises Le Guin's imagination.

D133 COMMIRE, ANNE, ed. "Le Guin, Ursula K." In Something About The Author. Vol. 4. Detroit: Gale Research, pp. 142-44.
 Entry contains four sections: personal, career, writings, sidelights, plus full page photo. Fourth section consists of three paragraphs in which Le Guin discusses the significance of fantasy and the value of the imagination, and asserts they are part of reality.

D134 COOLIDGE, ELIZABETH S. "A Vote to Keep the Prize for Worthy Children's Books." Boston Sunday Globe, 15 April, p. B-55.
 Argues for the significance of an NBA for children's literature. Finds The Farthest Shore, the current winner, representative of the quality. Commends her use of myths (Norse or Celtic), "stylized prose," and relevant

issues--ecology, death.

D135 DOTRICE, YVETTE. Review of The Farthest Shore. Evening
Standard, 22 November.
Thirteen-year-old reviewer responds to the relationship
between Ged and Arren. Novel makes her feel that "tucked
away somewhere these people may live."

D136 FANTASTES. "Enchantress of Earthsea." Cambridge Review (23
November), pp. 43-45.
Describes the particular appeal of following the career
of a living author--the tension of whether the new book
will be as good as the preceding, of whether the reader can
fulfill the demands of the new text. Acknowledges her
popularity in Great Britain and announces the beginning of
the critical process. Half the review is an overview of
her works. Her science fiction is not technologically
oriented; instead "her essential concerns are imaginative,
moral, and religious." Praises her style, description,
narrative ability, intellect, and "poetic resourcefulness"
in the use of language. Basic myths are usually borrowed.
"Her originality and fecundity" are impressive--all her
imaginary worlds are "solid" and "authentic." Second half
of article focuses on the principle by which she must be
evaluated: "the degree to which she affects the religious
views of her readers." All her works are Taoist fables and
must be judged by her use of that vision. City of Illusions, The Lathe of Heaven, The Farthest Shore are all
problematic books. The last two contain metaphysical discussions that are too cryptic, too personal, and do not
reach the reader. The Left Hand of Darkness and, more
especially, A Wizard of Earthsea are her most successful.

D137 FOX, GEOFF, ed. "Notes on 'Teaching' A Wizard of Earthsea."
Children's Literature in Education, no. 11 (May), pp. 58-
67.
Contains numerous suggestions by British teachers for
teaching the novel "through talk, choral work, drama, paint,
game making and the writing of prose and verse." Interspersed with transcriptions from tape of twelve-year-old
boys discussing the novel. Indicates that novel has been
used in several teaching workshops in England. Article
contains drawings by students.

D138 FRETZ, SADA. "Why Did They Win?" Book World (Washington
Post, part II, 13 May, p. 6.
Review of The Farthest Shore. National Book Award books
understandably selected, although none signals a new direction in children's book. Finds Earthsea's third volume not
of the same quality as the other two, but the award could be
viewed as commendation for the whole trilogy. Unfortunately,

the abstract themes do not rise "naturally" from the fantasy world, thus the novel is "top-heavy."

D139 GRAY, GERALDINE. "64 Books for Children." New Catholic World 216 (March/April):92.
Lists A Wizard of Earthsea as a moral fantasy recommended for children ages seven to twelve.

D140 HEEKS, PEGGY. "Triumphant Trilogy." Times Educational Supplement, 4 May.
Review of The Farthest Shore. After praising novel for its "power and meaning," she critiques the whole trilogy. A Wizard of Earthsea is the "richest in invention and incident"; The Tombs of Atuan "the sparest and tautest in plot"; and The Farthest Shore the clearest expression of the author's beliefs. She applauds the series' relevance: "We are ready for new parables, and here they are: we are in need of great adventure to lift us out of self and here in these breath-taking fantasies we find them, and mid-century heroes." Although comparable to Tolkien, Le Guin has not imitated anyone. Books combine her own ideas (rooted in "Existentialism and eastern philosophy") and myths ("Germanic sagas, Asian folk lore, Icelandic myth").

D141 HELLE, ANITA. "Portland Dreamworld." Oregon Times, November, p. 35.
Review of The Lathe of Heaven. Responds to the Portland setting and the characterization. Asserts that "only the consistency in character development saves the book from chaos, and serious implausibility." Specifies the book's science fiction elements—the "ingenious machine," the "alien threat" developed with surprise, and the return to normalcy at the end. Favors the satisfactory although tenuous ending and Le Guin's "humor and irony." Recommends it to Oregonians.

D142 KEMBALL-COOK, JESSICA. Review of The Tombs of Atuan. Mallorn [fanzine], no. 7.
Like the excellent first novel, it is concerned with "the conflict of Light and Dark"; but unlike the first, it is "inward looking." First half reminds her of Lovecraft. Praises Le Guin's descriptions, setting, and message about "the weight of freedom."

D143 KETTERER, DAVID. "The Left Hand of Darkness: Ursula K. Le Guin's Archetypal 'Winter-Journey.'" Riverside Quarterly 5 (April):288-97. Reprinted in New Worlds For Old: The Apocalyptic Imagination, Science Fiction and American Literature. Bloomington: Indiana University Press, 1974, pp. 76-90. [See D188.]
Criticizes novel as an example of fictions that develop

plots to serve a preselected mythic structure. Criticism
is based on Frye's principle that "the mythic basis of any
fiction . . . should exist irrespective of an author's in-
tentions and in a severely displaced relationship to the
story-line." The logic of Le Guin's plot events and the
rare Gethenian sexuality serve the mythic structure, not
the plot. Thus the plot events are not determined by their
own momentum nor are they affected by the Gethenian sexuality.

The remainder of the essay develops his argument that
the basic mythic pattern is death and rebirth, told through
the images of duality and unity and that this pattern is
also the heart of science fiction. Not only does Genly Ai
bring disunity to Gethen, he suffers disunity. The pattern
of death and rebirth is reinforced by the Gethenian myths.
The imagery of webs and weaving suggest not only the coming
of a new unity but also the coming of a unity out of the
act of writing. Praises the novel for writing about the
writing of science fiction. Concludes with his overall
criticism that "the plot is unfortunately subordinate to
the overly conscious use of mythic material." [See responses in letters--D129 and D156; and the later forum,
D262.]

D144   LEWIS, NAOMI. "Children's Books." Observer (London), 15
         April, p. 39.
              Review of The Farthest Shore. A "brilliant book" for
         children and adults. Concerns an "almost Homeric journey"
         through the islands. Extremely successful in inviting,
         like Tolkien, "a total belief in Earthsea place and time."

D145   [LEWIS, NAOMI.] "A Hole in the World." Times Literary Sup-
         plement, 6 April, p. 379. [Author identified by Bittner,
         "A Survey of Le Guin Criticism," fn. 8; see D533.]
              Review of The Farthest Shore. Foresees continuous
         critical discussion as to which is the greater book--A
         Wizard of Earthsea or The Farthest Shore (The Tombs of
         Atuan is on a different theme). Notes novel's series of
         "marvellous episodes" leading to a climatic scene with the
         "dead, re-risen sorcerer." Although a heroic adventure
         tale, its tensions come from unusual conflicts--"the con-
         tests are really of wit and will." She even avoids using
         conventional evil nonhuman character. "Unlike Kingsley,
         Macdonald, Kipling, C.S. Lewis, she does not take any overt
         political or theological stance." Lauds its "contemporary
         relevance" for the imbalance in Earthsea "comes from human
         greed allied to ill-used human knowledge (or sorcery)."

*D146   LEWIS, NAOMI. Observer, 15 May, p. 39. [Cited in Bittner,
         "A Survey of Le Guin Criticism," fn. 9; see D533.]

Part D: Critical Studies

D147 LUPOFF, RICHARD. "Lupoff's Book Week." Algol, no. 21 (November), pp. 42-43.
Review of A Wizard of Earthsea, The Tombs of Atuan, The Farthest Shore, From Elfland to Poughkeepsie. Cites the trilogy as an "unusual achievement." It should be considered as a three-act play. Fine in characterization, conflicts, and style. Elfland aptly describes the style that characterizes good fantasy. [See D153.]

D148 McINTYRE, VONDA N. Introduction to From Elfland to Poughkeepsie. Portland: Pendragon Press, pp. xiii-xviii.
Informally recounts her personal and professional admiration of Le Guin, particularly resulting from experiences with her in the University of Washington's Science Fiction Writers' Workshop. Impressed with her serenity and ability to critically analyze and discuss her own fiction. Praises the style, ideas, characterization, and setting in her fiction and lists her honors and awards. Describes her teaching ability with examples from the learning situations or "games" she used in the workshop.

D149 McNELLY, WILLIS E. "Archetypal Patterns in Science Fiction." CEA Critic 35 (May):15-19.
Urges that science fiction should no longer be neglected by Jungian critics. The Left Hand of Darkness is his longest detailed example. Briefly discusses the Jungian themes: "Light is the left hand of darkness; man is the left hand of woman; good is the left hand of evil. None can exist without the other." Argues that science fiction gave her the freedom to discuss human sexuality and the anima/animus relationship without "plunging over the precipice of semantics into the loaded language of homosexuality." Contrasts Le Guin with E.M. Forster's problem in Maurice. Concludes that "it is this very technique of building conjectural realities to examine human problems" that is the heart of science fiction.

D150 NYE, ROBERT. "Doings in Earthsea." New York Times Book Review, 18 February, p. 8.
Review of the Earthsea trilogy. Asserting the difficulty of writing new myths for children, he discusses the now complete Earthsea trilogy. After summarizing each of the three novels, he praises the first and faults the series. A Wizard of Earthsea is "an imaginary garden absolutely hopping with real toads"; but the remaining volumes include "lengthy passages that become tedious," do not include the detail of the first, and do not show the consistency of Ged's character. They do not compare with the energy of Tolkien's Lord of the Rings trilogy nor with the "informing theology" of C.S. Lewis's Narnia tales.

76

D151 _____. Review of The Farthest Shore. Books and Bookmen 18
 (July):106-7.
   All three Earthsea books move through several adventures
 to a climax that "is also a kind of initiation test." This
 last novel is concerned with endings and rebirths which are
 initiations for both Ged and Arren. Compares the finished
 series to Lewis and Tolkien and finds an "imaginative
 timidity" symbolized in each book by an avoidance: Ged
 pursued the shadow instead of confronting it; Arha followed
 Ged to an improved life; Ged shut the door in the land of
 the dead instead of going through it. Admits this criticism may be too severe for a children's series. A Wizard
 of Earthsea is best of the three.

D152 PACE, ERIC. "2 Book Awards Split for First Time." New York
 Times, 11 April, p. 38.
   Announcement of 1973 National Book Awards noting winner
 in children's books, The Farthest Shore.

D153 PORTER, ANDREW, comp. "Special Section: Ursula K. Le Guin's
 Universes." Algol, no. 21 (November), pp. 6-24. Reprinted
 as Dreams Must Explain Themselves; see C92. [Contains
 Le Guin's "Dreams Must Explain Themselves," "National Book
 Award Acceptance Speech," "The Rule of Names"; Douglas
 Barbour, "The Lathe of Heaven: Taoist Dream"; Jonathan
 Ward, "From An Interview." Issue also contains a review;
 see D147.]

D154 SEARLES, BAIRD. "Make Me A World." Village Voice, 12 July.
   Review of The Farthest Shore. Defines "pure fantasy" as
 that middle section of a spectrum that runs from science
 fiction to ghost stories. Surveys its history from William
 Morris and Lord Dunsany to recent books. Cites this novel
 and praises the Earthsea series which is "not flashy but
 beautifully conceived and written."

D155 SISCO, E.P. Review of The Lathe of Heaven. Kliatt Paperback
 Book Guide 7 (September):91.
   Quotes from "Thlon, Uqbar, Orbis Tertius," by Jorge Luis
 Borges. Recommends the novel, not only for its warning
 about easy solutions to world problems, but for its in-
 tricate plot, fine characterization, and word play.

D156 SMITH, SHERYL. Letter to the editor. Riverside Quarterly 6
 (August):90-91.
   Response to Ketterer essay (see D143). Asserts that he
 has read the novel only in light of his own theory. Argues
 that the novel is anthropological, not mythological.

D157 Top of the News 29 (June):302-3.
   Excerpt of Le Guin's National Book Award acceptance

speech [see C43] and of jury's statement.

D158   TOULSON, SHIRLEY.   "Fable and Fantasy: Childhood Haunts."
       New Statesman (25 May), p. 780.
          Review of The Farthest Shore. Series of incidents on
       Ged's and Arren's journey suggest reading this as a "socio-
       political myth." Devoid of the maps and names and language,
       it would be "a pretty run-of-the-mill parable."

                              1974

D159   ALDISS, BRIAN [W.] "SF."   New Review (London) 1 (October):
       65-67.
          Review of The Dispossessed. Warns reader that although
       her invented societies have parallels in contemporary
       political systems, her countries have an independent exis-
       tence. Novel effectively depicts the "ecological and social
       milieux" and complex political models. However, the char-
       acters are subordinate to the ideas. The Urrasti cocktail
       party exemplifies those scenes which are functional for
       the plot but not psychologically motivated. Although the
       novel is clearly significant, it is "joyless"--"one sneaks
       away from its worthy bulk with some relief."

D160   ALLEN, L. DAVID. "The Left Hand of Darkness." In Science
       Fiction: Reader's Guide. Lincoln, Nebr.: Centennial
       Press, pp. 184-97, passim. [See D122.]

D161   ANON. "About Metaphors." Manas 27 (4 December):3-4, 8.
          Review of "Science Fiction Tomorrow." [See C66.] Uses
       article as a springboard to discuss metaphor. Agrees with
       her comment that the value of science fiction is to use
       "irony, fantasy, and nonsense" to free the mind. Criticizes
       Robbe-Grillet's rejection of metaphor and his separation of
       man and things which leads to "a dull postscientific
       stoicism."

D162   ANON. "Easter Books: Quests and Tranquilities." Economist
       251 (13 April):69-70.
          Rejects judgments that children's literature is unim-
       portant and that the modern novel should follow what Roland
       Barthes has described as "a no-style, no-story" model like
       Camus's "L'Etranger." Observes that the epic is becoming
       more popular, its writers more skilled, and its audience
       both adult and child. Praises the Earthsea trilogy as a
       fine example. Identifies its style as "Bunyanesque Eng-
       lish." It seriously discusses the fusion of nature and
       technology, of "passion and realism."

D163   ANON. Review of The Dispossessed. Booklist 70 (15 June):1132.

Cites the novel for significance and appeal beyond science fiction.

D164   ANON. Review of The Dispossessed. Kirkus Reviews 43 (1 March):266.
          Marvels at her skill with a story that "could so easily have been so bad." Character, setting, and contrasting social systems are soundly developed. Praises her as "one of our finest projectionists of brave old and other worlds."

D165   ANON. Review of The Dispossessed. Publishers Weekly 205 (18 March):48.
          Central character confronts "the eternal human dilemma-- man as individual vs. man as part of a group."

D166   BARBOUR, DOUGLAS. Letter to the editor. Algol 11 (May):39.
          Praises issue no. 21 on Le Guin [see D153]. Recommends it and her article, "A Citizen of Mondath" [see C50], for understanding her as a writer. [See additional letters responding to this issue on pp. 40, 41, 46, 48.]

D167   _____. Letter to the editor. Algol 12 (November):48.
          Responds to McGuire's letter and disagrees with his criticisms [see D194].

D168   _____. "On Ursula Le Guin's 'A Wizard of Earthsea.'" River-side Quarterly 6 (April):19-23.
          Novel is not only for children; it contains the same "patterns of meaning (the Quest, the Tao, the creation of a total culture, and the use of light/dark imagery)" found in her other novels. As in City of Illusions, the quest is the plot. Taoism is reflected in the concept of unaction or acceptance of the order of the universe; and in the sense of Equilibrium. Ogion is "a kind of Tao-Zen teacher" and Ged is often the fallen Taoist; supported with quotes from the novel and Taoist books. The total culture is comprised of the centrality of magic, ecology, and culture. Imagery figures in the novel's epigraph which is similar to "Tormer's Lay" in The Left Hand of Darkness. But the meanings are more straightforward; in Earthsea, "darkness is associated with evil; light with good."

D169   _____. "Wholeness and Balance in the Hainish Novels of Ursula K. Le Guin." Science-Fiction Studies 1 (Spring): 164-73. Reprinted in Science-Fiction Studies: Selected Articles on Science Fiction 1973-1975. Edited by R.D. Mullen and Darko Suvin. Boston: Gregg Press, 1976, pp. 146-55.
          In addition to a shared space-time history, the Hainish novels (Rocannon's World, Planet of Exile, City of Illusions, The Left Hand of Darkness, "The Word for World is Forest")

are united by light/dark imagery. Discusses each, showing
that "good emerges from ambiguous darkness, evil from
blinding light." The last two novels show "her artistic
handling of balance as a way of life." In The Left Hand of
Darkness, the Handdara religion resembles Taoism. Uses
quotations from the Taoist books to show both are elusive
philosophies without creeds or institutions which emphasize
inaction and are preoccupied with "wholeness and like-
nesses." "The Word for World is Forest" uses the nature of
dreams and the interrelated culture and ecology to develop
a theme of balance. Athsheans present an image of "holistic
duality" in their equating reason and dreams; they are contrasted to the unbalanced, materialistic Terrans. She uses
the imagery in contrasting the three central characters.
Athshean sanity rests on the "awareness that balance must
be sought where dark and light meet and mix."

D170 BISENIEKS, DAINIS. "Tales from the 'Perilous Realm': Good
      News for the Modern Child." Christian Century 91 (5 June):
      618.
           Criticizes the prejudice of critics, publishers, and
      readers who ghettoize children's books, particularly fan-
      tasy. Quoting Tolkien, he argues that the storyteller re-
      covers "the richness of the created world" in contrast to
      unimaginative modern art of "concrete and glass and steel."
      Fantasy offers worlds and experiences beyond us and can
      "give the consolation of the happy ending." The best fan-
      tasy depicts a "full individualized" hero whose choices are
      inseparable from the self. Uses the Earthsea trilogy as
      one of his examples. Finds A Wizard of Earthsea to be the
      "most satisfying tale." Concludes with a strong criticism
      of "fashionable fiction" which he feels is the real ghetto.

D171 BRINEY, R.E. "SF in Review." Views and Reviews 6 (Fall):
      51-52.
           Review of The Dispossessed. Recommends it for its
      craft, rich story, and philosophical ideas--"a major novel
      which transcends any boundaries of genre."

D172 COOPER, SUSAN. "New High for Sci-Fi." Christian Science
      Monitor, 26 June, p. F4.
           Review of The Dispossessed. Praises its "combination
      of intelligence and imagination." Observes that the two
      worlds "are also the Janus-faces of our own world," with
      freedom problematic in each. Likes the chapter arrangement.

D173 del REY, LESTER. "The Reading Room." Worlds of If 22 (July-
      August):143-45.
           Review of The Dispossessed. After referring to
      Le Guin's works on the Ekumen as a "series," he briefly
      charts its growth in her writing. Recommends this novel

because of its value in providing information to the series.
However, novel is badly flawed in the last "ninety pages."
Shevek quits after his first failure with the Urrasti revolution and his going home with the Hainish is a "deus ex
machina." If the ending were rewritten, it would be an
excellent novel.

D174   DUFFY, DENNIS. "Utopia, Where the Traffic Problem is Only
         Partly Solved." Globe and Mail (Toronto), 31 August, p. 28.
            Review of The Dispossessed. Explains that "imaginative
         fiction" fulfills one of literature's principal functions,
         that is, maintaining "the flow of ideas within a culture"
         (Matthew Arnold). Novel focuses on the crisis of the
         anarchist society after "the original zing of the ideology
         that separates them from the rest of mankind has passed."
         Ideas are developed through the experiences of Shevek. Her
         imperfect utopia is a "bold vision" which consistently
         "feels right" and the resolution of its problems "remains
         open" at the conclusion. Issues are well handled and "take
         on a new vigor."

D175   EDWARDS, MALCOM. Review of The Dispossessed. Science Fiction
         Monthly 1, no. 11:25.
            Claims that with this novel she has transcended the "sf
         label and established herself as an important novelist"
         (as Aldiss, Ballard, Vonnegut did before her). Novel is
         well constructed, "removed from the usual sf technique of
         fast and loose narrative and discussion." Describing "a
         Utopia with feet of clay," she escapes the obvious conflict
         between the perfect society and the imperfect people. Her
         planets share only the human race with Earth, thus she
         "frees herself from the weight of the legacy of our history
         and institutions, and can thus build precisely the worlds
         she needs to build." The novel's debate over power sys-
         tems is weighted toward Anarres. Novel is "extremely well
         written" with believable characters, a fine combination of
         narrative and debate, and "authentic-sounding" science.

D176   EVERS, RICHARD. Review of The Dispossessed. Libertarian
         Review 3 (November):5.
            Praises it as a "philosophical novel that powerfully
         presents a heroic vision of life." Shevek's quest develops
         into a challenge to Shevek's own integrity. Skillful de-
         piction of Anarresti society; the novel does not propagan-
         dize--"the central ideas of mutual aid and moral choice
         come alive . . . in key relationships . . . and in the very
         fluidity of relationships, the directness of speech and
         atmosphere of trust, the unspoken knowledge that each one
         is free and responsible." Suggests that the "syndicalist
         economy" is impractical. Identifies the concept of per-
         manent revolution as the key to "the dramatization of
         utopian life."

D177 FINDSEN, JUDY. "An Unambiguous Utopia." <u>Cincinnati Enquirer</u>,
7 July.
 Review of <u>The Dispossessed</u>. Identifies Le Guin as "a
philosopher; an explorer in the landscapes of the mind."
Praises her political extrapolation, story line, and
imagery.

D178 GEIS, RICHARD. "Ursula Major: A Minor Review of <u>The Dis-
possessed</u>." <u>Alien Critic</u> 3 (November):35–37.
 Praises it as one of the best recent novels and suggests
it may become a cult book like Heinlein's <u>Stranger in a
Strange Land</u>. Well conceived and detailed in characters
and societies. Describes Le Guin's style as restrained,
with major events done "off stage." Thus some of her
passages are too "tame" and her major characters are too
controlled. [For response, see D243.]

D179 GUINN, NANCY. "Science Fiction Future." <u>Seer's Catalogue</u>
(Albuquerque), April.
 Review of <u>The Dispossessed</u>. She has accomplished the
difficult task of envisioning a positive future. Observes
that we see our own culture through "the eyes of the gentle,
thoughtful alien," Shevek, who has no concept of profit and
possession. Praises the writing style which is not de-
pendent on "progressive techniques or tricks."

D180 HALLIDAY, MARK. "This Utopian Fiction is a Tale of Two
Planets." <u>Providence Journal-Bulletin</u>, 20 October.
 Review of <u>The Dispossessed</u>. Equates Le Guin and James
Michener in their concern for the human race, their civic-
mindedness. Novel is about cultures, not individuals, thus
the characters are ideas and "ring hollow." Shevek, for
example, "serves as the Individual Principle, the healthy
mind that casts off socialized nonsense." Recommends the
novel, but warns that it shares the defect of the genre—
"once you take on the whole shape of future society you're
bound to sound like a creatively-written textbook."

D181 HARTWELL, D.G. "Thrilling Wonder Stories." <u>Crawdaddy</u>, p. 22.
 Review of <u>The Dispossessed</u>. The "health" of the science
fiction publishing field is illustrated by the quality of
writers and the care in the design and format of the hardcover books. This novel is a fine example and "could be
Le Guin's 'break-out' book--catapulting her, like Vonnegut,
into mass literary consciousness." Utopian mode is difficult but Le Guin handles it well by always focusing back on
how the central character is affected. Compares the structure to the Victorian novels which developed parallels and
"convergence" by alternating chapters. Claims the novel
will be read and reread, "belonging in the select company
of works such as Zamiatin's <u>We</u> and Huxley's <u>Brave New World</u>,

works which have informed our consciousness in this century."

D182 HEALD, TIM. "Recent Fiction." Daily Telegraph (London), 19
September.
     Review of The Dispossessed. Explains that novel reveals
much about societies more extreme than ours and "of the
individual's response to them." Her arguments are stark.
"Like most parables, however, it makes up in strength what
it lacks in complexity."

D183 HIPOLITO, JANE. "Flatland and Beyond: Characterization in
Science Fiction." In Science Fiction: The Academic Awakening (A CEA Chapbook). Edited by Willis E. McNelly.
[Distributed as supplement of CEA Critic 38 (November):18-
21.]
     Cites The Left Hand of Darkness as an excellent example
of science fiction that develops characters, while Flatland
(Abbott) illustrates science fiction of ideas.

D184 HUTCHINSON, TOM. "Science Fiction." Times (London), 19
September.
     Review of The Dispossessed. Like The Left Hand of Dark-
ness, it uses the symbols of science fiction "for contem-
plation of metaphysical ideas." Like Earthsea, it involves
the reader in a believable imaginary world. Story is well
told and ideas are complex, such as "how even Kropotkinite
anarchists can make prisons without wanting to, and jails
where they did not expect."

D185 KAITZ, MERRILL. "The Dispossessed: A Review." Papers Inc.
(Framingham, Mass.) (November), p. 24.
     Novel deserves top awards. Similarities to contemporary
political systems are clear (Anarres is like "Mao's China"),
but book is more than mere allegory. Fine characterization
of Shevek, "a reactionary revisionist, a Dubcek." Relations
between the sexes are "revolutionary, compassionate, and
concrete." Points out two minor flaws--too much explanation at the beginning, alternation of chapters becomes
"mechanical."

D186 KAUFMAN, JERRY. "Haber Is Destroyed on the Lathe of Heaven."
Starling [fanzine], no. 27 (January), pp. 35-40.
     Opening with a quotation from Le Guin that novels need
to shift from Confucian to Taoist, he asserts that the
opposition of Confucian and Taoist is the "heart and
marrow" of The Lathe of Heaven. Gives brief overview of
Taoist books and philosophy but not Confucian. Claims Orr
is a Taoist who has lost his serenity and tries to regain
it; Haber, his opposite, wants to gain power and change
nature. Uncertain what Lelache's role is; she may represent

"the balance of nature" since she is a mixture of male/
female, light/dark. Characters, however, are not "fully
realized . . . because each has been created to represent
an idea." Orr seems to be the novelist's voice yet he contradicts Le Guin's Vancouver speech [see C31]. Orr is
against all technology while Le Guin urged a balance between technology and knowledge of ecology. Concludes with
personal views.

D187 KEMBALL-COOK, JESSICA. Review of The Farthest Shore. Fantasy
Worlds 1, no. 10 (January).
Surprised by the subject of the last volume of the
trilogy--"an elegiac tale, parallelling the last part of
Beowulf." Inconclusive about the middle section of the
novel--it lags in "intensity," yet its subject is the
draining of "vitality and magic" from the world. The language and atmosphere are "the work of one of the greatest
living writers of fantasy." Praises the entire trilogy and
ranks it with the work of Garner and Tolkien. "Le Guin
demonstrates . . . the purpose of fantasy writing: the
quest as image for the search for self-knowledge, and the
rejection of . . . our ever-real world in order to depict
a situation where necessary values may more sharply be
brought to our notice."

D188 KETTERER, DAVID. New Worlds for Old: The Apocalyptic Imagination, Science Fiction and American Literature. Bloomington:
Indiana University Press, pp. 76-90, passim. [See D143.]

D189 LANE, RONNIE M. "Bridging 'Civilized' Worlds." Grand Rapids
Press, 16 June.
Review of The Dispossessed. Asserts it surpasses The
Left Hand of Darkness; lists the many topics in this novel
that "boldly takes on some of the most important issues of
our day." Notes its power, its ability to entertain and
to provoke. Le Guin is "basically romantic in outlook."

D190 La ROUCHE, ROBERT. "Value The 'Other.'" St. Louis Post Dis-
patch, 3 November.
Review of The Dispossessed. States that Le Guin writes,
neither as a woman or a man, but as "an integrated personality who understands social and personal complexities and
balances." Novel avoids polemic by "relating the abstract"
to very believable characters, especially Shevek. Notes
the ambiguity of the novel's political stance and concludes
"the answer for society lies in the individual's congruence
with self."

D191 LIVINGSTON, DENNIS. "Science Fiction Survey." Futures 6
(December):523-24.
Review of The Dispossessed. Heralds it as a "classic of

the utopian genre" because it combines both good writing
and an "imaginative social vision." Details four characteristics of Anarres which will appeal "to readers in
search of alternate ways of living": (1) "the people are
not rich, but they are happy"; (2) the society "is thoroughly
ecology-minded, both by choice . . . and by necessity";
(3) "women have complete equality with men"; (4) "the
society is not antitechnology, but has very carefully in-
corporated those devices which will enhance its philosophy
of being." Resolution of conflicts is imaged as breaking
down walls.

D192 LUPOFF, RICHARD. "Lupoff's Book Week." Algol, no. 23 (November), pp. 32, 34.
Review of The Dispossessed. Unabashedly impressed with
the novel. Certain aspects remind him of naive Soviet
Union fiction before Lenin's death and of some of C.S.
Lewis's moralizing. Novel is flawed but Le Guin's ambition
is outstanding.

D193 McARDLE, PHIL. "The Joy of Anarchy." Baltimore Sun, 30
June, book sect.
Review of The Dispossessed. Praises the development of
ideas and of characters. Comments on the history of the
anarchist political philosophy, noting its poor survival
record which contrasts with people who have been attracted
to it--"George Orwell, Aldous Huxley, Herbert Read, and
Kenneth Rexroth." Laments that Kropotkin's vision of
mutual aid which Le Guin has detailed can only be imagined
in another year, another world.

D194 McGUIRE, PATRICK. Letter to the editor. Algol 11 (May):46.
Disagrees with Barbour's assessment of The Lathe of
Heaven [see D130]. Criticizes the novel's "neo-Taoist
sermonizing" and the flat characterization of Haber. [See
D167 for Barbour's reply.]

D195 MILLER, DAN. "The Gift of Wisdom, in a Futuristic Setting."
Chicago Daily News Panorama, 22-23 June, p. 8.
Review of The Dispossessed. Coming from the "humanistic
tradition," the novel concerns a "quest not to gain something, but to give something."

D196 NICHOLLS, PETER. "Showing Children the Value of Death."
Foundation 5 (January):71-80. Reprinted in SF Commentary,
nos. 41/42 (February 1975), pp. 75-79.
Review of The Farthest Shore. With writing as fine as
Le Guin's and Alan Garner's, it is useless to speak of
adult, as opposed to children's, literature. Justifies
reviewing the trilogy in a science fiction journal because
Le Guin's magicians are scientists and the rules of magic

are rigorous. Compares it to Tolkien's trilogy and finds
it better: "where Tolkien is expansive, Ursula Le Guin is
condensed"; she has "deeper resources of language" which
he supports by comparative quotes. He praises her sharp
images but criticizes her lightly for an occasional unnecessary adjective. Identifies her as a metaphysician in
light of her major theme of mutually necessary dualities
and is reminded of Donne and Yeats. She is clearly "un-
Christian." Strong similarities to her science fiction.
Praises her for writing with both intelligence and emotion
and looks forward to her next book.

D197 NIXON, PETER. "The Best Read of 1973." Children's Literature
in Education, no. 14 (September), pp. 18-20.
Review of The Farthest Shore. Quotes part of his conversation with an eleven-year-old student about the novel.
Student recognizes the undercurrent of ideas about balance
and equilibrium; novel suggests to him scenes of contemporary life. They discuss convincing relationship of Arren
and Ged and the "reality" of this fantasy.

D198 NOWELL, ROBERT. "Secular analogue." Tablet (London), 23
November.
Review of The Dispossessed. Asserts it is flawed because "the author's imagination has built up a situation
he is unable to find any satisfactory solution to." Praises
the setting, the characterization, the social conflict and
the fact that they all blend in her major theme of "freedom
and responsibility." Review concludes with praise for the
lack of "easy answers" to the social problems. "Miss
Le Guin has given us a powerful secular analogue to St.
Paul's great distinction between the freedom of grace and
the bondage of law."

D199 NYE, ROBERT. "Family Matters." Guardian (London), 9 December.
Review of The Dispossessed. Labeling the novel "noisy
with ideas," he faults it for weak characterization and
action. Compares it unfavorably to David Lindsay's A
Voyage to Arcturus.

D200 PIERCE, J.J. Review of The Dispossessed. Renaissance
[fanzine] 6 (June/July):5-6.
Compares her to Cordwainer Smith: "both were striving
. . . to reconcile two systems of value in science fiction:
those of evolution and tradition, of change and permanence."
Prior to Smith, the two separate viewpoints were upheld by
Wells and C.S. Lewis. This novel is in the vein of recon-
ciliation. Shevek is not only believable, he is "perhaps
the first convincing portrait in modern SF of a utopian
man, one who takes for granted that the ideal should be the
real." His search for the time theory expresses his and

the author's belief that the "ideals of change and permanence" can be unified. The world of Anarres is authentic; but the world of Urras is "less successful." Its virtues and vices "are either too arbitrary, or too predictable," because it is too obviously the opposite of Anarres, too obviously like Earth. Just as The Lathe of Heaven was flawed because the Taoism was too explicit and "The Word for World is Forest" was flawed because Davidson was too clearly a villain, so The Dispossessed is flawed because the "foil for her utopia isn't convincing enough."

D201 PLATT, CHARLES. Review of The Dispossessed. Locus, no. 162 (20 July), pp. 3-4.
       Compares it to The Lathe of Heaven in that it offers no easy solution. Because it focuses on the nature of the individual and society, it is relevant now and will be relevant long after Asimov and Clarke are not; thus it fulfills the characteristics of the best science fiction.

D202 POHL, FREDERICK. "SF East: an SF Safari to Redland." Galaxy 35 (November):62-78.
       Describes a long visit to Eastern Europe, discussing science fiction in many countries. To illustrate contemporary American science fiction, he describes three novels which will never appear in Soviet block countries: Delany's Dahlgren, Russ's The Female Man, and Le Guin's The Dispossessed. [See response, D220.]

D203 ROGAN, HELEN. "Future Imperatives." Time 104 (5 August):84-85.
       Review of The Dispossessed. Praises the "sinewy grace" of her style; emphasizes Shevek's criticism of Anarres that leads him to Urras and to "re-examine his philosophy of life." Predicts the novel will win both the Hugo and Nebula.

D204 SCHOLES, ROBERT. "The Good Witch of The West." Hollins Critic 11 (April):1-12. Reprinted with an additional introduction and conclusion in Structural Fabulation: An Essay on Fiction of the Future. Notre Dame: University of Notre Dame Press, 1975, pp. 77-99. Section reprinted in Science Fiction: History, Science, Vision. Edited by Robert Scholes and Eric S. Rabkin. London: Oxford University Press, 1977, pp. 75-79.
       Initiates the critical attention her excellent fiction deserves by examining A Wizard of Earthsea and The Left Hand of Darkness. Earthsea trilogy is better then Lewis's Narnia tales. Rather than simply restating a known legend (the Christ story) and relying on the reader's conditioned response, she bases the legends on a broader metaphysic. She posits a dynamic, balanced universe, not dependent on a

creator, whose ethic is ecology. <u>Wizard</u> shows the power of
individual redemption. <u>Left Hand</u> is her finest work, however, because it shows the complexities of culture and
society. It uses the alien encounter better than most
science fiction, features the characters, and examines how
our perceptions of the world are formed. She weaves together both political and personal issues--"everything is
summed up in the relationship between the two main characters, and the narrative is shaped to present this relationship with maximum intensity."

D205 SEARLES, BAIRD. "'The Dispossessed': Visit From a Small
        Planet." <u>Village Voice</u>, 21 November, pp. 56, 58.
        After a brief overview of twentieth-century science
fiction, showing its movement from "a craft to an art," he
cites <u>The Left Hand of Darkness</u> as a "pivotal" novel which
demonstrated the ability of science fiction to broaden the
human horizon and to educate. This new novel is equally
good. He praises its fine detail of the "viable anarchist
society" including the invention of a new language, the
absorbing drama, the believable characters who are products
of their culture. Observes that "Ms. Le Guin does not
necessarily offer definitive answers, but she certainly
clarifies the questions."

D206 SEYMOUR-SMITH, MARTIN. "Thinking Italian." <u>Oxford Mail</u>, 9
        December.
        Review of <u>The Dispossessed</u>. Urges categorizing it not
as science fiction but as utopian fiction because she is
primarily interested in "the possibilities for metaphysical
and . . . politico-sociological explorations" which science
fiction genre cannot offer. Novel of character and situation, not ideas.

D207 SLATER, IAN. Review of <u>The Dispossessed</u>. <u>Fantasiae</u> 2 (Septem-
        ber):6-7.
        Counter to his own editorial policy, he reviews a science
fiction book because of its importance which stems from its
"high literary quality" and its persuasive description of a
functional anarchist society. He provides context by reviewing Hainish history. Observes that "part of the book
becomes an analysis of the meaning of Hell" as Terrans,
Hainish, Anarresti, and Urrasti present conflicting evaluations of Urras. Novel makes the reader feel Shevek's shock
over the consumer society. In a footnote, recommends <u>The</u>
<u>Anarchists</u>, edited by Irving L. Horowitz, for a survey of
anarchist thought.

D208 STURGEON, THEODORE. "<u>Galaxy</u> Bookshelf." <u>Galaxy</u> 35 (June):
        97-98.
        Review of <u>The Dispossessed</u>. High praise for her style,

story, and characters. Novel is both an exploration of
another social system and a biography of a man with whom
the reader empathizes.

D209 TOWNSEND, JOHN ROWE. <u>Written For Children: An Outline of
English-Language Children</u>'s Literature. Philadelphia:
Lippincott, pp. 251-52.
   In the context of discussing 1960's fantasy, he describes
the Earthsea trilogy, along with works by Alan Garner,
Lloyd Alexander, Joan Aiken, Rosemary Harris, Helen
Cresswell--all of whom write fantasy without catering to
children. Le Guin's theme is relevant to a world of science
and technology: "the greater the power the greater the
responsibility, and the vital balance cannot lightly be
disturbed."

D210 TUCHMAN, JAN. "Stellar Bookends." <u>Colorado Daily</u>, 3 September.
   Review of <u>The Dispossessed</u>. Different from and better
than <u>The Left Hand of Darkness</u> and <u>The Lathe of Heaven</u>.
Le Guin is especially talented in creating "characters with
whole personalities," and "suspenseful story line," as well
as developing "societal politics and the physics of the
universe." Observes that she is the only major science
fiction writer "who would cast the great thinker and revolutionary leader as a woman."

D211 WALKER, PAUL. "In A Critical Condition." <u>Luna Monthly</u>, no.
55 (October), pp. 16-17.
   Review of <u>The Dispossessed</u>. Defines and characterizes
"the paranoid novel" and reviews several current examples.
A post-World War Two response to "Hitler, Stalin, and
McCarthy," it grew out of a recognition that "genuinely
evil" people could gain political power and that technology's
"existence and growth" was "irrestible." Its basic idea is
that "somewhere out there someone is in charge" and that
someone is "in pursuit of power for its own sake." "Right-
wing paranoia" novels, like <u>Winter Kills</u> by Richard Condon,
criticizes but offers no solutions, suggesting that there
is no remedy. "Left-wing paranoia" is the utopian novel
which sees "the only solution as an escape into simplistic
fantasy." <u>The Dispossessed</u> is "brilliantly successful."
The criticism is offered in the Urras chapters and Anarres
is a realistic solution. Not only is it a novel of ideas,
it is also to be praised for its setting, characterization,
and structure.

D212 WALLACE, DOREEN. "Another Inhabited Planet." <u>Eastern Daily
Press</u> (Norwich), 27 September.
   Review of <u>The Dispossessed</u>. Fails to see the relevance
of chapter arrangement. Wishes this and other science fiction "had the cutting edge of their first exemplar, Swift.

Satire is more exhilarating to read than earnestness."

D213 WARWICK, MAL. Review of The Dispossessed. Locus, no. 167
      (20 November), p. 5.
          Finds it an outstanding book, although the plot is
      slowed down by discussion of ideas. The resolution, the
      easily found passage for Shevek back to Anarres, is "dramat-
      ically unsatisfying."

D214 WEBB, KAYE. "Children's Writer's." Observer (London), 3
      November, p. 26.
          Believes that A Wizard of Earthsea has established a
      new standard by which to judge children's fantasy. It has
      a wholeness that belies the process of creation, yet "is
      achieved with such artful simplicity." Whole trilogy is a
      "major contribution."

D215 WHALEY, STEPHEN V., and COOK, STANLEY J. "Man and His Chil-
      dren: Generations of Change." In Man Unwept: Visions
      from the Inner Eye. New York: McGraw-Hill, pp. 277-82.
          Introduces section in which "Nine Lives" appears by dis-
      cussing parent-child relationship, as represented in the
      Romantics, on the one hand, and the Victorians, on the
      other. Analyzes that relationship in stories by D.H.
      Lawrence, Collier, Kuttner, and Le Guin.

D216 WILLIAMSON, JACK. "SF in the Classroom." Science Fiction:
      The Academic Awakening (A CEA Chapbook). Edited by Willis
      E. McNelly. Distributed as supplement to CEA Critic 38
      (November):11-14.
          The Left Hand of Darkness appears on his list of the
      dozen most used books in the classroom.

D217 WORDSWORTH, CHRISTOPHER. "Hopes and Dreams." Observer (Lon-
      don), 6 October, p. 30.
          Review of The Dispossessed. Compares its clarity of
      setting and people to the Earthsea trilogy. Likes its
      attention to detail. "This eidolon of a future immense
      with hope and hazard has a firmamental sincerity and the
      solid fuel of a first-rate narrative."

1975

D218 ADAMS, PHOEBE-LOU. Review of The Wind's Twelve Quarters.
      Atlantic Monthly 236 (December):118.
          Recommends her for those who dislike science fiction be-
      cause "her knack of translating recognizable states of mind
      into fantastic action brings her close to the old fairy
      tale field."

D219 ANON. Review of The Dispossessed. Solidarity Newsletter
no. 12, pp. 1, 3.
Praises its convincing alien worlds, characterization,
and style; but is particularly intrigued with the libertarian ideas on Anarres. Speculates that she "must either
be a libertarian, or she has done a superb job of research
getting into the libertarian mind."

D220 BANKIER, JENNIFER. "Socialism and The Dispossessed, or a
Study in Selective Perception." Witch and The Chameleon 3
(April):4-8.
Disagrees with two commentators who suggested the novel
would be banned in the Soviet Union [see D192 and D202].
Actually, it explicitly criticizes capitalism and depicts
a functioning socialist society. Supports her assertion
with quotes and a comparison of the PDC with the power of
the employer in modern America. If the book were banned in
the Soviet Union, it would be for Shevek's criticism of the
centralized, authoritarian socialist state of Thu which is
like Russia. Concludes by speculating on the sympathies of
different readers which leads to seeing different things in
the novel. [For Le Guin's favorable response, see C91.]

D221 BARBOUR, DOUGLAS. Letter to the editor. SF Commentary, nos.
44/45 (December), p. 92.
Reply to Turner's review of The Dispossessed [see D288].
Objects to his assumption about how a novel is written. It
is risky to state that Le Guin consciously selected the
frame for it before she started writing or to divide the
novel into its fictional elements. Such an approach limits
Turner's reading of the novel, although Barbour does agree
with many of his comments.

D222 _____. "Wholeness and Balance: An Addendum." Science-Fiction
Studies 2 (November):248-49. Reprinted in Science-Fiction
Studies: Selected Articles on Science Fiction 1973-1975.
Edited by R.D. Mullen and Darko Suvin. Boston: Gregg
Press, 1976, pp. 278-79.
A note to his earlier article on the Hainish novels
[see D169]. Asserts that The Dispossessed fits the pattern
of her other Hainish novels by using the "paradoxical
light/dark pattern," as well as an image series peculiar
to the novel.

D223 BIERMAN, JUDAH. "Ambiguity in Utopia: The Dispossessed."
Science-Fiction Studies 2 (November):240-55. Reprinted in
Science-Fiction Studies: Selected Articles on Science Fic-
tion 1973-1975. Edited by R.D. Mullen and Darko Suvin.
Boston: Gregg Press, 1976, pp. 279-85.
Argues for reading the novel in the context of modern
utopias. "It is a prizeworthy contribution to the debate

about the responsibility of knowledge, of the visionary and of the scientist, in a planned society." Proposes her utopia is ambiguous in two senses. First, "the place is only ambiguously good." Scarcity of Anarres calls into question all assumptions about plenty and paradise in utopia, as well as the role of the flourishing genius. Second, the lifestyle is based on ambiguity in that "inevitable social and environmental changes" necessitate new choices by the individual. "Le Guin establishes continuing choice as the human condition, burden and joy." Concludes by discussing the novel in relation to her previous works. Previously, personal actions were not as central to the individual and social issues; the protagonist/outsider viewed a nonutopian society and offered no alternative vision. In the Earthsea trilogy, she moved forward by using an individual at the center of things who makes the crucial moral choices. Shevek is distinctly different because he is shaped by his utopian social and political environment. Predicts hopefully that her next novel will examine the Hainish people.

D224 CANARY, ROBERT H. "New Worlds for Old?" Science-Fiction
      Studies 2 (July):130-33.
          Part of the Ketterer Forum [see D262 and D326]. Rejects
      Ketterer's theory that science fiction is essentially
      apocalyptic. Includes a one-paragraph response to
      Ketterer's chapter on Le Guin. Ketterer's emphasis on
      archetypal patterns causes him to ignore the plot element
      that involves Ai and Estraven's relationship and the "permanent
      dualities" of Gethen. Thus Ketterer misses the
      novel's essential unity.

D225 CASSEL, ANN L. "Civil Liberties and Science Fiction: The
      Civil Rights and Feminist Movements Reflected in Selected
      Writings of Ursula K. Le Guin." Discovery: The Journal of
      the Humanities and Social Sciences of University College,
      Rutgers, pp. 1-7.
          Discusses Planet of Exile, The Left Hand of Darkness,
      and "The Word for World is Forest" to show her concern for
      racial and sexual equality. Planet depicts the necessity
      of cooperation and peaceful coexistence between the two
      races, a condition Le Guin sees as "the hope and salvation
      of the world." Left Hand is her best novel, "a classic of
      compassion and insight" into this topic. "World" is the
      most explicit exploration of the damages of racism. Cassel
      quotes frequently from a letter she received from Le Guin
      in 1974, using it to conclude her article: "Racism, sexism,
      political injustices, governmental oppression and the
      power of any elite or individual, are anathema to me. . . .
      I am left in the middle, voting Democratic and swearing;
      thinking non-violent anarchism and dreaming; and writing

down some of my curses and dreams."

D226 CHAUVIN, CY. "The Two Sides of Ursula K. Le Guin." Khatru 2
      [fanzine] (May), pp. 41-43.
           Asserts her fantasy and science fiction cannot be con-
      sidered separately because they share too many characteris-
      tics. Demonstrates his thesis by examining her earliest
      short stories, "April in Paris" and "The Dowry of
      Angyar" and one novel, City of Illusions. Notes Le Guin's
      first three novels show influence of Andre Norton and they
      are similarly flawed in that some elements of the environ-
      ment and culture do not quite fit together. Justifies
      Le Guin's blending of fantasy and science fiction by first
      citing Roger Zelazny's statement that the fantastic is to
      be accepted as both "plausible and mysterious." Second,
      he argues that they blend inward and outward, past and
      future which is the source of power in her fiction.

D227 _____. "The Future in Books." Amazing Science Fiction 49
      (July):113-14.
           Review of The Farthest Shore. Heralds it as the best
      fantasy or science fiction novel for 1972. Commends its
      detailed environment, strong style, and excellent character-
      ization. Warns readers not to be misled by the juvenile
      label.

D228 COMMITTEE OF THE YOUNG ADULT SERVICES DIVISION. "Best Books
      for Young Adults, 1974." Booklist 71 (15 March):747-48.
           The Dispossessed is included in an annotated list of
      thirty-five books, selected by this division of the American
      Library Association.

D229 COSGRAVE, MARY SILVA. "Outlook Tower." Horn Book Magazine 51
      (June):297-98.
           Review of The Dispossessed. Notes the fine contrast
      between the two worlds--a "speculative and provocative
      novel."

D230 DAMROSCH, BARBARA. "What's New From Venus?" Village Voice,
      7 July, pp. 39-40.
           Strongly criticizes old science fiction as being sexist
      fiction for the adolescent male. Like other popular fic-
      tion, books by men are always about "A Man Rises to the
      Challenge." Books by women are about "Something Terrible
      Is Happening to a Woman." Current science fiction has be-
      come more androgynous and speculative. Sturgeon's Venus
      Plus X was an early novel; Le Guin's The Left Hand of
      Darkness is a "rare achievement." "The best contribution
      women make to s f is their respect for the emotional vul-
      nerability that keeps us all human."

Part D: Critical Studies

D231 DANZIG, ALLAN. Review of Wild Angels. Science Fiction Review Monthly, no. 4 (June), p. 2.
  Fine, brief analysis of the concerns of her fiction that reappear in her poetry--concrete imagery, invented places, humanism, and tradition. Cites "Coming of Age" as the most ambitious and ultimately hopeful.

D232 DELAP, RICHARD. Review of A Wizard of Earthsea. Delap's F & SF Review, no. 6 (September), pp. 18-19.
  Praising the artistry in all of her fiction, he finds this novel a book for both adults and juveniles. The major and minor characters are sharply drawn and move in close accord with the "vigorous plot." The episode with the old couple on the deserted island is a sensitive account of "communication and love and humanity."

D233 del REY, LESTER. "The Siren Song of Academe." Galaxy 36 (March):69-80. Reprinted in Antaeus, nos. 25/26 (Spring/Summer), 1977, pp. 312-22.
  Contribution to a discussion of academia and science fiction which was preceded by the following: (1) Ben Bova, "Teaching Science Fiction," Analog 93 (June):5-6, 8, 176-78; (2) James Gunn, "Teaching Science Fiction Revisited," Analog 94 (November):5-6, 8, 10, 175-78; (3) see C77. It was followed by C88. Objects to the cliché, "Science fiction ghetto" used by both Gunn and Le Guin. Arguing from personal experience, he rejects the label. After answering Gunn's essay, he turns to Le Guin's. He argues with her standards for science fiction, but disagrees with her negative assessment of Golden Age Science Fiction. He asserts that science fiction writers have always treated contemporary social issues. Argues that science fiction is and is not escapist. He is most sensitive to her urging writers and fans to listen to the new academic criticism and recommends that everyone read C.S. Lewis's An Experiment in Criticism. He welcomes criticism, but vows it will not affect the way he writes and he doubts that there are any capable critics of science fiction.

D234 DISCH, TOM. Letter to the editor. SF Commentary, nos. 44/45 (December), p. 89.
  Reply to Turner's review of The Dispossessed; [see D288]. Agrees with Turner's assessment but adds that the novel should ultimately be viewed as a Bildungsroman. Anarres is the "classroom stage of the hero's education" and Urras is the "Real World" in which the ethical theory must be acted out. Thus, Anarres and Urras are not just two different worlds in the utopia/dystopia argument. Le Guin reflects contemporary theories (such as Melanie Klein's) about the significance of family relationships in the formation of character.

94

D235 FREDERICKS, S.C. "A Unique Critical Method." Science-Fiction
     Studies 2 (July):134-37.
          Part of the Ketterer Forum [see D262 and D326]. In-
     trigued with Ketterer's depiction of the significance of
     the apocalyptic imagination, but rejects it as a definition
     for the science fiction genre. Although not mentioning
     Le Guin directly, he does criticize Ketterer's use of
     Frye's principle as prescriptive and asserts that Ketterer
     is biased against writers who use myth deliberately.

D236 GILLESPIE, BRUCE. "A Trip to the Group Mind . . . Australian
     S F Writers' Workshop." SF Commentary, nos. 44/45 (Decem-
     ber), pp. 9-10.
          · Recounts the planning and organizing of the workshop
     which Le Guin had suggested be held in conjunction with the
     World SF Convention in Melbourne--the problems of obtaining
     funding, a site, and publicity. Focusing on Le Guin as
     director, he relates the activities, mood, and accomplish-
     ments of the workshop.

D237 _____. "Ursula Le Guin: Explorer of New Worlds." Educational
     Magazine (Australia) 32, no. 3.
          Explains the World Science Fiction Convention to be held
     in Melbourne and introduces Australians to Le Guin's fic-
     tion. Summarizes the three Earthsea volumes and suggests
     readers are attracted to her as a "superecologist" who
     stresses the necessity for equilibrium. Surveys her other
     novels and rise of her reputation. All her protagonists
     learn by not trying to control others.

D238 GRIMSTAD, KIRSTEN, and RENNIE, SUSAN, eds. ". . . And the
     new Science Fiction." In The New Woman's Survival Source-
     book. New York: Knopf, pp. 131-33.
          General article on the absence of significant treatment
     of male-female relationships in science fiction, followed
     by strong criticism of Le Guin's sexism. Science fiction,
     as a speculative genre, is flawed by its failure to treat
     women as anything more than "Mother and Server of Man."
     Argues that science fiction by women is often distinguished
     by a greater sensitivity to ethical issues and to change
     as a result of human (not machine) capability. Praises
     Le Guin's style and narrative ability but finds her female
     characters before The Dispossessed to be "the crudest patri-
     archal stereotypes: treacherous seductress, sex object,
     sweet young thing; above all, adjuncts to men, who are the
     dreamers and doers." The Left Hand of Darkness is acutely
     disappointing because the hermaphrodites are really males.
     The writers mistake Genly Ai's naive sexism for Le Guin's
     own. They are therefore amazed at the depiction of equal-
     ity for women in The Dispossessed.

Part D: Critical Studies

D239 HAMILTON-PATERSON, JAMES. "Allegorical Imperatives." Times
      Literary Supplement, 20 June, p. 704.
          Review of The Dispossessed. Overall, novel is too
      earnest and the allegory is too obvious. Urras is too
      close to America and Anarres is "the China that Western
      utopians like to believe in."

D240 HARTWELL, DAVID G. Review of The Dispossessed. Science Fic-
      tion Review Monthly, no. 5 (July), p. 3.
          Heralds it as a classic, ranking with We and Brave New
      World. Recounts its publishing history and discusses the
      novel's structure. Novel's ambiguity rests on the inability
      of either society to deal successfully with Shevek, the
      genius.

D241 HIGGINS, JUDITH. "Publishing Children's Paperbacks: A Talk
      With Puffin's Kaye Webb." Publishers Weekly (24 February),
      pp. 67-68.
          Le Guin's work referred to in this interview with the
      editor of Puffin, Penguin's paperback line of children's
      books. Discusses standards for children's books and dif-
      ferences between American and British market.

D242 HILL, DAVID W. "The Mythology of Control in The Left Hand of
      Darkness." N.p., tapette. One cassette tape, forty min-
      utes, of paper delivered at Worlds of Science Fiction Con-
      ference, Claremont College, Pomona, Calif. Deposited in
      Spaced-Out Library, Toronto.
          Insists author consciously attacks the myth of control,
      prominent in the science fiction adventure story. She uses
      the conventions of the adventure story to undercut it. She
      thus criticizes contemporary culture which is "preoccupied
      with control and a belief in its efficacy." Novel is also
      concerned with the writing of a science fiction novel, that
      is, Ai is self-consciously interpreting his experiences; so
      he functions as reader, writer, and protagonist. Ai's
      experiences teach him the shortcomings of the principle of
      control. The Handdara religion, for example, points up the
      limits of predictive knowledge: "Their desire for igno-
      rance is an attempt to avoid the stagnation that comes from
      our impulse to control the future through predictive knowl-
      edge." But the Yomesh cult with its assertion of total
      knowledge, results in a totalitarian state. In Le Guin's
      world, growth results from accepting "the uncertainty which
      produces a spontaneous, shadowed, surprising, open, and
      therefore evolutionary future."

D243 HOWARD, DENYS. Letter to the editor. Science Fiction Review
      (The Alien Critic) 4, whole no. 13 (May):33.
          Response to Geis's review of The Dispossessed [see D178].
      Argues that if the Odonian society has no gender roles then

the proheterosexual message should not be so strong. Les-
bians are not depicted and homosexual males appear "only
in cursory scenes." He reports asking Le Guin about this
major flaw, but her answer that homosexuality was not part
of her experience, has angered and alienated him. [For
Le Guin's response, see C126; for Howard's reply, see D333.]

D244   HUNTINGTON, JOHN. "Public and Private Imperatives in Le
       Guin's Novels." Science-Fiction Studies 2 (November):237-
       43. Reprinted in Science-Fiction Studies: Selected Arti-
       cles on Science Fiction 1973-1975. Edited by R.D. Mullen
       and Darko Suvin. Boston: Gregg Press, 1976, pp. 267-73.
          His thesis is that Le Guin's protagonist "has difficulty
       reconciling his public, political obligations with the
       bonds he has developed as a private individual." This
       dilemma leads the character, novel, and novelist into an
       examination of "different political structures." Analyzes
       the novels chronologically to show her different perspec-
       tives on the problem. Rocannon's World, typical of the
       early novels shows that "the success of the heroic guest
       entails personal loss." The Left Hand of Darkness reduces
       the urgency of public action and emphasizes the private
       world; its tale, "Estraven the Traitor," epitomizes the
       "discrepancy between the public and private worlds." She
       keeps the two worlds in balance, but in the next works she
       does not. The Lathe of Heaven shows the failure of public
       action; "The Word for World is Forest" shows that under
       adverse political systems, public action must take prece-
       dence over private action. All of the works are probing
       "for the point at which the public and private imperatives
       intersect, for the act that will allow them to be unified,
       if only momentarily." The Dispossessed is a breakthrough
       because it depicts "the private world almost totally as a
       function of specific political systems."

D245   JAMESON, FREDRIC. "World-Reduction in Le Guin: The Emer-
       gence of Utopian Narrative." Science-Fiction Studies 2
       (November):221-30. Reprinted in Science-Fiction Studies:
       Selected Articles on Science Fiction 1973-1975. Edited by
       R.D. Mullen and Darko Suvin. Boston: Gregg Press, 1976,
       pp. 251-60.
          The multiple narrative modes and themes in The Left Hand
       of Darkness raise the issue of the novel's unity. In set-
       tling the issue, Jameson describes the unique method of
       "world construction" which she uses. Most narrative thought
       experiments in science fiction use either analogy or extrap-
       olation; Le Guin uses "world-reduction": "a principle of
       systematic exclusions, a kind of surgical excision of em-
       pirical reality, . . . in which the sheer teeming multi-
       plicity of what exists . . . is deliberately thinned and
       weeded out. . . ." This technique is also the central

feature of all four of the novel's themes: ecology, religion, ambisexuality, and social systems. To illustrate only the last, Jameson argues that The Left Hand of Darkness is "the attempt to rethink Western history without capitalism." This novel functions also as a criticism of the imagined utopia and thus is the "proving ground" for The Dispossessed. Utopia as a "no-place," "untormented by sex or history," is demonstrated to be impossible in this novel--Karhide's development is indeed advancing.

D246 JONAS, GERALD. "Of Things To Come." New York Times Book Review, 26 October, pp. 48-49.
      Review of The Dispossessed. Characterizes all her novels as being "anthropological" and "seamless" because they involve the following: the creation of a world, including physical characteristics; the creation of a protagonist who is a product of that society on that world. This novel is a fine utopia because Anarres, even though flawed, is both "plausible and likeable." Shevek, in his experience on Urras, learns what "every good Odonian should always have known: There is no universal prescription for Utopia," that is, the strengths of Anarres cannot be transported to another world.

D247 KELLER, D. Review of The Wind's Twelve Quarters. Fantasiae 3 (November/December):15.
      Applauds the gathering together of Le Guin's fine short fiction, accompanied by "her own fascinating and witty comments."

D248 KETTERER, DAVID. "In Response." Science-Fiction Studies 2 (July):139-46.
      Part of the Ketterer Forum [see D262 and D326]. Restates his intention in New Worlds for Old and responds to the theoretical criticisms. Includes a detailed response to Le Guin's objections beginning with the suspicion that she has not read the entire book and so has misunderstood his definition of apocalyptic. He reasserts the apocalyptic nature of The Left Hand of Darkness. Although pleased that Le Guin acknowledges her plot does not "reflect" Gethenian sexuality, he argues that she did not recognize that "my whole argument amounted to an attempt to heal this breach." Admits he was ignorant of Le Guin's Taoism and failed to clarify the difference between mythic structure and mythic content.

D249 LEFANU, SARAH. "Ursula Le Guin: Science Fiction." Spare Rib [UK fanzine] (May), pp. 40-42.
      Review of The Dispossessed. Credits her with the rare ability to create unique characters for her alternate worlds. Her protagonist-as-exile offers a perspective from

which to explore normalcy in social, political, and sexual relationships. Supports with analysis of The Left Hand of Darkness and The Dispossessed, crediting her with focusing on "the dialectics between modes of production, sexuality, and consciousness." Feels she does not develop her ideas on sexuality to their logical conclusions. She limits her imagination by two principles: the primacy of the concept of balance and the use of a single central character. "The political potential . . . is lost in the mysticism of an individual consciousness."

D250 LEIBER, FRITZ. "From Asgard to Elfland." Fantastic 24 (February):113-17.
      Review of From Elfland to Poughkeepsie. Recommends it to writers and readers as an outstanding essay on language of modern fantasy. As he summarizes the essay, he adds his own discussion and examples in support of her assertions. Disagrees with her statement that fantasy is "only a construct built in the void, with every joint and seam and nail exposed." Does acknowledge his objection may be his own reservations about totally unleashing his subconscious.

D251 LEVIN, JEFF[REY H.]. "Ursula K. Le Guin: A Select Bibliography." Science-Fiction Studies 2 (November):204-8. Reprinted in Science-Fiction Studies: Selected Articles on Science Fiction 1973-1975. Edited by R.D. Mullen and Darko Suvin. Boston: Gregg Press, 1976, pp. 234-38.
      The first extensive list of her publications. Accuracy enhanced by his access to Le Guin's library. Listing is divided into three categories: collections, stories and novels, and general (nonfiction--primarily essays, interviews, and reviews). Items within each category are arranged chronologically; contains all known publications of each item, including foreign editions. No secondary material is included.

D252 MACKENZIE, JIM. "The all-too-familiar outer world." Nation Review (Melbourne), 26 September-2 October, p. 1285.
      Review of The Dispossessed. Series of questions designed to induce the reader to read this novel. Concludes praising it as story, social criticism, and literature of ideas.

D253 McNELLY, WILLIS E. "'Sci-Fi': State of the Art." America 133 (8 November):304-7.
      Overview of contemporary science fiction to demonstrate its high quality. Le Guin is named and praised. The Left Hand of Darkness and The Dispossessed offer us ways to "distance ourselves from ourselves."

D254 McINTYRE, VONDA N. "The West Coast Nebula Banquet." SFWA

Bulletin (July), pp. 8-9.

Informal account of the banquet. Because the official award ceremony was in New York, balloons were substituted for the Nebulas. Le Guin won two for *The Dispossessed* and "The Day Before the Revolution."

D255 MILLER, DAN. "Future Perfect Turns to Past Tense." *American Libraries* 6 (March):169.

Review of *The Dispossessed*. In an overview of recently published primary and secondary books in science fiction, he notes the genre's escape from the ghetto. Cites Le Guin's novel as "a brilliantly conceived and stunningly executed philosophical novel."

D256 _____. "The Hugo and Nebula Awards." *Booklist* (1 November).

Announcement of Hugo and Nebula awards with Le Guin cited several times.

D257 _____. "Science Fiction." *Chicago Daily News Panorama*, 8-9 November, p. 10.

Review of *The Wind's Twelve Quarters*. Declares "Le Guin fashions ideas like a goldsmith: intricate, involved and confident" and knows when to couch them in science fiction and when in fantasy. Collection valuable for illustrating her artistry, her development as a writer, and the relationship between these stories and her novels.

D258 MILLER, P. SCHUYLER. "The Reference Library: The Place of Man." *Analog* 94 (January):170-72.

Review of *The Dispossessed*. Identifies it as one of the Hainish novels which aptly illustrate that the whole universe is man's potential habitat if he can adapt to its conditions. Praises the strong characterization and hopes that it will be widely read by the youth because it can teach them about human nature and show the corruption of anarchy.

D259 MINES, SAMUEL. "Beyond the Bug-Eyed Monster." *Washington Post*, 14 September, H.

Review of *The Dispossessed*, *A Wizard of Earthsea*, *The Tombs of Atuan*. Praises the high quality of science fiction literature which has appeared in the last two decades. Cites Le Guin as a new author. *The Dispossessed* is well written, although "slightly ponderous," and is reminiscent of the still-popular historical novel. Two volumes of the trilogy are mentioned as being "written in a rich and fruity style suited to the theme."

D260 NUDELMAN, REFAIL. "An Approach to the Structure of Le Guin's SF." Translated by Alan G. Myers. *Science-Fiction Studies* 2 (November):210-20. Reprinted in *Science-Fiction Studies:*

Selected Articles on Science Fiction 1973-1975. Edited by
R.D. Mullen and Darko Suvin. Boston: Gregg Press, 1976,
pp. 240-50.
Drawing examples most frequently from The Left Hand of
Darkness, he discusses the nature of Le Guin's "artistic
originality." Two fundamental characteristics of her
textual structure are "radial linkage" and "iconicity."
Her novels are interconnected, not sequentially but
radially; that is, each story moves "from a single centre
[the League]" outward toward the particular planet and
story. "The essential structural principle" is iconicity,
that is, the particular narrative serves as an equivalent
for (an image of) the abstract idea. Le Guin's recurring
central idea is the groping for a lost unity in an atmosphere of "separateness, fragmentation, alienation." On all
levels of the text ("the universe--the world of the individual planet--the islets of life on it--the individual
person") this groping occurs. Thus "its structure becomes
a sign of its message." The plot structure is characterized by the cyclic journey. Myth and fairy tale plots,
"involving a formal return to their starting point, . . .
[are] tautological," whereas Le Guin's journeys "bring into
the world a change" which then becomes the basis for
further change. Her overall concept reflects her Taoist
philosophy and her deep social commitment in searching for
a solution to man's fragmentation.

D261 O'DONNELL, GUS. Letter to the editor. SF Commentary, nos.
44/45 (December), pp. 90-91.
Reply to Turner's review of The Dispossessed [see D288].
Asserts the novel fails because it does not create a "recognisable" political world. Le Guin has divided people too
sharply into groups by political beliefs. Followed by
editor's comments (pp. 91-92) that O'Donnell's standards
are for naturalistic fiction.

D262 "On David Ketterer's New Worlds For Old." Science-Fiction
Studies 2 (July):130-46.
Contains Robert H. Canary, "New Worlds for Old?"; S.C.
Fredericks, "A Unique Critical Method"; Le Guin, "Ketterer
on The Left Hand of Darkness"; David Ketterer, "In Response."
Revision of papers presented at a session of the 1974
Science Fiction Research Association Conference, University
of Wisconsin, Milwaukee. [For the chairman's introduction,
see D326.]

D263 PORTER, DAVID L. "The Politics of Le Guin's Opus." Science-
Fiction Studies 2 (November):243-48. Reprinted in Science-
Fiction Studies: Selected Articles on Science Fiction 1973-
1975. Edited by R.D. Mullen and Darko Suvin. Boston:
Gregg Press, 1976, pp. 273-78.

Discusses and categorizes the fiction solely as a "distinct medium of political communication." Lists three themes that come out of her political perception--the relationship of good and evil, the illusions of superior accomplishment, and the role of the individual in the face of catastrophic change. Suggests her political thinking has evolved from an early existential phase, through a Taoist phase, to a more recent phase of anarchism. This maturation "represents a significant section of a whole generation of white radical American intellectuals, from the early 1960s to the present." Also discusses political insights that are particularly relevant to American society. Essay includes interesting catalogs of her works and footnotes that suggest the political context of the sixties and seventies.

D264 POWER, COLLEEN. Review of The Wind's Twelve Quarters. Library Journal 100 (15 October):1951.
Praises the collection--"her worlds are haunting psychological visions molded with firm artistry"--and looks forward to Le Guin's next ten years.

*D265 PRIEST, CHRISTOPHER. "Cool Dreamer." Maya [fanzine], no. 7, pp. 19-23. [Cited in Bittner; see D532.]

D266 RAPPAPORT, KAREN. Review of The Farthest Shore. Science Fiction Review Monthly, no. 9 (November), p. 15.
Faults the novel for having little action and too much "pseudo-philosophical" discussion, as well as having no significant female characters.

D267 REGINALD, R. Contemporary Science Fiction Authors: First Edition. New York: Arno Press, pp. 156-57.
Lists five novels, one short story, a brief biographical sketch, and Le Guin's answer to the question why she writes science fiction.

D268 ROSENBAUM, JUDY. Review of Dreams Must Explain Themselves. Science Fiction Review Monthly, no. 10 (December), pp. 9-10.
Takes pleasure in the author's revelations about her creation of Earthsea.

D269 _____. Review of The Tombs of Atuan. Science Fiction Review Monthly, no. 8 (October), p. 2.
Praising the entire trilogy, she observes this volume is an "interlude" in the epic. Significant is its view of Ged from someone else's viewpoint--"this is the closest we may ever get to the sensation of seeing ourselves as others see us."

D270 ROTTENSTEINER, FRANZ. The Science Fiction Book: An Illus-

trated History. New York: Seabury Press, p. 151.
Brief mention in a catchall essay at the end. States
her best work is in fantasy.

D271 RUNYON, CHARLES. Letters to the editor. Science Fiction
Review (The Alien Critic) 4, whole no. 13 (May):59-61.
Apologizes for an angry letter he sent Le Guin, a copy
of which he sent to Geis. He has since discovered she was
angry with Geis, not himself, and that she referred to a
Runyon piece that irritated many people. His earliest letters
to Le Guin and to Geis are also printed.

D272 RUSS, JOANNA. "Books." Fantasy and Science Fiction 38 (March):
41-44.
Review of The Dispossessed. Although Le Guin "is poten-
tially a writer of masterpieces," this novel is seriously
flawed because of "inauthenticities" on both planets.
Urras is too clearly a one-to-one correspondence with contemporary countries; it contains unreal scenes, particularly
the "mass protest in A-Io"; and its social system is incon-
sistent, particularly in portraying male and female behavior. Russ suggests that Le Guin is "still in the process
of finding her voice." Recommends that "Big, Public Subjects" are not her forte; her talent is lyrical. Suggests
she drop the male protagonist and every topic she is not
interested in.

D273 _____. "Reflections on Science Fiction: An Interview with
Joanna Russ." Quest: A Feminist Quarterly 2 (Summer):40-
49.
In this interview which draws out Russ's thinking on her
own writing and feminist concerns, she reveals her admiration for Le Guin in a brief digression and explains her
angry criticism of her as a "disappointed adoration." [See
D272.]

D274 SARGENT, PAMELA, ed. "Introduction: Writers in Science Fiction." In Women of Wonder. New York: Vintage, pp. xiii-
lxiv.
Discusses her as one of the women who began in the
sixties. After a reference to "Nine Lives," she reviews
The Left Hand of Darkness. Focuses on sexual nature of
Gethenians and resultant social mores. Includes lengthy
footnote of excerpts from the Le Guin-Lem exchange on the
novel [see C32 and D59].

D275 SEARLES, BAIRD. Review of A Wizard of Earthsea. Science Fiction Review Monthly, no. 7 (September), pp. 4-5.
Praises the novel, detailing its intricate background
for a retelling of the sorcerer's apprentice story.
Searles, however, personally prefers a more glamorous
fantasy.

Part D: Critical Studies

D276 SLATER, I. Review of Dreams Must Explain Themselves. Fantasiae 3 (November/December):15.
      Finds the Ward interview uninformative but praises the
   remaining selections, especially Le Guin's essay.

D277 SMITH, JEFFREY D., ed. "Women in Science Fiction: A Symposium."
   Khatru [fanzine], nos. 3-4 (November).
      Symposium of eleven authors, conducted by letters from
   9 October 1974, to 8 May 1975. Besides Le Guin's contributions [C112], there are references and responses to her by
   the other authors who include Suzy McKee Charnas, Samuel R.
   Delany, Virginia Kidd, Vonda N. McIntyre, Raylyn Moore,
   Joanna Russ, James Tiptree, Jr., Luise White, Kate Wilhelm,
   and Chelsea Quinn Yarbro.

D278 SULLIVAN, CHARLES WILLIAM. "Cultural Myths: Ellison, Le Guin
   and Delany." N.p., tapette. One cassette tape, thirty-two
   minutes, of paper delivered at Worlds of Science Fiction
   Conference, Claremont College, Pomona, Calif. Deposited at
   Spaced-Out Library, Toronto.
      Opens with assertion that science fiction examines myths,
   that is, what we believe in, the underlying assumptions of
   a culture. Studies three authors--Harlan Ellison examines
   individual assumptions, Le Guin "examines the conflicts
   between one culture and another," Delany looks at the nature
   of cultural reality itself. [Note: equipment failure pre-
   vented hearing the entire tape.]

D279 SUVIN, DARKO, ed. "The Science Fiction of Ursula K. Le Guin."
   Special Issue of Science-Fiction Studies 2 (November):203-
   74. Reprinted in Science-Fiction Studies: Selected Articles on Science Fiction 1973-1975. Edited by R.D. Mullen
   and Darko Suvin. Boston: Gregg Press, 1976, pp. 233-304.
      Contains: Darko Suvin, "Introductory Note"; Jeff Levin,
   "A Select Bibliography"; Ursula K. Le Guin, "American SF
   and the Other"; Rafail Nudelman, "An Approach to the Structure of Le Guin's SF"; Fredric Jameson, "World-Reduction
   in Le Guin: The Emergence of Utopian Narrative"; Ian
   Watson, "The Forest as Metaphor for Mind: 'The Word for
   World is Forest' and 'Vaster Than Empires and More Slow'";
   John Huntington, "Public and Private Imperatives in Le
   Guin's Novels"; David L. Porter, "The Politics of Le Guin's
   Opus"; Douglas Barbour, "Wholeness and Balance: An Adden-
   dum"; Judah Bierman, "Ambiguity in Utopia: The Dispos-
   sessed"; Donald F. Theall, "The Art of Social-Science Fic-
   tion: The Ambiguous Utopian Dialectics of Ursula K.
   Le Guin"; Darko Suvin, "Parables of De-Alienation:
   Le Guin's Widdershins Dance." [See C121.]

D280 SUVIN, DARKO. "Introductory Note: The Science Fiction of
   Ursula K. Le Guin." Science-Fiction Studies 2 (November):

203-4. Reprinted in Science-Fiction Studies: Selected
Articles on Science Fiction 1973-1975. Edited by R.D.
Mullen and Darko Suvin. Boston: Gregg Press, pp. 233-34.
 Discusses rationale for Philip K. Dick and Ursula K.
Le Guin as subjects for the first special issues of the
journal. Both are major authors, using quite different
methods and styles, but criticizing the same problem: the
"alienation, isolation and fragmentation pervading the neo-
capitalist society of the world of the mid-20th century."
Notes this issue is incomplete, particularly in the absence
of an essay integrating her fantasy and science fiction.

D281 _____. "Parables of De-Alienation: Le Guin's Widdershins
Dance." Science-Fiction Studies 2 (November):265-74. Reprinted in Science-Fiction Studies: Selected Articles on
Science Fiction 1973-1975. Edited by R.D. Mullen and Darko
Suvin. Boston: Gregg Press, 1976, pp. 295-304.
 Thesis is that "the main thrust and strength of Ursula
K. Le Guin's writing lies in the quest for and sketching of
a new, collectivist system of no longer alienated human
relationships, which arise out of the absolute necessity
for overcoming an intolerable ethical, cosmic, political
and physical alienation." Briefly traces her evolving
maturity, then focuses on her latest story, "The New
Atlantis," a juxtaposition of the new and the old political
systems. Its unique features include: 1) an ambiguity in
the accomplishments and failures of the scientist and his
friends; 2) an ambiguity in the genesis of the new consciousness. The ambiguities in the story are, as in her
other work, dynamic; there is "always a lefthand skate or
sweep, a counter-clock helix, a widdershins dance that goes
against the dominant and alienated received ideas of our
civilization." Criticizes a strain of "petty-bourgeois
intellectualism" that often comes out in her myths and
mysticism. Praises her work since 1969 for exploring "the
deep value shifts of our age," particularly the shift from
"capitalist alienation" to "classless de-alienation."

D282 _____. "SF and The Left Hand of Darkness: An Interview."
Interview conducted by Cathleen Toiny and Madlyn Ferrier.
Seldon's Plan [fanzine] 7 (February-March):6-17.
 Questions draw out Suvin's views on the relationship between science fiction and modern drama, the definition of
science fiction, the nature of his classes on science fiction. Comments on the novel are scattered throughout the
interview. All of them come back to his central point that
science fiction must be based on a "true novelty" which in
this novel is the effect on society of the absence of
sexual roles. Thus the novelty of the ice trip consists
not of the setting but of the communication that develops
between the two aliens. Novel suffers from a lack of dis-

cussion of the economic system, but that is a failing
common to recent American science fiction.

D283 TAYLOR, ANGUS. Letter to the editor. SF Commentary, nos.
      44/45 (December), p. 90.
          Reply to Turner's review of The Dispossessed [see D288].
      Challenges his assessment; Anarres is the utopia of the
      novel, and the novel is quite optimistic. Fears Turner's
      misreading comes from his self-proclaimed ignorance of
      political science. Suggests Le Guin has been influenced by
      Marx, Mao, Kropotkin.

D284 _____. "The Politics of Space, Time, and Entropy." SF Com-
      mentary, nos. 44/45 (December), pp. 24-28. Reprinted and
      revised in Foundation, no. 10 (June 1976), pp. 34-44.
          Introductory discussion of Le Guin and Philip K. Dick as
      examples of very different ideas about the nature of the
      universe and man's relationship to it. Uses Le-Guin's The
      Dispossessed and "The Word for World is Forest" extensively,
      Dick's Ubik and Now Wait for Last Year. Both authors,
      however, affirm the same position: "that a reified social
      structure is a mystification, and . . . that a proper
      stance must be one of individual self-responsibility coupled
      with community solidarity."

D285 THEALL, DONALD F. "The Art of Social-Science Fiction: The
      Ambiguous Utopian Dialectics of Ursula K. Le Guin."
      Science-Fiction Studies 2 (November):256-64. Reprinted in
      Science-Fiction Studies: Selected Articles on Science Fic-
      tion 1973-1975. Edited by R.D. Mullen and Darko Suvin.
      Boston: Gregg Press, 1976, pp. 286-94.
          Central assertion is that "all her novels . . . are
      utopian in the specific sense of creating some relative
      perfection as a contrast with the world of the reader."
      Thus, the key characteristic, which she shares with the
      utopian tradition, is ambivalence. Characters, ideas, and
      societies comment on and evaluate each other, as well as
      evaluate the reader's world. One specific technique
      Le Guin uses to achieve this complex perspective is "the
      stranger visiting a new world." One sign of her unfailing
      interest in utopia is "the history and nature of the Ekumen."
      The particular theme which illustrates Le Guin's interest
      in utopianism and her knowledge of the "humane sciences" is
      that of communication. Uses The Left Hand of Darkness and
      The Dispossessed to illustrate. Concludes by comparing her
      to the Polish philosopher, Leszek Kolakowski, and his
      acceptance of the principle of inconsistency.

D286 TIPTREE, JAMES Jr. [Alice Sheldon]. "The Time Machine."
      Universe SF Review [fanzine], no. 5 (September/October),
      p. 2.

Review of <u>The Lathe of Heaven</u>. Deeply affected by the
novel, she names its more unusual qualities. First, things
happen in an "ambience of quietness, mystery, and pre-
cision"; yet it contains a real horror, leaving her won-
dering "how much of my own activity is Haber like." Second,
it has an initially simple plot which becomes a series of
"collapsing time-frames." Faults of novel do not count;
predicts it is a forerunner of a new development in
Le Guin's writing.

D287 TURNER, GEORGE. "From Paris to Anarres: The Le Guin Retrospective." <u>SF Commentary</u>, nos. 44/45 (December), pp. 20-
23, 28.
Review of <u>The Wind's Twelve Quarters</u>. Examines stories
as evidence of the artist's development. The first third
consists of "formative" stories which introduce ideas but
are not outstanding by themselves. Last of them is "Winter's
King," science fiction with the mood of fantasy. The remainder (which he divides into two groups, 1969-1971 and
1973-on) are fine stories, showing her experimentation and
moving into new areas of science fiction. "Nine Lives" is
her first "true" science fiction story; the psychomyths
depict what is "just beyond the edge of psychological
visibility." "The Day Before The Revolution" demonstrates
a new quality in Le Guin--the ability to draw a complete
character. Turner digresses into a discussion of characterization, arguing that it is, appropriately, secondary
in science fiction.

D288 _____. "Paradigm and Pattern: Form and Meaning in <u>The Dis-
possessed</u>." <u>SF Commentary</u>, nos. 41/42 (February), pp. 65-
74, 64.
Initially evaluates the novel as significant both as a
contemporary novel and a modern novel. Argues that it be
judged for the "form and meaning," not for what the reader
believes ought to be there. The novel is not political but
philosophical. Novel's pattern conveys the theme; characterization is secondary. Large section of the article is
devoted to mapping out the chapter structure and demonstrating how it develops two plots united by one hero and
one theme: "the need for meaningful communication." Compares it to <u>Daniel Deronda</u> which also relied on the hero
"as the connecting link, and for the same purpose--the
display of two cultures--Jewry and upper-middle-class
English, in similarity and opposition." His single criticism is that the "women's-libbery" is overdone on Urras.
[For responding letters, see D221, 234, 261, and 283.]

D289 WATSON, IAN. "The Forest as Metaphor for Mind: 'The Word for
World is Forest' and 'Vaster Than Empires and More Slow.'"
<u>Science-Fiction Studies</u> 2 (November):231-37. Reprinted in

107

Science-Fiction Studies: Selected Articles on Science Fiction 1973-1975. Edited by R.D. Mullen and Darko Suvin. Boston: Gregg Press, 1976, pp. 261-67.
Establishes the double theme of "The Word for World is Forest": political exploitation and the psychological sanity and harmony of a culture. Establishes the metaphoric quality of the Athshean forests; they become "a kind of external collective unconscious." Then argues that the story "is oriented politically and ecologically," which requires verisimilitude, not metaphor. As a result, the forest metaphor has "a surplus of energy and idea . . . which cannot find a full outlet here." On the other hand, "Vaster" makes use of "the paranormal element from the Hainish cycle as a way of validating the forest-mind which is a verisimilar actuality rather than a metaphor." Explores other forest minds in science fiction and finds only Stapledon's sympathetic in tone with Le Guin's. "Vaster," he argues, is Le Guin's attempt to find the best "locale" for her "authentic 'mystical' strain," similar to the way The Lathe of Heaven functioned as a "discharge of paranormal elements" for the Hainish cycle [see D290]. A brief final paragraph asserts that the treatment of forest minds in these two stories is a step "in a development from ur-SF to the mystico-political theory of time and society in The Dispossessed."

D290 _____. "Le Guin's Lathe of Heaven and the Role of Dick: The False Reality as Mediator." Science-Fiction Studies 2 (March):67-75. Reprinted in Science-Fiction Studies: Selected Articles on Science Fiction 1973-1975. Edited by R.D. Mullen and Darko Suvin. Boston: Gregg Press, 1976, pp. 223-31.
Charts six Hainish novels to show that her first four move forward in future time and show increased use of paranormal abilities; her last two ("The Word for World is Forest" and The Dispossessed) move backward in future time and show decreased use of the paranormal. The Lathe of Heaven falls at the change point and is a writing out of the paranormal ability. She uses "the Dickian mode to discharge this particular accumulation of energy" and thus "clears the way for The Dispossessed." Compares George Orr to Dick's ordinary protagonists in The Three Stigmata of Palmer Eldritch, Ubik, and A Maze of Death.

D291 _____. "What Do You Want--The Moon?" Foundation, no. 9 (November), pp. 75-83.
Review of The Dispossessed. A truly significant novel, not only as "social statement," but also as "a breakthrough to a new level of science fiction." Review consistently analyzes and praises its "distancing effect" and the depth and unity of its narrative structure and content. Its

realistic detail truly "alienates--sets apart for political
and epistemological inspection." Anarres is offered as an
authentic social model, explored on "many levels: the
linguistic, the educational, the economic, the sexual."
The concept of revolution as process (or "balance-by-move-
ment") has no name in our society. Concept is supported by
all the elements of the novel--"balancing binary oppositions" (e.g. freedom from and freedom to), social dynamics,
Shevek's science, and narrative structure. Includes an
informative discussion of Terran physics and math which
precede and support Le Guin's speculations. Thus, the
science, like the society, is both familiar and alienated.

D292 WOOD, MICHAEL. "Coffee Break For Sisyphus." New York Review
of Books, 2 October, pp. 4-5.
       Review of The Dispossessed. Begins with an unsympathetic
review of Robert Scholes's Structural Fabulation. Discusses The Left Hand of Darkness briefly and then asserts
this novel is stronger "since it links sexual discrimina-
tion with politics and ideas about property." Concept of
women in Anarresti society well done. Quotes closing concept that one can go home again, "as long as you understand
that home is a place where you have never been" and suggests
that all science fiction is like this. It provides "genuine
but cerebral joys" in an escape from reality to which the
reader must return.

D293 WOOD, SUSAN. "Locus Looks at Books." Locus, no. 181 (17
November), p. 4.
       Review of The Wind's Twelve Quarters. Significant for
the high quality of fiction and insight into Le Guin's work.
This, along with the novels, reveals that "a passionate concern with human conduct is the strength and weakness of all
her work." Best stories fuse "Character and idea, emotion
and intellect" (like "Nine Lives"); least successful ones
are didactic (like "The Ones Who Walk Away from Omelas").
Praises the writing and the revision of "Winter's King."

D294 YBARRA, I.R. Review of The Dispossessed. The Match! 6 (January):10.
       Announces his own preference for not owning property and
welcomes this novel because it shows how it could work.
Recognizes both societies are flawed, the Anarchist and the
Statist, and asserts that the ambience of the two is the
real focus of the novel.

1976

D295 AMIS, MARTIN. "Science Fiction." Observer (London), 4 April,
p. 27.

Review of <u>The Wind's Twelve Quarters</u>. Identifies three
periods of Le Guin's writing: "the early Arthurianisms,
through the middle period psychodramas, to the later . . .
'psychomyths.'" Praises the middle group for doing more
dramatizing than stating. Best pieces are as disconcerting
as her "best novel, <u>The Lathe of Heaven</u>."

D296 ANGELL, ROGER. "Greetings, Friends! (After Frank Sullivan:
1893-1976)." <u>New Yorker</u> (27 December), p. 25.
Poem in the style of and as tribute to Sullivan.
Le Guin is the first person named and toasted.

D297 ANON. Review of <u>Nebula Award Stories Eleven</u>. <u>Kirkus Reviews</u>
44 (15 December):1322.
Finds the collection unbalanced in "approaches and
themes."

D298 ANON. Review of <u>Orsinian Tales</u>. <u>Booklist</u> 73 (15 September):
122.
Criticizes the stories for not being as good as her
science fiction. Characters and plots are inadequate for
"the intellectual and emotive burdens assigned them."

D299 ANON. Review of <u>Orsinian Tales</u>. <u>Kirkus Reviews</u> 44 (15 July):
809. Reprinted:44 (15 August):912.
Compares the tales to her science fiction--both have
"the persistent accumulation of detail about a society's
past, present, geography, ecology." Title suggests "the
Illyria (Yugoslavia) of Duke Orsino in <u>Twelfth Night</u>."

D300 ANON. Review of <u>Very Far Away From Anywhere Else</u>. <u>Kirkus
Reviews</u> 44 (1 July):739.
Praises her portrayal of the teenagers without mockery
or self-congratulation; notes her inner world is "as sharply
realized . . . as her Other ones."

D301 ANON. Review of <u>Very Far Away From Anywhere Else</u>. <u>Vanguard</u>
(Canada) (November/December).
Puzzles out an assessment of the characterization.
Characters seem too idealized, too talented and candid for
American high school seniors, yet their supporting relation-
ship is refreshingly hopeful. Praises her ability to
handle this story about moving beyond the faded American
dream.

D302 ANON. Review of <u>The Word for World is Forest</u>. <u>Kirkus Reviews</u>
44 (1 February):158.
Judges it to be secondary to her other works; states it
"shows signs of a previous fragmentary incarnation as a
children's story."

Part D: Critical Studies

D303   ASH, BRIAN. "Ursula K. Le Guin." In Who's Who in Science
        Fiction. New York: Taplinger, p. 134.
                Sketches her science fiction writing career.

D304   BANNON, BARBARA A. Review of Orsinian Tales. Publishers
        Weekly 210 (26 July):69.
                Admires the enchanting and "beautifully written" stories
        which are not identified with any particular place. They
        are concerned with "liberty as an elemental human drive and
        love as solace."

D305   _____. "The Writer and SF." Publishers Weekly 209 (14 June):
        46-48.
                Le Guin is one of thirty writers who responded to ques-
        tionnaires. Their statements are used to discuss the label
        "Science fiction" and its value as literature, to illustrate
        their background in science and in science fiction, and to
        sample their ideas on the future of science fiction. [See
        C129.]

D306   BARBOUR, DOUGLAS. "Patterns and Meaning in the Novels of
        Ursula K. Le Guin, Joanna Russ and Samuel R. Delany, 1962-
        1972." Ph.D. dissertation, Queen's University (Canada).
                Relevant material includes chapter two, appendices one
        and two. Analyzes three novelists of the late 1960s to
        demonstrate the significance of their work and of four
        critical approaches to science fiction: the quest pattern,
        literary and cultural allusions, other world creation, and
        structure/style. His overview of Le Guin stresses her
        original use of the future history series and its effect.
        Discusses each of the four critical approaches by con-
        sidering her novels chronologically, demonstrating con-
        sistently that "The Word for World is Forest" and The Lathe
        of Heaven are different from the preceding novels.
                She first uses the personal quest, then the societal,
        and in The Left Hand of Darkness develops "a societal quest
        through personal quests." The last two works, however,
        show failed or antiquests. Taoism is the main cultural
        allusion. Her other world creation is marked by original-
        ity and the causal relationship between culture and ecology.
        Her style is distinguished by light/dark imagery which is
        connected to her "overall use of the Tao and her interest
        in balance."
                In conclusion, he describes her vision as an ethical one
        based on Taoism and concerned with humanizing technology.
        Her work improves as it depends less on the "popular con-
        ventions" of science fiction. Her more mystical statements
        in the last two novels may not be accepted by all readers.

D307   BENNETT, CARL. Review of From Elfland to Poughkeepsie. SF
        Booklog [fanzine], no. 8 (March/April).

Declares it is a necessary essay for the beginning
writer of fantasy and science fiction.

D308 BETSKY, CELIA. "An Animator of the Inanimate." Los Angeles
Times, 10 November, part IV.
Review of Orsinian Tales. Writes, not as a science
fiction writer, but as "a scientist of fiction, expert in
the alchemy of literary fantasy, necromancy and historical
evocation." Identifies the setting as Hungary and the
people as dispossessed. Praises her style, her ability to
make the inanimate animate, to evoke feeling. "She writes
about the redemptive qualities of love and of art."

D309 BRESLIN, JOHN B. "The Pleasures of Sci-Fic." America 134
(7 February):106-8.
Review of The Wind's Twelve Quarters. Discusses two
strengths: psychologically developing characters to show
"the limits of our emotions" and "projecting the past into
the future" to show the conflict between power and truth.

D310 BRIM, CHRIS. Review of The Wind's Twelve Quarters. Daily
Iowan (Iowa City), 15 April, p. 9B.
Praises the collection because so few stories are un-
noteworthy. Suggests there are "two main veins": "pure
escape fairytales . . . and grim little sardonic fables."
The best are those when she is "politically engaged" and
going beyond the limits of science fiction. The two
feminist stories are outstanding--"Winter's King" and "The
Day Before the Revolution"--the latter suggesting Tillie
Olsen's fiction.

D311 CAREW, VIRGINIA. "Le Guin--Artistic and Formal Maturity."
In The Noreascon Proceedings: The Twenty-Ninth World
Science Fiction Convention, Boston, Mass., September 3-6,
1971. Edited by Lwaliw Ruewk. Cambridge, Mass.: NESFA
Press, pp. 115-18.
Informal paper on The Left Hand of Darkness as a novel
demonstrating artistic maturity which readers and writers
ought to appreciate. Discusses teaching it in courses with
Catch 22, Antigone, and "The Love Song of J. Alfred
Prufrock." Argues that students' resistance to it (a re-
luctance to work hard to meet its demands) suggests it is
a classic.

D312 CLARK, JEFF. Letter to the editor. Seldon's Plan [fanzine]
7, whole no. 38 (March):33.
Criticizes Stanislaw Lem's handling of exposition in
Solaris and holds up Le Guin's The Left Hand of Darkness as
an alternative method.

D313 COGELL, ELIZABETH CUMMINS. Review of The Wind's Twelve

Quarters. <u>Delap's F&SF Review</u> (February), pp. 4-5.
Welcomes this first collection of short stories which
demonstrates both complexity and harmony (the stated goals
of the Ekumen in "Winter's King"). Headnotes show the
variety of her creative mind.

D314 COMISKEY, RAY. "Fantasy and Science Fiction." <u>Irish Times</u>
(Dublin), 5 May.
Review of <u>The Wind's Twelve Quarters</u>. Cites Le Guin as
one of the few who can write creative fantasy. Even the
early stories show "a sensitivity in the use of language
as charming as anything Wilde ever did." Later stories
increasingly suggest "varied interpretation"; "every silver
lining has a cloud." Praises her style, universality, and
characterization.

D315 COOK, ELIZABETH. <u>The Ordinary & The Fabulous: An Introduction
to Myths, Legends and Fairy Tales</u>. 2d ed. Cambridge:
Cambridge University Press, 182 pp.
Lists each of the three volumes of the Earthsea trilogy
in the bibliography of "Modern Hybrid Myth, Legend, and
Fantasy" with the note that they are "invented legend" like
Tolkien's.

D316 COOPER, SUSAN. "Newbery Medalist Susan Cooper Reviews New
Novels." <u>Christian Science Monitor</u>, 3 November, p. 20.
Review of <u>Very Far Away From Anywhere Else</u>. Labels it
"pure gold," and praises its criticism of the pressures on
young adults to conform.

D317 COSGRAVE, MARY SILVA. "Outlook Tower." <u>Horn Book Magazine</u>
52 (August):430-31.
Review of <u>The Wind's Twelve Quarters</u>. Discusses the
provocative nature of the stories. Cites those which are
related to her novels and two "haunting stories": "Things"
and "The Ones Who Walk Away From Omelas."

D318 _____. "Outlook Tower." <u>Horn Book Magazine</u> 52 (October):529.
Review of <u>The Word for World is Forest</u>. Notes the sensitive portrayal of exploitation and the ironic resolution
in which the Athsheans defeat the Terrans by warfare
learned from them. Cosgrave errs in some details.

D319 DALMYN, TONY. "Crossing The Wall." <u>Winding Numbers 3</u> [fan-
zine] 1 (March-May):11-15.
Review of <u>The Dispossessed</u>. Novel deals with "giving
up illusions and with coming to terms with the nature of
our existence as individuals in society." Asserts the
alternating chapters emphasize the similarities between the
two societies. Shevek journeys on three interrelated
levels: between societies, in intellectual development,

and in human development. Walls, finally, are an illusion.

D320   De BOLT, JOE, and PFEIFFER, JOHN [R.]. "The Modern Period,
       1938-1975." In Anatomy of Wonder: Science Fiction. Edited
       by Neil Barron. New York: Bowker, pp. 214-15, passim.
          Annotates The Dispossessed, The Lathe of Heaven, and The
       Left Hand of Darkness. Suggests comparing the latter to
       Frank Herbert's Dune, and The Lathe of Heaven to Borges's
       "The Circular Ruins."

D321   DELAP, RICHARD. Review of Dreams Must Explain Themselves.
       Delap's F&SF Review (May), pp. 17-18.
          Commends and quotes from the autobiographical essay.

D322   DICK, PHILIP K. "Man, Android and Machine." In Science Fic-
       tion at Large. Edited by Peter Nicholls. London:
       Gollancz, pp. 202-24.
          Refers to The Lathe of Heaven as one of our outstanding
       books because it depicts dreaming as being both internal
       and external.

D323   DILLARD, R.H.W. "Speculative Fantasy and the New Reality."
       Chronicle of Higher Education (23 February).
          Review of The Wind's Twelve Quarters. Announces it is
       an excellent introduction to "one of the most important
       American writers" and demonstrates her development from "a
       somewhat romantic dreamer to an articulate seer and sayer."
       Discusses contemporary science fiction and Le Guin's
       writing career. Asserts that "all realistic fiction . . .
       must necessarily be science fiction" in the sense that a
       writer's concept of reality is shaped by current science.
       The worlds she creates are like ours--"motion and change
       are the norm . . . , therefore, the primary values are
       always growth, balance, and harmony."

D324   EISENSTEIN, ALEX. "On Le Guin's 'American SF and the Other."
       Science-Fiction Studies 3 (March):97.
          Response to Le Guin's article [see C111]. Followed by
       Le Guin's answer [see C122]. [For Suvin's answer, see
       D366.] Objects to her sweeping generalizations and lack of
       "critical rigor." Half of the letter takes her to task for
       misreading Niven's short story, "Inconstant Moon." Labels
       her article "offhand slander" not helpful criticism.

D325   ELLIOTT, ROBERT C. "A New Utopian Novel." Yale Review 65
       (Winter):256-61.
          Review of The Dispossessed. Locates the novel in the
       utopian tradition and praises its contribution to the genre.
       It avoids some but not all of the genre problems. It is
       always difficult, for example, to describe "the good life"
       without becoming dull; it is easier to show "what it is

not," especially in this novel which could be viewed as
testing Socrates' description of the utopian simple life in
The Republic. She does avoid expository sections and provides a new perspective on the present. Scenes on A-Io are
the weakest. Shevek is a remarkable character, worthy in
any novel tradition. Chides the science fiction genre for
trying to include utopia; the science fiction label on this
novel led to its being ignored by reputable journals.

D326 GALBREATH, ROBERT. "Introduction to the Ketterer Forum."
      Science-Fiction Studies 3 (March):60-64.
          Describes the context of the forum on Ketterer's book,
      New World For Old [see D262], at the 1974 Science Fiction
      Research Association meeting, noting Le Guin's presence and
      the attention given The Left Hand of Darkness. Offers
      "general observations on several of the larger issues em-
      phasized in the exchange" over Ketterer's critical theory.

D327 GERSTENBERGER, DONNA. "Conceptions Literary and Otherwise:
      Women Writers and the Modern Imagination." Novel: A Forum
      on Fiction 9 (Winter):141-50.
          Uses Genly Ai's experience in trying to describe the
      alien world of Gethen as an analog to women writers trying
      to record a life that "exceeds the conceptualizations" of
      our society. Women writers face a literary tradition that
      has cannonized the male point of view, and they must do
      more than just record their own point of view. They must
      explore the concepts by means of myth and language, thereby
      offering a new vision. Analyzes Margaret Atwood's novel,
      Surfacing, as a fine example of what is needed. It has the
      same message as The Left Hand of Darkness: "to be wholly
      human is to be humanly whole." Other comparisons include
      protagonists who recognize the alienness of their sur-
      roundings, the limits imposed on concepts by language, and
      the myth of the "perilous journey."

D328 GRAVES, ELIZABETH MINOT. "Children's Books for the Bicen-
      tennial." Commonweal 103 (19 November):763.
          Very Far Away From Anywhere Else appears in this an-
      notated list.

D329 GUNEW, SNEJA. "To Light a Candle Is to Cast a Shadow: The
      Shadow as Identity Touchstone in Ursula Le Guin's Earthsea
      Trilogy and in The Left Hand of Darkness." SF Commentary
      48/49/50 (October/November/December):32-38.
          After an introduction which asserts that Le Guin uses
      the mythmaking impulse, particularly the symbolism of light
      and dark, to bring the reader into the imaginary world, she
      discusses the four novels. The shadow represents the area
      between darkness and light, the "twilight area" of choice;
      its "adjunct . . . is the 'name' or area of certainty with

respect to identity." In the trilogy, names indicate both
potential and identity. All the main characters learn the
necessity of balance, the significance of the act, the
necessity of acknowledging their own mortality. The Shadow
functions as a messenger or a hunter in their quests for
identity. Notes that later novels' passages have more sub-
stance; they balance "the message and the speaker's voice,"
a move from "exposition to communication."
   The Left Hand of Darkness emphasizes the nurturing as-
pect of darkness and the shadow has a different meaning,
"an area of individual integrity." [See D561 for expanded
version.]
   Concludes that Le Guin's redefining of the symbols has
led to the creation of a new mythology as well as to the
development of complex, full characters.

D330 HALL, JOAN JOFFE. Review of The Wind's Twelve Quarters. New
      Republic 174 (7 February):28-29.
         Distinguishes her from most science fiction writers in
      that she is concerned with the nature of future experience,
      not its causes; illustrates with "Nine Lives." Although
      mentioning story titles, Hall relies heavily on The Left
      Hand of Darkness to support two observations: that her
      fiction argues for "cultural relativism" and that her works
      provide feminist solutions. Finds her psychomyths less
      successful pieces, especially when compared to a science
      fiction story like "Field of Vision." Overall, finds an-
      thology not as good as her novels, "for Le Guin is superb
      at suspensefully sustaining long narrative sequences im-
      possible in short fiction."

D331 HAYES, SARAH. "Untypical Teenagers." Times Literary Supple-
      ment, 1 October, p. 1238.
         Review of A Very Long Way From Anywhere Else. Observes
      that Le Guin has picked up teenage stereotypes and changed
      them; her protagonists are intellectuals. Story evokes
      emotions well but remains "a very small slice of life."

D332 HOFFMAN, MARCIA R. Review of Orsinian Tales. Library Journal
      101 (1 October):2086.
         Recognizes that stories center on "insignificant people"
      and deserve the reader's unhurried attention. "Conversa-
      tions at Night" is the most memorable. Each shows "a
      turning point in the lives of its characters."

D333 HOWARD, DENYS. Editorial response. WAM! [fanzine], no. 6
      (May), pp. 4-5.
         Replies to Le Guin's letter [see C126] which answered
      Howard's previous letter [see D243].

D334 HUTCHINSON, TOM. Review of The Dispossessed. Times (London),

19 September.
Praises the novel for its perspective and for her
ability to draw believable imaginary worlds. Novel explores paradoxes of human political behavior; "it is a
well-told tale signifying a good deal."

D335 HYDE, PETER. Review of Dreams Must Explain Themselves and The
Dispossessed. Vector 72 (February), pp. 23-24.
Dismisses the map and NBA speech as "mere padding," but
is delighted with Le Guin's essay and short story. Praises
The Dispossessed as her best novel, noting particularly the
details by which Anarresti society reflects Odonianism.

D336 JONAS, GERALD. Review of Orsinian Tales. New York Times Book
Review, 28 November, pp. 8, 44.
Recognizes they are not science fiction but that they
share the concerns of her novels. Finds Orsinia a truly
imaginary country, not a disguised Hungary. Sense of
authenticity comes, not from her research, but from "the
primary act of imagination." Stories themselves examine
the role of the imagination, showing that it "destroys as
well as redeems."

D337 KEMBALL-COOK, JESSICA. "Earthsea and Others." New Society
38 (11 November):314-15.
Overview of her work for British audience. Notes the
Earthsea trilogy is already well known in England and
rivals works by C.S. Lewis, J.R.R. Tolkien, and Alan Garner.
It does not merely imitate these authors but uses fairy
tale elements as metaphors for human experiences, as noted
by Jung and Campbell. Her science fiction combines traditional hardware with the "ideals of romantic heroism."
Notes high quality of her writing and her popularity, asserting the vision common to all her novels is mystical--
"the philosophy of balance and reconciling opposites."

D338 KROEBER, KARL. "Sisters and Science Fiction." Little Magazine 10 (Spring-Summer):87-90.
Humorous, informal essay solicited by editors to accom-
pany Le Guin's "Brothers and Sisters." Dismisses both
biographical and genre criticisms as unhelpful in understanding her work. Biographical information is irrelevant
because the crucial act between her experience and a completed story is beyond the reach of the critics, that is,
the working of the imagination. The label, "science fiction writer" is inadequate; Le Guin is an "imaginative
author" who has used the science fiction pattern because
she is "an honest fantast unperturbed by the whims of the
New York Literary Establishment." Sees a lack of imagination in the modern novel and extends Bettelheim's analysis
of the value of fairy tale to adult literature: both

should be places where one "learns useful truths of human existence." The best science fiction "exhuberantly pretends freakishness to work back toward the essential nature of fiction."

D339 KULLESEID, ELEANOR. Liner Notes to filmstrip of The Tombs of Atuan, adapted by Norman Weiser [see B142].
   Designed as teacher's guide. In addition to a brief summary, it includes notes on labyrinths in mythology and history; reincarnation; women in religion; word study; suggestions for related activities such as research, games, and interviews.

D340 LAMPMAN, LINDA. "Ursula Le Guin Wins All the Marbles Again." Oregonian, 30 May.
   Review of The Word for World is Forest. Predicts this novel, too, will be an award winner. For the reader, it "provides a rich emotional and intellectual experience."

D341 La ROUCHE, ROBERT. Review of The Wind's Twelve Quarters. St. Louis Post-Dispatch, 23 March.
   Applauds the collection's retrospective nature and the author's comments. Characterization strong, especially in "The Day Before the Revolution."

D342 LAST, MARTIN. Review of The Wind's Twelve Quarters. The Science Fiction Review.
   This retrospective collection is marred by her "irresistible penchant for being didactic" so that every story (except "Nine Lives") has an "instructive form . . . extrinsic to the work itself."

D343 LEWIS, NAOMI. "No More Nannies." Listener 96 (11 November): 623.
   Review of A Very Long Way From Anywhere Else. Reviews it with several other young adult books on adolescent problems. Ending is hopeful; style and plot are sound.

D344 McCORMACK, WIN. "Anarchy in Outer Space." Oregon Times Magazine (February-March), p. 46.
   Review of The Dispossessed. Categorizes it as "social realism," not utopianism. Key challenge to anarchism is the emergence of a genius--does "the authority of public opinion . . . turn out to be just as coercive as the authority of the state it replaces"? It is a lesser novel than The Left Hand of Darkness because it is closer to being "an explicit political tract."

D345 McINTYRE, VONDA N. "Ursula K. Le Guin." Note on album cover of "The Ones Who Walk Away From Omelas" [see B65].
   Admires her versatility, originality, and personal

"unified and serene sanity." Asserts "there is no 'typical'
Le Guin story" and no permanent "plateau" of achievement.

D346 MILLER, DAN. "Science Fiction." Booklist 72 (1 January):615.
     Review of The Wind's Twelve Quarters. Cites the collec-
     tion for its quality, insights into her development, and
     relationship to her novels."

D347 MILLER, JANE. "Doubtful Improvements." Times Literary Supple-
     ment, 30 July, p. 950.
     Review of The Wind's Twelve Quarters. Observes that her
     comments on her own stories call attention to her role as
     inventor and thus ask for a different response from readers.
     The best stories dramatize her ideas, notably in "Nine
     Lives." Stories are not about hardware nor are they alle-
     gories; they seek questions, not answers.

D348 MOLSON, FRANCIS J. "Juvenile Science Fiction." In Anatomy of
     Wonder: Science Fiction. Edited by Neil Barron. New York:
     Bowker, p. 323.
     Annotates A Wizard of Earthsea and refers to the other
     two Earthsea novels. Praises the blending of myth and
     Jungian ideas.

D349 NELSON, ALIX. "Ah, Not to Be Sixteen Again." New York Times
     Book Review, 14 November, p. 29.
     Review of Very Far Away From Anywhere Else. Admits Owen
     is the protagonist but finds Natalie a "most interesting"
     young woman.

D350 PANSHIN, ALEXEI, and PANSHIN, CORY. SF In Dimension: A Book
     of Explorations. Chicago: Advent, 342 pp.
     Generally critical of Le Guin's work, especially The
     Left Hand of Darkness which they deem full of facts and
     data and telling but no showing. One favorable reference
     to The Dispossessed.

D351 PERRY, JOAN ELLEN. "Visions of Reality: Values and Perspec-
     tives In the Prose of Carlos Castaneda, Robert M. Pirsig,
     Ursula K. Le Guin, James Purdy, Cyrus Cotter and Sylvia
     Plath." Ph.D. dissertation, University of Wisconsin.
     Examines authors who are concerned with "the effect of
     values on human consciousness rather than with moral cri-
     teria . . . by which to assess or establish values." Uses
     Castaneda and Pirsig as touchstones by which to understand
     Le Guin's The Left Hand of Darkness and The Lathe of Heaven.
     Le Guin's novels advance the idea that "to see an alien
     vision in its own terms . . . is requisite to human sur-
     vival." This new seeing includes a "respect for and accep-
     tance of the unknown." Perry shows how much Ai must learn
     from Estraven, the alien. If Gethen is to accept the

Ekumen, then Argaven must accept the Envoy; but this can
only occur if the Envoy accepts Estraven. In The Lathe of
Heaven, Dr. Haber represents "the rigidity of rationality"
while Orr represents the acceptance of the unknown. The
two disagree on the best way to human survival, evidenced
in Haber's desire to eradicate problems as opposed to Orr's
desire to find solutions to existing problems. Love is the
crucial subjective experience for Orr just as it was for
Estraven.

D352 PLANK, ROBERT. "Ursula K. Le Guin and the Decline of Romantic
      Love." Science-Fiction Studies 3 (March):36–43. Reprinted
      in Science-Fiction Studies: Selected Articles on Science
      Fiction 1976–1977. Edited by R.D. Mullen and Darko Suvin.
      Boston: Gregg Press, 1978, pp. 148-55.
          Asserts The Left Hand of Darkness and The Dispossessed
      are different from her previous work in dominance of theme
      of ambisexuality. Her earlier novels treat three themes
      that are common motifs in science fiction and indicate
      psychological inadequacy: the individual struggle with
      delusion, reliance on paranormal mental abilities, and the
      quest. These two novels have a wide appeal because they
      deal with tensions over sexuality. Historically analyzes
      three sexual models, none of which guarantees happiness:
      romantic love, permissiveness, and ambisexuality. Le Guin
      is able to show the potential for happiness in the latter
      but the suffering tone of her novels indicates to the
      reader that the time for realizing happiness by ambisex-
      uality has not yet come.

D353 PODULKA, FRAN. Review of Orsinian Tales. Grand Rapids Press,
      14 November.
          Welcomes this collection of short stories by a fine
      author. Themes are sweeping, yet told out of individual
      lives and personal dilemmas. Her images are "sometimes
      unreal, Bergmanesque." Her "lucid, restrained style" is
      appropriate for the material. Two most notable stories are
      "Brothers and Sisters" and "A Week in the Country."

D354 REMINGTON, THOMAS J. "The Muse of SF." North American Review
      261 (Fall):87–89.
          Review of The Wind's Twelve Quarters. Opens with over-
      view of science fiction publishing industry; reviews three
      short story collections in light of their authors' pub-
      lishing history and reputation (Le Guin, Thomas Disch,
      Robert Silverberg). Praises Le Guin for not self-con-
      sciously referring to science fiction in her novels, but
      wishes her introductory remarks took her fiction more
      seriously. She demonstrates characteristics of quality
      science fiction in three categories--reworking myths
      ("Vaster Than Empires and More Slow"), blending the real

and the fantastic ("A Trip to the Head"), and reducing the fantastic to the "humdrum" ("Field of Vision").

D355 _____. "A Touch of Difference, A Touch of Love." Extrapolation 18 (December):28-41.
Asserts she uses science fiction motifs and conventions, not to gain an audience or a classification, but because they are organic to her themes. Urges more reading of her excellent short stories which also develop her theme of the self and other. Analyzes "Nine Lives," "The Word for World is Forest," and "Vaster Than Empires and More Slow" to demonstrate the three facets of this theme: "the loneliness of the self, the impossibility of understanding the self except through its relationship to the other, and the human need to establish that relationship through reaching out to the other in love." The last story is the most complex and operates on a symbolic and mythic level. Osden plays out the "King of the Wood" myth as outlined by Frazer. [See D389 for responses.]

D356 ROBB, CHRISTINA. "Political Fairy Tales Where the Princes Are Charming." Boston Globe, 10 December.
Review of Orsinian Tales. Stories are "political tales" set in an "imaginary Hungary." Cites "Brothers and Sisters" as the best story. Insightful discussion by grouping stories according to setting. Concludes by pointing out parallels between "The Barrow" and "Imaginary Countries," both of which utilize barons concerned with Norse legends.

D357 RUBINS, DIANE TEITEL. Teacher's Guide: Very Far Away From Anywhere Else. New York: Bantam, 2 pp.
Includes a summary of plot and theme, discussion questions, suggested activities, a brief biographical note, and excerpts from five reviews of the novel.

D358 SARGENT, PAMELA, ed. Foreword to "Nine Lives." In Bio-Futures: Science Fiction Stories About Biological Metamorphosis. New York: Vintage [paper], pp. 97-98.
Quotes from an article on cloning by James D. Watson and speculates about the less dramatic, more probable future uses of cloning. Notes that Le Guin's single surviving clone member portrays basic human experience "in a new light."

D359 SCHOLES, ROBERT. "Science Fiction as Conscience: John Brunner and Ursula K. Le Guin." New Republic 175 (30 October):38-40. [Issue includes C139.]
Finds them concerned with "founding a new morality and a new politics upon our new knowledge of the cosmos and the human situation in it." In this way, they are doing what Joyce did in a more limited way, creating a new "'conscience

for the race.'" Unlike Brunner's naturalism, Le Guin's
fiction is more like fantasy and her style is more lyrical.
The Left Hand of Darkness is her best single work which,
despite criticism by radical feminists, does make reader
aware of sexual stereotyping in personality, human relationships, and culture. Pleas for a recognition of value
of such writers.

D360 SICILIANO, SAM JOSEPH. "The Fictional Universe in Four Science
        Fiction Novels: Anthony Burgess's A Clockwork Orange,
        Ursula Le Guin's The Word for World is Forest, Walter
        Miller's A Canticle for Leibowitz, and Roger Zelazny's
        Creatures of Light and Darkness." Ph.D. dissertation,
        University of Iowa.
            Discusses the novel as one of four science fiction
        pieces exemplifying both the diversity and quality of
        modern science fiction. Discusses three levels of meaning:
        the story itself, its parallels to the contemporary world,
        its mythic references to the fall from innocence. Although
        there are strong parallels to actual historical events such
        as the American role in Vietnam, he urges that the novel
        portrays the universal condition of an oppressed people,
        the condition of the natural wilderness, the actions of
        conquerors who are also destroyers. The mythic element
        operates in two ways. Davidson and Selver are likened to
        gods and the story is that of Eden, "the fall from inno-
        cence and introduction of evil." Davidson, Selver, and
        even Lyubov are gods because they are larger than life. In
        addition, Selver is a god in that he translates the vision
        of the dream into action. The story suggests many parallels
        to the Eden story. Athshe represents Eden, Davidson the
        serpent, Selver an Eve or a savior who cannot be reborn.
        Its resolution also parallels Eden in that evil cannot be
        drained back out of the world. Concludes by praising
        Le Guin's characterization, complex levels of meaning, and
        storytelling ability.

D361 SIMMONS, STEVE. Letter to the editor. Seldon's Plan [fan-
        zine] 7, whole no. 38 (March):33-34.
            Response to Suvin interview [see D282]. Finds the ab-
        sence of economics understandable in The Left Hand of Dark-
        ness but not in The Dispossessed.

D362 SLUSSER, GEORGE EDGAR. The Farthest Shores of Ursula K.
        Le Guin. The Milford Series: Popular Writers of Today.
        Vol. 3. San Bernadino, Calif.: Borgo Press, 60 pp.
            This is the first analysis longer than an essay. Con-
        centrates on her novels from Rocannon's World to The Dis-
        possessed with a minimal biography and a bibliography which
        lists first editions only. In an introductory overview,
        he identifies two modes of development. First, her emphasis

is changing from "the celebration of balance and toward the
problematics of balance" which strengthens the role of the
individual. Second, as the novels become more complex, the
form changes and she experiments with point of view. Includes chapters on "The Early Hainish Novels," "The Left
Hand of Darkness," "The Earthsea Trilogy," and "The Dispossessed."

The first three novels establish the two poles of her
perspective: the "celebration of balance and cosmic order"
and man's discovery that it is difficult "to predict, to
control" the direction of that order. The Left Hand of
Darkness draws specific societies for the first time. Ai
finds the sexual nature of the Gethenians a barrier for
accepting their difference. Ai matures as he learns to
accept differences. Ambiguity emerges as "the true state
of things." Novel ends with death and uncertainty about
the future.

Earthsea trilogy develops the same themes as her science
fiction: "the problems of individual responsibility, of
folly, evil and the search for selfhood." It differs from
the pessimistic tone in her other writings of this period.
The Farthest Shore is a "genuine epic vision" that is
"quite un-Christian, un-Western, in its naturalism, its
reverence for the balance of life, and its refusal of
transcendental values." Final book shifts the focus from
artist (Ged) to ruler (Arren), thus setting the stage for
Shevek in The Dispossessed. Shevek is a scientist/artist
who learns to accept social responsibility. Novel also
explores what society's responsibility is to the exceptional
person. Man emerges as "the dynamic element in the universal balance." But the novel's ending is also uncertain.

Conclusion queries what her next direction will be.
Comments on "The Day Before the Revolution" and "The New
Atlantis," concluding "In these two stories, the individual
life ends in death, the collective existence in annihila-
tion."

D363   SMITH, CURTIS C. "Le Guin, Ursula K(roeber)." In Comtemporary
        Novelists. Edited by James Vinson. New York: St. Martin's
        Press, pp. 795-97.
        Biographical sketch includes jobs she has held. Publica-
        tions list is of first editions in the United States and
        United Kingdom. Analytical essay focuses on her appeal to
        different audiences. Earliest novels appeal to the science
        fiction reader and are space opera, but with foreshadowings
        of later concerns. Next work brings her out of the "science
        fiction ghetto." Her audiences will continue to change.

D364   STUMPF, EDNA. "A Queen of the Night Turns Time's Flight Back-
        ward." Philadelphia Inquirer, 21 November.
        Review of Orsinian Tales. Praises the stories as "the

delicate, well-polished wood-carving of a woman who has
created whole forests with words." Argues strongly for
noting the science fiction tradition out of which she comes
and has never denied. Judges her novels are her main
achievements. She has used and added to the conventions of
the genre.

D365 SUTHERLAND, ZENA. "Tell Me, Where is Fantasy Bred?" Saturday
Review 55 (25 March):109.
The Tombs of Atuan is one of several books cited in
support of an affirmative answer to the question, "Isn't
anyone writing good fantasy any more?"

D366 SUVIN, DARKO. "On Wolk, Eisenstein, and Christianson in SFS
#8." Science-Fiction Studies 3 (July):211-12.
Response to letters by Wolk [see D368] and Eisenstein
[see D324]. Answers Wolk's objections by reducing his
argument to a belief in total objectivity of the critic and
neutrality of the text. Identifies Wolk's critical attitude as "romantic, positivist, liberal, or individualistic."
Defends his own statements about fantasy and anarchism.
Accepts Wolk's criticism that essays too quickly pass over
individual works in order to emphasize Le Guin's evolution.
Apologizes for not including the note that identified
Le Guin's "American SF and the Other" as an intentional
polemic. Refers the reader to Le Guin's "more gracious and
more economical" reply to Eisenstein [see C120].

D367 TYLER, ANNE. "Books for Those Awkward, In-Between Years."
National Observer 15 (25 December):15.
Review of Very Far Away From Anywhere Else. Recommends
it as a book boys would enjoy. Notes that her sixth grade
child was "confused" by the sudden introduction of the sex
theme but suspects a teenager would accept it.

D368 WOLK, ANTHONY. "On the Le Guin Issue." Science-Fiction
Studies 3 (March):95-96.
Response to recent Le Guin criticism, including the
Le Guin issue [see D279]. [For Suvin's answer, see D366.]
Generally impressed but is uncomfortable with critics who
impose an a priori judgment on her art in terms of genre
and philosophy. Objects to Suvin and Watson finding, respectively, the fantasy and the paranormal less significant
than her other work. Finds anarchism privileged to the
extent that critics fail to see all the qualities of any
given work.

D369 WOOD, SUSAN. "The Propeller Beanie." Algol 13, no. 26,
(Summer-May):23-26. Reprinted as "The Clubhouse." Amazing
50 (June):124-30.
Report on Aussiecon, the 33rd World Science Fiction Con-

vention when Le Guin was guest of honor. Interspersed
with quotation from Le Guin's speech; [see C113]. Includes
information on Le Guin's participation in interviews and
panels.

D370 _____. Review of The Word for World is Forest. Delap's F&SF
Review (July), pp. 8-9.
Surprised at Le Guin allowing it to be reissued without
first revising it. Novel is too heavy handed, "a morality
play, a reworking of Genesis." The two cultures are presented as marked opposites. As a result, character development suffers and the work becomes a polemic, not a novel.
It lacks "moral and esthetic balance."

D371 WOODCOCK, GEORGE. "The Equilibrations of Freedom: Notes on
the Novels of Ursula K. Le Guin. Parts 1 and 2." Georgia
Straight 10 (21-28 October):4-5, 9; 10 (28 October-4 November):6-7.
Announces he will focus on The Dispossessed since that
is closest to his own interest in anarchism. Praises her
fundament of knowledge, her clear style, reminiscent of
nineteenth-century writers of travel books, and her persistent interest in human and environmental ethics. The
Lathe of Heaven and The Dispossessed are different from her
other novels in depicting settings and examining problems
closer to the contemporary world. The latter, in examining
anarchism's challenge to "authoritarian predispositions" on
the left and right, appropriately conveys a greater sense
of bewilderment in style and solutions because it is dealing
with current issues. The Lathe of Heaven criticizes simplistic answers to world problems of overpopulation and
racism.

1977

D372 ANON. Review of Orsinian Tales. Choice 14 (March):63.
Recommends it as "first-rate" literature. Notes that
the pieces are tales rather than stories; characterizes
them as being about individuals, not archetypes; being
"products of human memory more than human imagination";
dealing with dilemmas that are "more momentous than tragic
in dimension"; and containing "recollections of the real
[rather] than representations of the abstract."

D373 ANON. Review of Planet of Exile. Kirkus Reviews 45 (15
December):1339.
Discusses how novel illustrates Le Guin's main interest,
that is, the shaping of a society by environmental and
cross-cultural influences.

D374 ANON. Review of <u>Very Far Away From Anywhere Else</u>. <u>Babbling</u>
      <u>Bookworm</u> 5 (March):[4].
          Summarizes this story of "the turbulence of the adoles-
      cent years."

D375 ANON. Review of <u>Very Far Away From Anywhere Else</u>. <u>Bulletin</u>
      <u>of the Center for Children's Books</u> 30 (January):77.
          Praises the style and clarity of her depiction of the
      characters and their relationships, as well as "the prob-
      lems of the young intellectual."

D376 ANON. "Ursula K. Le Guin." Liner notes on <u>"Gwilan's Harp"</u>
      and "Intracom": Read by the author. [See B74.]
          Biographical sketch, fiction awards, dates of residency
      in Oregon and England.

D377 ASH, BRIAN, ed. <u>The Visual Encyclopedia of Science Fiction</u>.
      New York: Harmony Books, passim.
          Contains references to her in sections by various
      authors on sex themes, environmental themes, inner space,
      and current trends in science fiction.

D378 ASIMOV, ISAAC, ed. "Ursula K. Le Guin." In <u>The Hugo Winners</u>.
      Vol. 3. New York: Doubleday, pp. 223-24, 469-70.
          Ostensibly introductions to "The Word for World is
      Forest" (Hugo winner for Novella in 1973) and "The Ones
      Who Walk Away From Omelas" (Hugo winner for Short Story in
      1974). However, since he has never met her he discusses
      instead the 1973 World Con, the increasing number of women
      writers, and how he happened to see a photograph of Le Guin.

D379 BICKMAN, MARTIN. "Le Guin's <u>The Left Hand of Darkness</u>: Form
      and Content." <u>Science-Fiction Studies</u> 4 (March):42-47.
          Uses the novel to show how form and content can be
      blended in science fiction "in a functional, organic, and
      aesthetically meaningful way." Ai selects and arranges all
      material, enabling the reader to share his same learning
      experience; thus the structure "is not so much a way to
      tell the story as it is the story itself." The pattern is
      one of unity and diversity, the very lesson Ai must learn.
      The novel structure follows a thesis-antithesis-synthesis
      movement, as well as a movement between myth and reality.
      Only Ai and Estraven find true unity through differences;
      Tibe's unification of Karhide is false, for example, as is
      Orgoreyn's enforced unity which has removed "uniqueness and
      individuality." The movement between myth and reality ex-
      plores the multiplicity of perspectives, ending with Ai's
      story to Estraven's son in which Ai's real story is going
      to become a myth.

D380 BISHOP, MICHAEL. Review of <u>The Left Hand of Darkness</u>. <u>Delap's</u>
      <u>F&SF Review</u> (March), p. 26.

Announces novel has become a classic and confesses how
extensively it influenced his own first novel. Cites
criticisms with which he disagrees and states his own,
primarily that the ice journey becomes boring and that Ai's
and Estraven's control of sexual tension is too easily
achieved.

D381   BLUMBERG, MYRNA. "Clear-eyed Ironic Survival." London Times,
       8 June.
            Review of Orsinian Tales. Praises the collection by a
       "serious inspirational" author. It is "an allusively
       beautiful monument to politics, self-respect, wit, lyricism,
       and limitless aspirations." Disturbed by the use of "storm
       and bloodshed" as "fertilizing" experiences.

D382   BOYER, ROBERT H., and ZAHORSKI, KENNETH J., eds. "Ursula
       Kroeber Le Guin." In The Fantastic Imagination. New York:
       Avon, pp. 297-98.
            Introduction to "The Rule of Names." Biographical
       sketch notes her reputation as a teacher in the Science
       Fiction Writers' Workshop at the University of Washington.
       Story is adept at foreshadowing, and it contains several
       elements she later develops in the Earthsea trilogy.

D383   BRADLEY, MARION ZIMMER. "My Trip Through Science Fiction."
       Algol 15 (Winter):10-20.
            Describes the personal significance of The Left Hand of
       Darkness.

D384   BUHLE, PAUL. "A Writer Who Expands the Limits of Outer Space."
       Seven Days 1 (11 April):37-38.
            Review of The Word for World is Forest and Orsinian
       Tales. Heralds her critique of Western civilization--the
       "threat of the all-absorbing state to the fulfillment of
       humanity's simplest dreams: to love, to dream, to make a
       living in a cooperative fashion." Underlying this conflict
       in her work is the myth of a simpler life that is a source
       of both optimism and sadness. Praises Word for treating
       the broad issue of space colonization, finding it more
       significant than Bradbury's Martian Chronicles. Tales,
       however, is not as successful. It is "non-science fiction,"
       a genre that left her no room for fantasy. Characteriza-
       tion and settings are weak; the most memorable protagonists
       are "nobles and intellectuals" who suffer from "ineffectual
       lovesickness and a Sartrean sense of dilemma." However,
       Le Guin is unique in not portraying an antiutopian vision
       but a "reconciliation" vision, combining her Taoism, femi-
       nism, and mysticism. [Issue also contains C147.]

D385   CARPIO, VIRGINIA. "The Best in 1977: Books for Young Adults."
       Catholic Library World 49 (December):196-99.

Includes Very Far Away From Anywhere Else in an annotated
list of thirty-three titles, selected for "literary quality"
and "their effectiveness in motivating young adults to read
and on their relevance to the lives of adolescents."

D386 CARTER, PAUL A. The Creation of Tomorrow: Fifty Years of
Magazine Science Fiction. New York: Columbia University
Press, passim.
Several references in chapter seven on women in science
fiction which concludes with a discussion of The Dispossessed
which placed the issues of sexuality in a socio-political
context.

D387 CASSELBERRY, DIANE. "A Rich New Selection that Helps Teach."
Christian Science Monitor, 2 November, p. B1.
Article describes the newly established Center for the
Study of Children's Literature at Simmons College. Includes
the director's argument for the value of this literature
and her list of suggested books. In the fantasy category,
A Wizard of Earthsea is one of three books listed.

D388 CASSILL, R.V., ed. "Ursula K. Le Guin: The New Atlantis."
In The Norton Anthology of Short Fiction: Instructor's
Handbook. New York: Norton, pp. 128-30 [paper].
Describes the novel as satirizing an "increasingly
meddlesome and . . . inefficient government" which is en-
croaching on "private choice, initiative, and enterprise."
By implication, Le Guin suggests that the primary way to
resist this encroachment is through daydream. The itali-
cized passages are "a whopper," a daydream described as
nearly like music as prose can come. Story ends with
"certain uncertainty" which he compares to the closing
lines of Shelley's Prometheus Unbound.

D389 CLARESON, THOMAS [D.]. "The Launching Pad." Extrapolation 18
(May):100-6.
Prints two responses to Remington's essay on Le Guin
[see D355]--one by Harlan Ellison and one by Robert
Silverberg, Remington's reply to Ellison, and Clareson's
comments. The discussion centers on Remington's statements
about what was said at a panel discussion involving Ellison,
Silverberg, and Le Guin on the topic of science fiction
categorization. Clareson quotes Le Guin from his tape of
the discussion.

D390 CLARK, STEPHEN. "Technophilia and Other Afflictions." Times
Literary Supplement, 14 January, p. 42.
Review of Nebula Award Stories 11. In the context of
reviewing eight science fiction anthologies, he finds this
one "disappointing." SFWA did not pick the year's best.

Part D: Critical Studies

D391 COGELL, ELIZABETH CUMMINS. "Setting as Analogue to Charac-
      terization in Ursula Le Guin." Extrapolation 18 (May):131-
      41.
          Uses five Hainish stories (Rocannon's World, Planet of
      Exile, City of Illusions, The Left Hand of Darkness, "The
      Word for World is Forest") to show Le Guin's increasingly
      complex use of setting, "from straightforward geographical
      influence to influence on myth, ritual, and ways of per-
      ceiving the world." Discusses each of the stories. Con-
      cludes that Le Guin has integrated setting with two themes:
      that "each species' perception of reality" is shaped by its
      environment and that the "harmony of man and nature is
      necessary for racial survival and development."

D392 COSGRAVE, MARY SILVA. "Outlook Tower." Horn Book Magazine
      53 (April):198-99.
          Review of Orsinian Tales. Compares the stories to those
      of Isak Dinesen; praises the "insight and compassion" with
      which Le Guin develops her themes.

D393 CUNNINGHAM, VALENTINE. "Black Pudding." New Statesman (10
      June), p. 787.
          Review of Orsinian Tales. Imaginary world setting is
      too contrived; the stories' "realism is often too raffishly,
      too louchely imagined." Consequently, the stories have
      only "would-be humane themes of love, freedom, and fidelity
      in the hostile world of anti-contingent politics."

D394 DARCH, MARILYN. Review of Very Far Away From Anywhere Else.
      Children's Book Review Service 5 (January):47.
          Judges it to be a "poor book" with flat characters.

D395 DEITZ, PAULA. "'Outside the Dreams, Outside the Walls.'"
      Ontario Review, no. 6 (Spring-Summer), pp. 106-8.
          Review of Orsinian Tales. Insightful analysis of setting
      and theme. Locale detailed until, as in Middlemarch,
      reader visualizes "an actual map" of the region. Settings
      shift from one time period to another; thus reader carries
      into a new story a memory of past events. Prominent fea-
      ture of the setting is the architectural detail, evidenced
      in the contrast between urban crowding and rural openness
      or in seeing ruins of a building from a previous story.
      Her major theme is "the borders and boundaries of the land
      and of the mind." "The stunning climax of each story is
      the pivotal moment at which the persons cross over to a new
      level of awareness, a kind of freedom, leaving behind the
      constriction of their previous state." Transitions also
      reflected in imagery--descriptions of the shift from night
      to day or summer to winter. Characters who can make the
      transitions are often the young, particularly the women,
      "brave and determined, who know what to do." Although the

collection is not marked by moments of happiness, it does
portray "the inner joy of maturity and the subsequent re-
lease into full awareness."

D396   de JONGE, ALEX. "July SF." Spectator, 30 July, p. 22.
Review of The Word for World is Forest. Novel is sadly
dated in its allusions to Vietnam and its one-sided presentation (there are no Vietcong). The villain is little more
than a former space opera hero. Summarizes the conclusion
thus: "Eventually the green men overrun us despite all our
advanced technology, and make their planet safe from exploitation."

D397   DELANY, SAMUEL R. "To Read The Dispossessed." In The Jewel-
Hinged Jaw. Elizabethtown, N.Y.: Dragon Press, pp. 239-
308.
His central criticism is that there is an imbalance between foreground and recit so that the "didacta" often re-
place the foreground. There are discrepancies and contradictions between the ideas behind the novel and what is
portrayed in actual scenes. Thus, causes of certain kinds
of social behavior are inadequately discussed and key scenes
are missing. His second focus is that this imbalance is
particularly damaging in science fiction where the author'
is restructuring a universe. Writing science fiction requires more analysis as part of the creative act than mun-
dane fiction. The published fiction, however, should
transcend both ideology and autobiography.
In support of his argument he discusses key images in
the novel, some of which reinforce the meaning and some of
which do not. He discusses Shevek's succumbing to the
erotic feelings of Urrasti furniture and the sexual teasing
of Vea as false because Shevek had not learned the erotica
of that culture. He discusses crucial scenes which Le Guin
should have written, notably the first time Shevek uses
Urrasti money to purchase something, the discovery by
Shevek and Takver that his manuscript was being mutilated
by Sabul, and the psychological readjustments required when
Shevek shifts lovers from Bedap to Takver.
Delany discusses the nature of science fiction, arguing
that science fiction's function is "to take recognisable
syntagms and substitute in them, here and there, signifiers
from a wholly unexpected paradigm."
Concludes by noting that Le Guin's place is secure in
science fiction because of the impact her works have had.
His type of criticism will improve her writing by making
her more aware of language and increasing the energy of her
fiction. The Dispossessed is admirable for its ambition;
it is flawed in trying to accomplish the goals.

D398   DIXON, BOB. "The Supernatural: Religion, Magic and Mystifi-

cation." In <u>Catching Them Young: Political Ideas in
Children's Fiction</u>. London: Pluto Press, pp. 120-64.
    A Marxist interpretation of the history of children's
religious fiction which began with John Bunyan's <u>Pilgrim's
Progress</u>. After tracing the development, he discusses six
modern authors (J.R.R. Tolkien, Alan Garner, Ursula Le Guin,
Madelein l'Engle, Richard Adams, C.S. Lewis) to show the
continuation of the ideology in this tradition. Argues
that they are subtle propagandists for "political quietism,
antagonism toward ordinary people, royalism, patriotism,
original sin and selfishness." Modern fantasy helps the
writer and reader escape from pressing "moral and political
problems." Le Guin's Earthsea trilogy is portrayed as
being against change, especially in the social order, and
being elitist. Her "titanic battles between good and evil
remind me of the (admittedly cruder) struggles in the
United States comic books." Strongest criticism is directed
at C.S. Lewis.

D399 ECCLESHARE, JULIA. "As If By Magic." <u>New Statesman</u> (20 May),
      p. 686.
    Review of <u>Earthsea</u>. Praises the trilogy and cites it as
a book that revamped the image of wizards as "bogey-men"
into "quasi-religious controllers of the forces of good and
evil."

D400 ERLICH, RICHARD D. "On Barbour on Le Guin." <u>Science-Fiction
      Studies</u> 4 (November):317-18.
    Note comments on parallels between Le Guin and D.H.
Lawrence, most specifically in the imagery surrounding "the
love- and sex-life of Shevek and Takver" in <u>The Dispossessed</u>
and of Birkin and Ursula in <u>Women in Love</u>. Speculates that
both are influenced by Chinese philosophy.

D401 FISHER, MARGERY. "An Old Favourite." <u>Growing Point</u> 16 (May):
      3118-19.
    Review of <u>Earthsea</u>. Discusses what can be discovered
by reading the trilogy in one volume: that there are two
basic cultures in Earthsea, one Mediterranean and one
American Indian; that its meaning depends on suggestive
imagery; that it is more accessible than <u>Lord of the Rings</u>;
and that its relevance is Ged's "human desire to instruct
and strengthen."

D402 _____. "Personality Problems." <u>Growing Point</u> 15 (January):
      3040-42.
    Review of <u>A Very Long Way From Anywhere Else</u>. High-
lights the point of view, the "offhand voice" of seventeen-
year-old Owen that allows the reader to hear a great deal
about his inner and outer worlds and makes possible a com-
pressed story.

Part D: Critical Studies

D403 FRAZIER, BOB. "Poetry in the Major S.F. Novel." Speculative
      Poetry Review, no. 2, pp. [27-28].
         Noting several examples of poetry used in science fiction
      novels, he divides them into four categories: attachment,
      enhancement, supplement, and content. Places "Tormer's
      Lay" from The Left Hand of Darkness in the enhancement
      category, that is, poetry not necessary for understanding
      the novel.

D404 FRIEND, BEVERLY. "Virgin Territory: The Bonds and Boundaries
      of Women in Science Fiction." In Many Futures, Many Worlds:
      Theme and Form in Science Fiction. Edited by Thomas D.
      Clareson. Kent, Oh.: Kent State University Press, pp.
      140-63.
         Extensive updating of her 1972 essay [see D87]. Dis-
      cusses the androgynes of Le Guin's The Left Hand of Dark-
      ness, but notes that the main focus is on "Genly Ai's re-
      action to them." Concludes by asserting that after Joanna
      Russ, "Sturgeon and Le Guin's answers seem a little pat."

D405 GARFITT, ROGER. "In Praise of Limestone." Times Literary
      Supplement, 10 June, p. 697.
         Review of Orsinian Tales. Puzzles over how to cate-
      gorize and evaluate the stories, as well as Le Guin's
      choice of Europe for their background. Labels the book her
      "first venture into the mainstream of literature," but adds
      that she does not "entirely eschew fantasy." His serious
      question about its quality as fiction involves Le Guin's
      choice to create "an imaginary world" which "is surely not
      as difficult nor as necessary a task as making imaginative
      sense of one's own world." European background complements
      the austerity of the setting and perhaps gives Le Guin the
      distance she needs in order to criticize America. Praises
      their detailed setting and characterization, as well as
      their "moral power, a refreshed sense of human dignity."

D406 GIOLITTO, JUDITH. "Lofty Themes in Short Stories." South
      Bend (Indiana) Tribune, 3 April.
         Review of Orsinian Tales. Praises the couching of
      "lofty" themes ("the struggle for personal and political
      freedom and the human need for love") in the lives of "men
      and women as vaguely familiar as faces in an old photograph
      album." Ultimate optimistic tone comes from the images and
      the emotions of the characters.

D407 HEINS, ETHEL L. Review of Very Far Away From Anywhere Else.
      Horn Book Magazine 53 (February):57-58.
         Identifies its appeal as the criticism of "conformity,
      hypocrisy and . . . anti-intellectualism." Praises it as
      "a small jewel."

D408 HORNUM, BARBARA G. "American Values and World View as Reflected in Science Fiction." Ph.D. dissertation, Bryn
Mawr.
Examines American science fiction to show that it "sets
up alternative, fictional models of future cultures and
uses this heuristic device to reflect and portray the
values, folk ideas and world view of contemporary America."
Le Guin's novels are used as examples in four chapters.
Chapter four, "Male-Female Relationships" uses The Left
Hand of Darkness as one of a few novels that do not maintain male-female stereotypes. Chapter nine, "The Political
System" uses the same novels and classifies Le Guin as a
writer who, although fearful of the political future, sees
more optimistic alternatives.
Chapter ten, "The Economic System," draws on The Dispossessed to show Le Guin's ability to criticize both
societies. Chapter twelve, "The Family System," points out
her uniqueness in probing "perhaps more than any other
science fiction writer," the relationship between social
institutions (especially the family) and resultant personality. She uses Left Hand and The Dispossessed.

D409 KLEIN, GERARD. "Le Guin's 'Aberrant' Opus: Escaping the Trap
of Discontent." Translated by Richard Astle. Science-
Fiction Studies 13 (November):287-95. Reprinted in Science-
Fiction Studies: Selected Articles on Science Fiction 1976-
1977. Edited by R.D. Mullen and Darko Suvin. Boston: 1978,
Gregg Press, pp. 313-21.
Argues that she is unique among American science fiction
writers on the question of the "future unity of human
civilization." She posits not "discontent and pessimism,"
but a plurality of cultures and a plurality of solutions to
problems. Discusses the original Hainish condition and
concludes that for her "history is neither a succession nor
an accumulation of experiences, but a confrontation of experiences." Her fiction supports cultural relativism and
thus challenges the concept of an ideal society, a belief
in the "objectivity of the social realm," and the quest for
a "total social science." Her ethics is central to all her
works and is the "taking account of the behaviors, points
of view, and ethics of others." Most of his examples come
from The Left Hand of Darkness.
Discusses The Lathe of Heaven as an examination of the
role of the unconscious (subjectivity) and its significance
in solutions between the rational and the unconscious individual mind. Her exterior model is the science of ethnol-
ogy which leads her to extol cultural diversity. Concludes
with the conjecture that her unique point of view is a result of being a woman. Not obsessed with acknowledging
"the power of the phallus," she can posit "a world without
a central principle, without a unifying system, without
domination."

D410 KNIGHT, DAMON. Letter to the editor. SFWA Bulletin 12
(Summer):21-22.
  Response to Le Guin's letter on the Lem affair [see
C144]. States that the honorary SFWA membership was created
for Tolkien. [Followed by the editor's statement that
since both sides have aired their viewpoints, there will be
no more letters published on the Lem affair.]

D411 KORN, ERIC. "So Many Notions to the Page." Times Literary
Supplement, 8 July, p. 820.
  Review of The Word for World is Forest. Although dated
by its depiction of the Vietnam War, the novel is valuable
beyond contemporary history for its fine drawing of the
Athshean psychology and change. The novel is "a lament for
the loss of Angkor Vat."

D412 LUNDWALL, SAM J. Science Fiction: An Illustrated History.
London: London Eds., p. 79.
  Discusses The Dispossessed as the "best example of the
traditional Utopia described in terms of modern sociology."
In spite of some preaching, it is unique in including within each utopia its own "seeds of destruction" and in recog-
nizing human fallibility. The Dispossessed "is certainly
among the best and most mature modern Utopias in the traditional style."

D413 M., J. Review of A Very Long Way From Anywhere Else. Junior
Bookshelf (UK) 41 (April):116-17.
  Welcomes it as "the most sensitive book" read in 1976,
particularly because of the values that emerge in the two
relationships--between boy and parent, boy and girl.

D414 McINTYRE, VONDA N. "Ursula K. Le Guin: 'Using The Language
With Delight.'" Encore 1 (April/May):6-7.
  Recounts early publishing history and notes her current
influence, especially in her compassionate humanism and
delight in language. Her serenity does not rule out a
sharp wit in her fiction. Interspersed with quotations
from Le Guin.

D415 McNELLY, WILLIS E. Review of Nebula Award Stories Eleven.
America 136 (23 April):381-82.
  Discusses the collection as showing the health of the
short story and the new developments in science fiction;
notes the careful editing of Le Guin.

D416 MELVIN, KENNETH B.; BRODSY, STANLEY L.; and FOWLER,Jr., Raymond
D., eds. "Ursula K. Le Guin." In Psy-Fi One: An Anthology
of Psychology in Science Fiction. New York: Random, pp.
232-33.
  Introduction to "The Diary of the Rose." Discusses the

issue of the professional imposing social control. Cites
One Flew Over the Cuckoo's Nest as an example. Le Guin's
story examines two themes: the therapist's "developing
awareness of the interactions of psychotherapy and social
control" and psychotherapy's future techniques.

D417 MEYERS, WALTER E. "Orsinian Tales." In Magill's Literary
      Annual, 1977. Edited by Frank N. Magill. Englewood Cliffs:
      Salem Press, pp. 601-4.
         Finds it inferior to her previous, praiseworthy work.
      Setting, characters, and plot are all deficient. The
      message of "Imaginary Countries"--to leave imaginary
      places--contradicts the whole collection.

D418 MILLER, DAN. "Science Fiction." Booklist 73 (1 July):1635.
         Review of Rocannon's World. Discusses the novel's sig-
      nificance as an early presentation of alien life and of the
      Hainish culture.

D419 NASSO, CHRISTINE, ed. "Le Guin, Ursula K(roeber)." Contem-
      porary Authors. Vol. 21-24. 1st rev. ed. Detroit: Gale
      Research Co., p. 526.
         Bio-bibliographical information arranged in three cate-
      gories: Personal, Career, and Writings. Incorrect marriage
      date listed.

D420 NICOL, CHARLES. "Finding Le Guin's Right Hand." Science-
      Fiction Studies 4 (March):86.
         Review of The Farthest Shores of Ursula K. Le Guin [see
      D362]. Praises it as a good survey of and introduction to
      her work. Faults it for inadequate survey of published
      criticism. Scholars will have to take into account his
      discussion of The Dispossessed and the Earthsea trilogy.

D421 NILSEN, ALLEEN PACE. "Books for Young Adults: A Roundup of
      Good Books." English Journal 66 (September):86.
         Review of Very Far Away From Anywhere Else. Names three
      unique features: a boy's viewpoint of romance; teenagers
      who feel different because they are intellectuals; a sin-
      cere treatment of a boy-girl friendship. Quotes a librarian
      who praises the book's depth and brevity.

D422 NOVITSKI, PAUL DAVID. "Pendragon Press: An Interview with
      Chuck Garvin and Jeff Levin." Pacific Northwest Review of
      Books, premier issue (Winter):1, 6-8.
         Article/interview includes details on the establishment
      of this press for fantasy and science fiction works. In-
      dicates the significance of From Elfland to Poughkeepsie as
      their first publication. "The Water is Wide" has led them
      beyond the genre limits. Publishers discuss how they
      select paper color and texture, using "The Water is Wide"
      as an example.

D423 O'BRIEN, DENNIS J. Review of The Earthsea Trilogy. Common-
      weal 104 (9 December):797.
          Appears in article, "Critics' Choices for Christmas."
      Commends her ability to make magic believable. Identifying
      the key to her magic as naming, he contrasts Earthsea to
      modernity which "can be seen as the loss of names, the in-
      ability to summon any spirit at the core of the things and
      events." Believes The Tombs of Atuan is the best.

D424 OFFUTT, ANDREW. "How It Happened: One Bad Decision Leading
      to Another." Science-Fiction Studies 4 (July):138-43.
          Response to various pieces in Science-Fiction Studies on
      the Lem affair; Offutt was the Membership Chairman of SFWA
      who officially revoked Lem's honorary membership. Irri-
      tated that Le Guin and others did not write to him for in-
      formation on the actions of SFWA. [See C146, D441, D425.]

D425 "On the Ouster of Stanislaw Lem from the SFWA." Science-
      Fiction Studies 4 (July):126-44.
          Only two entries mention Le Guin [see D424 and D433].
      Contains: Brian W. Aldiss, "What Dark Non-Literary Pas-
      sions . . ."; Stanislaw Lem, "Looking Down on Science Fic-
      tion: A Novelist's Choice for the World's Worst Writing"
      [reprint of his 1975 article which allegedly initiated the
      SFWA dispute]; Pamela Sargent and George Zebrowski, "How
      It Happened: A Chronology of the 'Lem Affair'" [see D433];
      Pamela Sargent, "Comment and Conclusions"; George Zebrowski,
      "Why It Happened: Some Notes and Opinion"; Jack Dann and
      Gregory Benford, "Two Statements in Support of Sargent and
      Zebrowski"; Andrew Offutt, "How It Happened: One Bad De-
      cision Leading to Another" [see D424]; R.D. Mullen, "I
      Could Not Love Thee, Dear, So Much. . . ." [Followed by
      additional information from James Gunn in "On the Lem
      Affair," Science-Fiction Studies 4 (November):314-16 and
      his "A Clarification," Science-Fiction Studies 5 (July):
      198.]

D426 PARISH, MARGARET. "Fantasy." English Journal 66 (October):
      90-92.
          Le Guin's work has called attention to the error in
      classifying fantasy as children's literature. Quotes C.S.
      Lewis for support and notes that the Earthsea trilogy is
      sometimes marketed as children's literature and sometimes
      as adult literature. Her audience is anyone who likes
      fantasy, although the theme of initiation is especially
      appealing to young adults. Includes reactions of three
      readers: Richard Erlich, English professor; Liam Lavery,
      fifth grader; Elizabeth Fannin, high school student.

D427 PARKER, HELEN NETHERCUTT. "Biological Themes in Modern Science
      Fiction." Ph.D. dissertation, Duke University.

Tracing the biological theme, she provides a "thematic
and stylistic overview" of the genre. Le Guin is one of
four authors discussed in chapter six who use "interaction
between human beings and aliens . . . to develop a far-
reaching analogy between the two different life forms, and
to comment through that analogy on man's present and possible future situation." The others are Stanley Weinbaum,
Isaac Asimov, and John Brunner. In The Left Hand of Darkness, "Gethenian biology functions . . . as the central and
most arresting symbol of the concept of unity in duality."
This concept is reinforced by the novel's structure,
imagery, and plot situation. Praises her skill, style, and
depth of insight, indicative of the quality of modern
science fiction. [Misspells Genly Ai.]

D428 PARRINDER, PATRICK. "The Black Wave: Science and Social Consciousness in Modern Science Fiction." Radical Science
Journal, no. 5, pp. 37–61.
      Traces the "literary and ideological developments" of
recent science fiction which possesses an "increasing
social and political awareness." Examines novels by Lem,
Arkady and Boris Strugatsky, and Le Guin to "illustrate the
radical directions." The fine psychological development of
Shevek (The Dispossessed), scientist and anarchist, shows
the problems of maintaining individual and social freedom,
"equality and permanent revolution."

D429 PARTNOW, ELAINE, ed. "Ursula K. Le Guin." In The Quotable
Woman 1800–1975. Los Angeles: Corwin Books, p. 397.
      Of the nineteen quotes, nine are from The Left Hand of
Darkness, nine are from The Lathe of Heaven, and one is
from The Dispossessed.

D430 PEARSON, CAROL. "Women's Fantasies and Feminist Utopias."
Frontiers: A Journal of Women Studies 2 (Fall):50–61.
      Analyzes the "numerous areas of concensus" among eight
feminist utopias--Mary E. Lane's Mizora: A Prophecy,
Charlotte Perkins Gilman's Herland, Marge Piercy's Woman
on the Edge of Time, Joanna Russ's The Female Man,
Le Guin's The Dispossessed, Dorothy Bryant's The Kin of
Ata Are Waiting for You, James Tiptree Jr.'s "Houston,
Houston, Do You Read?", Mary Staton's From the Legend of
Biel.
      The similarities are discussed under two general topics:
the criticisms of the "patriarchal society" and the depic-
tions of an alternative model--the home. Pearson suggests
both come out of women's experience because they have been
victims and they have been builders of homes, based on co-
operation not competition. The Dispossessed and "Is Gender
Necessary?" are frequently cited and quoted. [Pearson mistakenly lists the first author and novel as Mary Bradley

Lane, Mizara: A Prophecy.]

D431   POURNELLE, JERRY. Letter to the editor. SFWA Bulletin 12
       (Summer):20-21.
             Response to Le Guin's letter [see C146]. States she is
       wrong in asserting that Lem was expelled from SFWA. In-
       stead, he was offered a better form of membership. Resent-
       ment among members stems from Lem's rudeness in not trying
       to debate the nature of American science fiction within
       SFWA.

D432   SANDERS, JOE. Review of Nebula Award Stories Eleven. Delap's
       F&SF Review (July), pp. 29-30.
             Recommends the book for libraries who want the complete
       series; otherwise, the book is not unique. Most of the
       stories are readily available in other anthologies and this
       year's winners are not outstanding.

D433   SARGENT, PAMELA, and ZEBROWSKI, GEORGE, "How It Happened: A
       Chronology of the 'Lem Affair.'" Science-Fiction Studies
       4 (July):129-34.
             A chronological account of Stanislaw Lem's relationship
       with SFWA, from 17 March 1973, to January 1977. Le Guin's
       participation is described in four entries: 8 March 1976;
       19 March 1976; 7 April 1976; August-January 1976-1977. She
       protested the revoking of Lem's honorary membership.

D434   SCHOLES, ROBERT, and RABKIN, ERIC S. Science Fiction: His-
       tory, Science, Vision. London: Oxford University Press,
       pp. 75-80, 226-30, passim.
             First section discusses her as one of the outstanding
       writers of the sixties [see D204]. Delineates the major
       conflicts between opposing ideas and social systems in The
       Lathe of Heaven and The Dispossessed. No assessment is
       made since she is in the middle of her writing career.
       Second section discusses The Left Hand of Darkness as an
       exploration of multiple relationships. Novel demonstrates
       science fiction's unique ability to literalize metaphors:
       "The alien encounter . . . becomes the obvious metaphor
       for relations between the human sexes."

D435   SCHWEITZER, DARRELL. "The Vivisector." Science Fiction Re-
       view, no. 20 (February), pp. 36-38.
             Review of Orsinian Tales. Dubs them not science fiction
       and not quality Le Guin. Finds "Brothers and Sisters" very
       poor because it is dull, lacks a unified point of view and
       memorable characters. Praises "The Fountains." Suggests
       the book is Le Guin's attempt at a Dubliners. Recommends
       reading only six of the stories; the rest lack "emotional
       intensity and focus" and have weak characters.

D436 SHIPPEY, T.A. "Archmage and antimage." Times Literary Supple-
      ment, 15 July, p. 863.
           Review of Earthsea. Observes that the first novel opens
      by confronting and dispelling two current rationalizations
      about magic: (1) that it is an analogue of science
      (Frazer) and (2) that it is a cathartic for fear
      (Malinowski). Futhermore, she covertly disproves sci-
      entists' (particularly Francis Bacon) belief that things
      are more significant than words. Notes that the underlying
      myth of the trilogy is Book VI of the Aeneid, the trip into
      "Shadowland." Ideas, narrative, and Ged's development are
      all interwoven in the first volume. The second volume
      dramatizes "the distinction between the lacrimae rerum of
      the universe and the institutionalized cruelty of ritual
      which men invent to try to palliate it." Final volume,
      which draws its picture of eternity from Crime and Punish-
      ment, completes the trip to the land of death. Le Guin uses
      fantasy as it should be used--to treat themes beyond realis-
      tic fiction but without lapsing into allegory or myth.

D437 _____. "The Magic Art and the Evolution of Words: Ursula
      Le Guin's Earthsea Trilogy." Mosaic 10 (Winter):147-63.
           Asserts the trilogy is an excellent modern fantasy, ex-
      emplifying and handling modern semantic problems. The
      sharp distinctions now made between science, magic, and
      religion give the writer of fantasy a special problem and
      a special opportunity. First, magic will have to be ex-
      plained and perhaps defended in order to overcome the
      reader's preconceptions. Thus, in the first volume, both
      Ged and the reader gradually learn that magic has intellec-
      tual, moral, and scientific boundaries. It is unlike
      science in that personal genius is crucial to its operation.
      Second, the explanation of magic becomes a commentary on
      the contemporary world, suggesting that current "truths"
      are neither total nor universal.
           Her theme in the first volume is that "being . . . is
      more than use. . . . To speak, one must be silent." Her
      philosophy thus respects "separate existences within the
      totality of existence," including even darkness and death.
      Further, the novel can be viewed as a criticism of current
      myths, especially those that view nature as a machine to
      be worked on.
           The second volume is about the nature of religion,
      pointing up man's fears which make gods crueler and stronger.
      Arha wins her freedom from the human religion, but not with-
      out the loss of mother and friend. The third volume con-
      tinues the trend to grimness and more familiar world. Just
      as the Kargs are more like us than the mages, so the weak-
      ening Earthsea is like "America in the aftermath of Vietnam."
      In her exploration of the fear of death, she shows that the
      real devastation is caused by a loss of faith. Le Guin

asks the reader to believe in magic even though it promises
no afterlife.

D438   STEIN, RUTH M. "Book reMarks: A Personal View of Current
       Juvenile Literature." Language Arts 54 (April):442-43.
           Review of Very Far Away From Anywhere Else. Outstanding
       feature is the characterization of the young adults; other-
       wise, theme and plot are not original.

D439   SUTHERLAND, FRANK. "Science Fiction: Its Tales, Techniques,
       and Creators." Nashville Tennessean, 6 March.
           Review of Nebula Award Stories Eleven. Applauds the
       SFWA's selection of winners and Le Guin's selection from
       the runnersup. Criticizes her inclusion of two nonfiction
       articles at the expense of two stories.

D440   SUTHERLAND, ZENA, and ARBUTHNOT, MAY HILL. Children and Books.
       5th ed. Glenview, Ill.: Scott, Foresman & Co., pp. 207-8.
           After describing the trilogy, cites Le Guin's ability to
       develop character; compares her style ("serious, spare,
       precise") to modern idiom.

D441   SUVIN, DARKO. "A First Comment on Ms. Le Guin's Note on the
       'Lem Affair.'" Science-Fiction Studies 4 (March):101-2.
           Response to Le Guin's criticism of SFWA over their re-
       voking Lem's honorary membership [see C146]. Asserts her
       statement raises the issue of writers' unions turning from
       "useful to baleful." The Lem affair suggests that SFWA may
       be about to shift from a trade union to the side of bureau-
       cracy, dedicated to maintaining the status quo. Questions
       what SFWA and SFRA response should be. Urges individual
       responses to Le Guin through Science-Fiction Studies. [For
       replies, see D424, D425, D480.]

D442   SYKES, PETER. "The Game of the Names." Oxford Times, 18
       March.
           Review of Earthsea. Finds the trilogy "stiff with alle-
       gory." Fine use of language; in spite of being fantastic,
       the world is believable.

D443   WINGROVE, DAVID. "Juvenalia? A Child's View of Earthsea."
       Vector 81 5 (May-June):4-7.
           Review of Earthsea. Asserts that Schopenhauer's de-
       rision of women is analogous to our derision of juvenile
       literature. Le Guin's trilogy is not textbookish nor
       allegory; instead it presents the child with a philosophy
       he/she can understand. The concepts of balance, acceptance
       of evil, the necessity of death, self maturation, freedom
       and constraint are all within the child's understanding,
       especially as Le Guin develops them. Praises Le Guin over
       Tolkien because she is "progressive," where he is "regres-
       sive."

D444 WOLFE, GARY K. "The Known and the Unknown: Structure and
Image in Science Fiction." In Many Futures, Many Worlds:
Theme and Form in Science Fiction. Edited by Thomas D.
Clareson. Kent, Oh.: Kent State University Press, pp. 94-
116.
Argues that "one of the key oppositions of all science
fiction [is] the opposition between the known and the unknown." This tension is reflected in shared images (or
icons) and give the genre its "'sense of wonder.'" He discusses The Dispossessed and its images of barriers; he compares the novel's structure to Clarke's The City and The
Stars.

D445 WOOD, SUSAN. Review of Very Far Away From Anywhere Else.
Pacific Northwest Review of Books (Winter), pp. 5,8.
Summarizes the novel to suggest its similarity to
"trendy 'young adult' books" on "'real life' problems" and
then asserts it is different because it is authentic in
setting, characterization, and situation. Maintains that
readers, including Le Guin, identify with Owen. Only awkwardness is in the wrongly chosen title which does not
call attention to Owen's imaginary country and frontier,
Thorn.

1978

D446 ANNAS, PAMELA J. "New Worlds, New Words: Androgyny in
Feminist Science Fiction." Science-Fiction Studies 5
(July):143-56.
Because science fiction is structured like a scientific
experiment in which alternatives are imagined, it has the
potential for being a revolutionary literature. Feminist
writers have recently begun using it to explore avenues of
social change. Since The Left Hand of Darkness, many have
seen androgyny as an appropriate political response.
Discusses many of Le Guin's novels. The Left Hand of
Darkness is Le Guin's fullest exploration of the androgyne;
The Lathe of Heaven, The Word for World is Forest, and The
Dispossessed "use the device of contrast between a men-
tality which is dualistic and one which is androgynous" on,
respectively, an individual, a species, and a social level.
Views Shevek's time theory as complementary to androgyny
since "it denies separation and duality." Article dis-
cusses other feminist pieces, including Joanna Russ's The
Female Man and Marge Piercy's Woman on the Edge of Time.

D447 ANON. Review of City of Illusions. Kirkus Reviews 46 (1
April):396.
Labels it "tentative and imperfect Le Guin," but remarks
on the "generous ardor and judiciousness" of the writing.

141

D448 ANON. Review of <u>Millennial Women</u>. <u>Bulletin of the Center for Children's Books</u> (November), p. 46.
"Eye of the Heron" is the outstanding story in style, narrative, and portrayal of the "timeless . . . struggle between good and evil."

D449 ANON. Review of <u>Millennial Women</u>. <u>Kirkus Reviews</u> 46, part II (1 May):516-17.
Sharply critical of the volume for not living up to the vision promised in Marilyn Hacker's opening poem. Le Guin's "Eye of the Heron" is dismissed: "With its overkill of earnest understatement, it is nearly a parody of this writer's best work."

D450 BAINBRIDGE, WILLIAM SIMS, and DALZIEL, MURRAY. "The Shape of Science Fiction as Perceived by the Fans." <u>Science-Fiction Studies</u> 5 (July):165-71.
Initiates the quantitative study of the structure and content of science fiction with a "quantitative analysis of the relationships perceived by readers [130 editors of American fanzines and their associates] among twenty-seven authors and several types of literature." Le Guin is one of the authors. Data presented in four tables.

D451 BANNON, BARBARA A. Review of <u>Planet of Exile</u>. <u>Publishers Weekly</u> 213 (9 January):73.
Praiseworthy for its "emotional power and strongly depicted setting."

D452 BENESTAD, JANET. Review of <u>Planet of Exile</u>. <u>Best Sellers</u> 38 (May):41.
Cites the style, imagination, and disinclination to preach of this exploration of "problems of racial prejudice and person bigotry."

D453 BITTNER, JAMES W. "Persuading Us to Rejoice and Teaching Us How to Praise: Le Guin's <u>Orsinian Tales</u>." <u>Science-Fiction Studies</u> 5 (November):215-42.
Pieces together the chronology of Le Guin's composing and publishing the Orsinia material to show that it is the "bedrock" of her science fiction and fantasy. His overview of the collection demonstrates her use of the circular romance quest which not only structures an individual story and the arrangement of the tales, but also reinforces her ethical concerns and her historical awareness.
The country of Orsinia is like her other invented lands in combining the real with the imaginary and in functioning as a <u>paysage moralise</u>. The blurring of the familiar and the fantastic is consistent with her perception of the world where demarcations between concepts are blurred because she sees "both-and" instead of "either-or." This is

most obvious in her insistence on the blurring of truth and imagination, legend and fact. Even the topography of Orsinia stresses flux: karst is rock dissolved by water. Finally, her moral values reflect the same world-in-process. Points up her similarity to W.H. Auden and Rilke: all three use "concrete settings and naturalistic landscape detail to express moral values and emotions."

Second half of the essay is a detailed examination of two stories written in 1960: "Imaginary Countries" is the "central tale" and "An die Musik" is an early statement of her conflict "between her deep devotion to art and her strong commitment to ethical principles." After detailing the biographical influences on and parallels in "Imaginary Countries," he discusses its centrality as a story about "the circularity of fantasy."

"An die Musik" is an early thought experiment that raises questions about the function of art and of the artist. It demonstrates that the "raison d'être" of art is "to persuade us to rejoice and to teach us how to praise." The essay contains numerous comparisons to other works of art (poetry, fiction, music), extensive documentation, information from private correspondence with Le Guin.

D454   BOYER, ROBERT H., and ZAHORSKI, KENNETH J., eds. "Ursula Kroeber Le Guin." In Dark Imaginings: A Collection of Gothic Fantasy. New York: Delta, pp. 167-68 [paper].
       After tracing her writing career and awards, discusses her special place in High Fantasy. In addition to her, only Macdonald and Tolkien wrote both short stories and novels. Praises From Elfland to Poughkeepsie as a "handbook of style for the fantasy writer." Introduces "Darkness Box" with comments on style, detail, and imagery.

D455   _____. "Ursula K. Le Guin." In The Fantastic Imagination II: An Anthology of High Fantasy. New York: Avon, pp. 215-16 [paper].
       Sketches her biography and her professional writing career, including the awards and critical attention by scholars. Introduces "April in Paris," commenting on her special ability to blend realism and fantasy, humor and seriousness.

D456   BRYFONSKI, DEDRIA, and MENDELSON, PHYLLIS CARMEL, eds. "Le Guin, Ursula K(roeber)." In Contemporary Literary Criticism: Excerpts from Criticism of the Works of Today's Novelists, Poets, Playwrights, and Other Creative Writers. Vol. 8. Detroit: Gale Research Co., pp. 341-43.
       Identifies the novel as her primary mode, the Earthsea trilogy as children's literature. Includes excerpts from D325, D330, D359 (wrongly attributed to Derek de Solla Price), and D336.

D457 BUCKNALL, BARBARA J. "Androgynes in Outer Space." In <u>Critical Encounters: Writers and Themes in Science Fiction</u>. Edited by Dick Riley. New York: Ungar, pp. 56-69, 179.

Claims the idea of androgyny made the novel popular and won it the awards. Androgyny offers a vision of unity and freedom from undesirable emotions. Novel explores the "psychological, philosophical, and even religious" ramifications of androgyny. Incest is a major theme of fidelity and betrayal. Because the family and hearth structure is so fundamental on Gethen, Bucknall asserts "that sex between Gethenians must always be closer to sex between brother and sister . . . than any other sexual bond." Thus loyalty to Ai becomes a betrayal of the family. The novel's myths illustrate incest and connect it with love and betrayal. Compares <u>The Left Hand of Darkness</u> to <u>Tombs of Atuan</u>, but mistakenly believes <u>Tombs</u> preceded <u>Left Hand</u>. Crucial points of the essay are not always fully explained.

D458 CHRISTNER, HENRY. "Tranquil, Direct Style of Writing is Displayed." <u>Fredericksburg Free Lance-Star</u>, 30 September.

Review of <u>City of Illusions</u>. Cites the novel as an example of her prize-winning style. Notes the slow plot and criticizes its "superficial similarities to 'Star Wars.'" [Reviewer apparently unaware that <u>City</u> was first published in 1967.] Praises the journey scenes and the probability of her future society.

D459 COGELL, ELIZABETH CUMMINS. "The Middle-Landscape Myth in Science Fiction." <u>Science-Fiction Studies</u> 5 (July):134-42.

Points out that both the myths of the apocalypse and of the middle landscape in science fiction "express current cultural tensions." Selects one novel to represent each of the three kinds of apocalypse charted by John R. May: <u>Earth Abides</u>, primitive; <u>Love in the Ruins</u>, Judeo-Christian; <u>The Lathe of Heaven</u>, secular. Discussion of <u>Lathe</u> notes the middle landscape is an urban society trying to survive natural chaos and manmade chaos; the middle way, represented by Orr, is that of Taoist humanism. Haber and Orr are contrasted by a double series of three slogans. Concludes by asserting the viability of the two myths, especially when used within the same novel.

D460 De BOLT, JOE. "A Le Guin Biography." <u>Empire</u>, no. 13 (7 April), pp. 23-28. Reprinted in <u>Ursula K. Le Guin: Voyager to Inner Lands and to Outer Space</u>. Edited by Joe De Bolt. Port Washington, N.Y.: Kennikat, pp. 13-28, 198-200.

The only essay-length biography. A careful piecing together of statements in essays, interviews, newspaper articles "without rude invasion of Le Guin's life or dubious psychologizing about her works." Includes an account of her childhood, her developing writing career, her family life in Portland, her sense of her own writing. Concludes suggesting her life story could be subtitled, "An Ambiguous Success" as she has recognized the tension between her desire to be moralistic and to be aesthetic.

D461 del REY, LESTER. "The Reference Library." Analog 98 (November):173.
Review of Three Hainish Novels. A good collection which provides background for Le Guin's later novels. Finds City of Illusions the "strangest"; praises characterization in all three.

D462 De MONTREVILLE, DORIS, and CRAWFORD, ELIZABETH D., eds. "Ursula K. Le Guin." In Fourth Book of Junior Authors & Illustrators. New York: H.W. Wilson, pp. 221-23.
Brief biographical sketch, followed by a summary of how she came to write the Earthsea books. Discusses her science fiction with detail on The Left Hand of Darkness. Concludes with brief mention of Very Far Away From Anywhere Else.

D463 DOCTOR, KEN. "Home Truths and Illusions." Willamette Valley Observer, 22 December, p. 12b.
Review of City of Illusions and Very Far Away From Anywhere Else. Cites her as a "master storyteller." Observes that the journey is a "trip from mindlessness to the final mind-game," which ends the book too neatly. Very Far shows a similar "concern for human dignity." Although the book is "hopeful," "it is as much about the failure of adulthood as it is about the idealism of youth."

D464 ELLIOTT, GEORGE P. "Fiction and Anti-Fiction." American Scholar 47 (Summer):398-406.
Discusses the quarrels over evaluations of and categories in modern fiction, asserting it is more a problem for the critic than the writer and reader, and is especially pronounced in academia and the New York literary establishment. Central conflict is between fiction and anti-fiction, terms he defines and discusses. Concludes that the quarrel is now over and all fiction has benefitted. Names and praises new publications by Stanley Elkin, John Gardner, John Cheever, Le Guin (Orsinian Tales), Wallace Stegner.

D465 ESTES, SALLY C. "Wonder Women: Science Fiction From the Distaff Side." Daily Facts, 5 June, p. C4.
Review of Planet of Exile and City of Illusions. Planet, a novel about intolerance, convincingly portrays "the alien landscape and the interactions between" two different human settlements. Agrees with Le Guin that the villains of City are not convincing, "but the characterization of the hero and the unraveling of his experiences more than compensate."

D466　FANZONE, JOSEPH.　"Four From the Further Realms of Reality."
　　　　　Baltimore Sun, 19 March.
　　　　　　　Review of Planet of Exile.　Identifies it as a pre-
　　　　　figurement of her greater novels and wishes for a "much
　　　　　more detailed treatment."

D467　FRANSON, DONALD, and DeVORE, HOWARD.　A History of The Hugo,
　　　　　Nebula, and International Fantasy Awards.　Dearborn, Mich.:
　　　　　Misfit Press, 129 pp.
　　　　　　　Primarily lists nominees and winners for each year that
　　　　　each award has been given (Hugo, 1953-1979; Nebula, 1965-
　　　　　1978).　Author index allows user to locate all thirty-five
　　　　　nominations for Le Guin.

D468　GEIS, RICHARD.　"I Hear Voices. . . ."　Science Fiction Review
　　　　　7 (May).
　　　　　　　Review of "Gwilan's Harp" and "Intracom" Read by the
　　　　　author.　Recommends it both for her dramatic reading ability
　　　　　and her delightful liner notes.

D469　GILDEN, MEL.　"Genesis of Le Guin's 'Left Hand.'"　Los Angeles
　　　　　Times, 17 September, p. 12.
　　　　　　　Review of City of Illusions.　Notes flaws such as the
　　　　　mixture of fantasy and science fiction, contrived plot
　　　　　events.　But her descriptions and characterizations are
　　　　　strong.　Contains the "roots" of The Left Hand of Darkness
　　　　　in "the clash between two cultures and the man caught in
　　　　　the middle."

D470　GROVE-STEPHENSEN, PHILLIPPA.　Review of Orsinian Tales.
　　　　　Paperback Parlour 2 (August).
　　　　　　　Identifies them as "understated tales"; they are imagina-
　　　　　tive and well crafted but are not science fiction.　Notes
　　　　　that the capital city, Krasnoy, typifies the central
　　　　　struggle of the human spirit against oppression.

D471　HANNAY, DICK.　"Sci-Fi Roster:　No Star Bores."　Nashville
　　　　　Tennessean, 12 February.
　　　　　　　Review of Rocannon's World.　Acknowledges it as early
　　　　　Le Guin, but finds the fantasy "delightful" and the "quest-
　　　　　myth" appealing.

D472　HANNER, RICHARD.　"Writer no Sleeper--She's Alert to the Mys-
　　　　　teries of Darkness."　Palo Alto Times, 8 April.
　　　　　　　Announces a special citation from the Association for
　　　　　the Psychophysiological Study of Sleep has been awarded to
　　　　　Le Guin.　Describes a symposium held in her honor, "The
　　　　　Many Worlds of Dreaming."　Participants included Michel
　　　　　Jouvet (Lyons, France) and Rosalind Cartwright (Chicago).
　　　　　Le Guin commented on her debt to sleep researchers who
　　　　　cultivate the "intellectual zucchini."　"Then I hop over the

fence, and later say 'come buy my succotash.'"

D473 HELDENFELS, R.D. "Records Bring Fantasy To Life." <u>Daily Press</u> (Newport News, Va.), 7 May, p. E5.
Review of Caedmon Records' series of science fiction readings. Distinguishes Le Guin as a reader who performs. Her work gains in strength when heard in this way.

D474 HENAHAN, DONAL. "Naumburg-Winning Jubal Trio Gives Concert." <u>New York Times</u>, 4 February, sec. 1, p. 13.
Review of 2 February performance which included "the world premier of Joseph Schwantner's 'Wild Angels of the Open Hills' (1977)" based on Le Guin's poetry. Trio consists of Lucy Sheton, soprano; Sue Ann Kahn, flutist; and Susan Jolles, harpist. Reviewer calls it "high-water mark" of the concert. Describes Le Guin's poems as "elliptical but haunting verses" with "verbal images that are often Eliot-like." [See D495.]

D475 HERSHMAN, MARCIE. "Short Talks." <u>Boston Globe</u>, 5 February.
Review of <u>Planet of Exile</u>. Observes that the introduction calls attention to Le Guin's early feminism, thus "throwing the story in a new light."

D476 HIGGINS, STEEV. "Dispossession." <u>Vector 90</u> [UK fanzine] (November-December), pp. 39-42.
Review of <u>The Dispossessed</u>. Novel has several levels of meaning, all of which are related to the subject, a political utopia. It clearly functions as a novel because it focuses on Shevek and on a political system that is "about people." Defines Odonianism and contrasts it to the unreality and materialism of Urras. Calls Anarres a utopia, but a more believable one than other literary utopias. Praises her style.

D477 HOLDSTOCK, ROBERT. <u>Encyclopedia of Science Fiction</u>. New York: Mayflower Books, p. 181, passim.
After her surprising emergence in 1968 and 1969, she has become "a kind of touchstone, a symbol of sf's potential quality." Claims the 1970s have not been as productive for her.

D478 KIDD, VIRGINIA. Letter to the editor. <u>Locus</u> 11 (January-February):10, 13.
Insists on the correct spelling of Le Guin's name: Ursula K. Le Guin. Describes the Schwantner program of music set to <u>Wild Angels</u> and announces coming PBS production of <u>The Lathe of Heaven</u>.

D479 LAWLER, DONALD L. "Ursula K. Le Guin's 'Nine Lives.'" In <u>Instructor's Manual: Approaches to Science Fiction</u>.

Boston: Houghton Mifflin, pp. 64-66.
Recommends Le Guin's essay on "Nine Lives" [see C52] and
From Elfland to Poughkeepsie. Points out her skill in detailing the setting and using it to reinforce the themes of
remoteness and isolation. Themes are developed by clone
situation, as well as the friendship of Martin and Pugh.
Concludes with comment that in a post-Freudian society,
with a writer like Le Guin in the science fiction genre, we
can explore the dimensions of friendship ("love without
sexual overtones and the motivation of self-interest").

D480 "The Lem Affair (Continued)." Science-Fiction Studies 5
(March):84-87.
Further responses in the Lem Affair [see C146 and D441].
Contains: Philip K. Dick, "A Clarification"; Pamela
Sargent, "A Suggestion"; Darko Suvin, "What Lem Actually
Wrote: A Philologico-Ideological Note" [Suvin argues that
the English version of Lem's article was not a translation
but an adaptation; he illustrates with examples of poor
translation].

D481 LESTER, COLIN, ed. The International Science Fiction Year-
book. New York: Quick Fox, passim [paper].
Numerous citations and references.

D482 LLOYD, DAVID. "Another Best Seller?" Charlotte (N.C.)
Observer, 2 June.
Review of Planet of Exile. Responds to Le Guin's introduction in which she criticizes the question, "Where do you
get the ideas from?" It is the ideas that separate science
fiction from other kinds of literature, and it is the interweaving of ideas and story that separates the best science
fiction authors, like Le Guin, from the rest.

D483 MARMOR, PAULA K. Review of The Eye of the Heron. Fantasiae
6 (November-December):17.
Notes the similarity in subject matter to The Dispossessed, but ascertains this piece is much better. The
people are so believable that their motivations are clear
and "the political confrontations are more than intellectual
exercises." By contrast, The Dispossessed was a "cold"
work.

D484 MOLSON, FRANCIS J. "Le Guin, Ursula K(roeber)." Twentieth-
Century Children's Writers. Edited by D.L. Kirkpatrick.
New York: St. Martin's, pp. 755-57.
Information on life, teaching experience, and publica-
tions. Analytical essay compares the trilogy favorably to
Tolkien. Classifies it as "high or heroic fantasy,"
suitable for young adults because it shows "the centrality
of making ethical choices while growing up or coming of

age." Discusses three qualities that make it outstanding:
(1) uses Jungian ideas to justify using fantasy for a portrayal of maturation; (2) uses vivid detail to create a
believable "secondary world"; (3) uses a style that is
appropriate in pace and diction.

D485 MORNER, CLAUDIA J. Review of Planet of Exile. School Library
Journal 25 (November):82.
Asserts it is a novel of the sixties, reflecting the
issues of racism and love. Mistakenly records that their
winter is fifteen years long.

D486 NASH, LES. "Life in the Guise of Marriage." Courier-Journal
(Louisville), 28 May.
Review of Planet of Exile. In spite of standard science
fiction conventions, Le Guin's novel is successful. The
conventions become "symbols to imaginatively explore the
nature of marriage and sexuality." The union of the two
individuals symbolizes "union with the other and a con-
sequent expansion of our personal universe."

D487 PARISH, MARGARET. "Pick of the Paperbacks: Science Fiction."
English Journal 67 (February):117-18.
Review of The Left Hand of Darkness and The Word for
World is Forest. Calls attention to the variety and
quantity of paperback science fiction. That which was published in the last fifteen years is called "the second
revolution," focusing "as much upon the mind as upon the
machine." Illustrates with Dune and The Left Hand of Darkness. Most significant difference between the two is that
the first "shows a triumph of power, while Left Hand of
Darkness shows a triumph of empathy . . . that enables its
hero to overcome his xenophobic response to another culture."
Same anthropological perspective evident in Word. Discusses several novels and short stories by other authors.

D488 _____. "Of Love and Sex and Death and Becoming and Other
Journeys." English Journal 67 (May):88-90.
Review of Very Far [Away] From Anywhere Else. Discusses
it with several other titles in the context of recommended
books frankly treating teenage problems. Categorizes it as
not the best of Le Guin, notes that the characters are
kept at a distance; but finds it a strong book on the
"conflict between the need for love and the need for
identity and achievement."

*D489 PAUSACKER, JENNY. "Ursula K. Le Guin: The Earthsea Trilogy."
School Library Bulletin 10, no. 2:61-64. [Cited in the
annual bibliography of Women and Literature 7 (Winter
1979).]

D490 PERRIN, NOEL. "New World For Women." Inquiry Magazine (29
 May), pp. 26-27.
  Review of Planet of Exile and City of Illusions. Noting
  the increasing attention paid to women in science fiction,
  he welcomes the two hardcover editions of Le Guin's first
  two novels. Commends Planet because "Le Guin enters so
  fully into the minds of both groups, and makes you see both
  as right." Finds her apology for not making Rolery a more
  radical feminist unnecessary. City is "less successful."
  The tale of the journey is "marvelous," but the depiction
  of the Shing as villains is not completely convincing.
  Recommends both novels as a way to correct false impressions
  about science fiction.

D491 PURVIANCE, HARRIET. "Berkeley SF Seminar." Locus 11 (April):
 6.
  Describes the first four of ten lectures at UC Berkeley:
  "Facts About Science Fiction: The Writers Speak." Le Guin
  did not deliver a prepared speech but answered questions.
  Reporter paraphrases her description of her writing experience as being "a transcendental dream state of active
  imagination."

D492 ROBERTS, TOM. "Reading Science Fiction and Reading Interviews." In Speaking of Science Fiction. Edited by Paul
 Walker. Oradell, N.J.: Luna Publications, pp. 1-10.
  Lists and discusses five ways in which a science fiction
  story functions: as history, invention, telling, character,
  and mandala. Le Guin is mentioned in the second and discussed in the third. Notes her Hainish stories depend
  "heavily upon" Asimov's image of "a fallen-apart empire
  pulling itself together again." Praises her storytelling
  ability, citing the chapter structure and placement of the
  climax in The Dispossessed.

D493 ROTTENSTEINER, FRANZ. The Fantasy Book: An Illustrated History From Dracula to Tolkien. New York: Collier Books,
 p. 115 [paper].
  Urging she is the American rival of C.S. Lewis in fantasy for children, he finds A Wizard of Earthsea "rich in
  imaginative detail, if occasionally somewhat simplified."
  The trilogy is superior to her science fiction, but like
  her other writing in "warmth and balanced unity of feeling
  and intellect."

D494 SCHLOBIN, ROGER C. "An Annotated Bibliography of Fantasy Fiction." CEA Critic 40 (January):37-42.
  Includes the Earthsea trilogy.

D495 SCHWANTNER, JOSEPH. Program Notes. Stagebill 5, no. 5,
 (January).

Program notes for the 2 February 1978, performance of
his composition, Wild Angels, by the Jubal Trio [see B143].
Describes the work, a cycle of five songs which use a text
from Le Guin's poem. "The poems struck an immediate and
deep responsive resonance within me and I became excited by
the dramatic and musical possibilities envisaged by the
poem's vivid imagery."

D496 SHAPIRO, CECILE. "What Women Want: A Novel Answer to Freud."
      Bookviews 1, no. 12:28-31.
          Explores answers to the title's question in current
      novels by women authors. In discussing one topic, "the
      hazards of female anatomy," she wonders why "women do not
      fantasize a new biology more often" as Le Guin did in The
      Left Hand of Darkness. Describes the Gethenian androgynes
      and indicates the resultant society without "division of
      inhabitants . . . is one of the things women want."

D497 SENICK, GERARD J., ed. "Le Guin, Ursula K(roeber)." In
      Children's Literature Review: Excerpts from Reviews,
      Criticism, and Commentary on Books for Children and Young
      People. Vol. 3. Detroit: Gale, pp. 117-25.
          Identifies her as a writer for adults and young adults.
      Includes excerpts from her essay, "Dreams Must Explain
      Themselves" [C53] and from the following critical essays:
      D359, D150, D136, D204, D437, D72, D145, D57, D394, D402,
      D49.

D498 SPIGEL, SAUL. "Summer Sci-Fi." Hamden Chronicle, 27 July.
          Review of City of Illusions. Noticeably an early work
      of Le Guin; minor characters are not well developed and the
      plot is slow. Still, the novel "touches perceptively on
      the enduring human concerns of identity and reality."

D499 TYMN, MARSHALL B. "An Annotated Bibliography of Critical
      Studies and Reference Works on Fantasy." CEA Critic 40
      (January):43-47.
          Includes Dreams Must Explain Themselves and From Elfland
      to Poughkeepsie.

*D500 _____. Recent Critical Studies on Fantasy Literature: An
      Annotated Checklist. Council of Planning Librarians Ex-
      change Bibliography 1522. Monticello, Ill.: Council of
      Planning Librarians [paper]. [Cited in "The Year's Scholar-
      ship in Science Fiction and Fantasy: 1978," Extrapolation
      21 (Spring 1980):58.]

D501 URBANOWICZ, VICTOR. "Personal and Political in The Dis-
      possessed." Science-Fiction Studies 5 (July):110-17.
          Supports his claim that Le Guin is knowledgeable about
      and sympathetic toward anarchist theory and writers. He

names Peter Kropotkin, Herbert Read, and Paul Goodman. Announces his thesis: she stresses "that the personal and political growth of the individual must be not only compatible with but also complementary to each other." Shevek's growth comes out of that solitude and freedom he needs to do physics; he becomes aware of the defects of his society and the strengths of anarchist theory. Thus characterization, plot, structure, imagery, theme are all organically interrelated. The essay contains a fine discussion of the imagery of walls and the concept of physics. Urbanowitz summarizes his ideas when explaining a concept of Proudhon: "we are essentially social, so that the free exercise of personal initiative is not only compatible with but positively conducive to the benefit of society." Thus freedom cannot just be the negative, "freedom from," but must be the positive, "freedom to." Praises Le Guin's vision.

D502　"Ursula K(roeber) Le Guin." The Writers Directory 1976-1978. New York: St. Martin's Press, p. 626.
　　　　Summarizes her writing career; lists her as fantasy and science fiction writer, poet, and freelance writer.

D503　"Ursula Kroeber Le Guin." Who's Who in America. 40th ed. [1978-1979]. Vol. 2. Chicago: Marquis Who's Who, p. 1923. [Also listed in 41st ed., 1980-1981, vol. 2, p. 1987.]
　　　　Lists minimal biographical information, awards, organizational memberships, published books.

D504　WAGGONER, DIANA. The Hills of Faraway: A Guide to Fantasy. New York: Atheneum, pp. 219-20, passim.
　　　　Annotates the three Earthsea novels and The Lathe of Heaven. Notes that A Wizard of Earthsea is based on religious ideas from the Far East and the American Indians. Calls The Lathe of Heaven, "science fantasy."

D505　WIGGS, MARGARET E. "'Oldie' Ahead of Its Time." News-Sentinel (Fort Wayne, Ind.), 18 February.
　　　　Review of Planet of Exile. Seems taken with Le Guin's imagination. Although ahead of its time in 1966, it is now timely in the milieu of Star Wars and Close Encounters. Urges that this novel would "make a great movie."

D506　WILLIAMS, RAYMOND. "Utopia and Science Fiction." Science-Fiction Studies 5 (November):203-14. Reprinted in Science Fiction: A Critical Guide. Edited by Patrick Parrinder. London: Longman, 1979, pp. 52-66.
　　　　Clarifies the relationship between science fiction and utopia, using several categories and arguing that utopian fiction must clearly show the connection to realism. Discusses modern utopias and dystopias, noting their historical development and illustrating science fiction's move

away from the utopian tradition. The Dispossessed, therefore, is unusual in returning to the utopian tradition and
holding to science fiction characteristics. Novel is an
expression of our times in two ways: "the wary questioning
of the utopian impulse itself, even within its basic acceptance; the uneasy consciousness that the superficies of
utopia--affluence and abundance--can be achieved, at least
for many by non-utopian and even anti-utopian means."
Novel is unique in portraying a utopia flourishing in a
wasteland and in portraying an open utopia where no state
of "perpetual harmony and rest" is achieved. Her novel is
a sign of renewal of the "utopian impulse."

D507 WOOD, SUSAN. "Women and Science Fiction." Algol 16 (Winter):
9-18.
   Issue dated 1978-1979. Her thesis is that in light of
the attention focused on male dominance in science fiction,
there are more stories about "real women, real men" as well
as many articles on their absence in stories. In discussing
both phenomena, she cites The Left Hand of Darkness, quotes
from Le Guin's "American SF and the Other" [see C111], men-
tions The Dispossessed and offers Odo in "The Day Before
the Revolution" as a fine female character. Article supported with numerous examples; includes extensive notes and
a bibliography of women and science fiction.

D508 WYMER, THOMAS L.; CALDERONELLLO, ALICE; LELAND, LOWELL P.;
STEEN, SARA JAYNE; and EVERS, R. MICHAEL. Intersections:
The Elements of Fiction in Science Fiction. Bowling Green,
Oh.: Popular Press, pp. 15, 52, 65, 97-98, 122.
   In this textbook for introductory science fiction
courses, there are two brief discussions of her work and
several passing references.

                              1979

D509 ADAMS, PHOEBE-LOU. Review of The Language of the Night.
Atlantic Monthly 243 (May):95.
   Notes the repetition among essays, but finds the collection a fine argument for the seriousness of science fiction
and fantasy. Le Guin writes with "eloquence, humor, and
passion."

D510 ALLEN, KEITH. Review of The Earthsea Trilogy. Oregon Daily
Emerald, 18 January.
   Applauds it as a fine fantasy, combining "deep and complex characters" with "narrative simplicity." Middle book
is the weakest because it lacks the "mysticism" of the
first book and climaxes too early.

D511 _____. "Le Guin Reads From Work in Progress, Leaves Enrap-
tured Full House in Suspense." Oregon Daily Emerald, 31
January, p. 3.
News story of Le Guin's visit to the University of
Oregon as the Henry Failing Distinguished Lecturer. She
read from a novel she called "Threshold" because "I pur-
posely obscure the threshold" between "reality and imagination." [Novel was first published as The Beginning Place.]

D512 ALTERMAN, PETER [S.]. "Ursula K. Le Guin: Damsel With a
Dulcimer." In Ursula K. Le Guin. Edited by Joseph D.
Olander and Martin Harry Greenberg. Writers of the 21st
Century Series. New York: Taplinger, pp. 64-76, 225-26.
Discusses The Word for World is Forest and "Vaster Than
Empires and More Slow" as examples of "the similarity between Romantic and science-fiction visions of the mind of
man." Drawing on poetry by Blake, Wordsworth, and
Coleridge, he argues that Romantic poets and science fiction writers use similar "rhetoric and dialectic."
Two factors affect the rhetoric: an emphasis on "the
creative relationship between perceiving mind and perceived
object" and using nature, not just as a political metaphor,
but also as a metaphor for consciousness. Both factors are
clearly illustrated in Word. "Vaster" makes the relationship between nature and mind more active, comparable to
what Coleridge describes in "The Eolian Harp." In science
fiction, the metaphors are made to function on the literal
level, a characteristic that Lem and Russ have suggested is
definitive to science fiction.
The dialectic in Romantic poetry and the two stories is
a conflict between the imagination and natural objects:
"The humans cannot cast aside the demands of tangible nature;
nor can they allow this nature to be the only element of
reality." The resolution in romantic poetry and the two
stories is similar. First, the metaphor is made literal.
Second, intuitive analysis, rather than rational analysis,
is shown to be the way to knowledge. Selver and Osden are
both able to bridge the two worlds, "material and visionary"
"rational and irrational." Compares Davidson and Selver to
Blake's contraries, Urizen and Orc.

D513 AMERICAN PUBLISHERS, ASSOCIATION OF. America Through American
Eyes: An Exhibit of Recent Books That Reflect Life in the
United States, September, p. 57.
The Dispossessed is listed and annotated in this catalog
of the books, selected for the Moscow International Book
Fair. Kurt Vonnegut was chairman of the selection com-
mittee.

D514 ANGENOT, MARC. "The Absent Paradigm." Science-Fiction
Studies 6 (March):9-19.

Uses passages from The Left Hand of Darkness and The
Dispossessed to discuss the "essential rules and criteria"
which the reader uses to identify a text as science fiction.
He stresses the value of the semiotic approach in defining
science fiction.

D515   ANON. "Biographical Note." In Ursula K. Le Guin. Edited by
       Joseph D. Olander and Martin Harry Greenberg. Writers of
       the 21st Century Series. New York: Taplinger, pp. 247-48.
           Gives standard career information. Erroneously lists
       1951 as date of her marriage; correct date is 1953.

D516   ANON. Review of The Beginning Place. Kirkus Reviews 47 (1
       December):1393. Reprinted 15 December.
           Recommends the novel to intelligent readers from ages
       fourteen to ninety as an "impeccable parable." The novel
       is a "fantasy about the limitations of fantasy." Deems it
       some of her "best work"; "the allegorical implications of
       the story are touched on with an understated sweetness that
       can only be described as masterly."

D517   ANON. Review of The Beginning Place. Publishers Weekly 216
       (3 December):47.
           Heralds the novel as both similar to and different from
       her science fiction and fantasy "for this is a fantasy with
       a contemporary setting, written in a cool (and appropriate)
       style unlike any its author has used before."

D518   ANON. Review of The Language of the Night. Choice 16 (Sep-
       tember):834.
           Recommends the collection for all libraries because it
       is valuable for students of modern literature, as well as
       serious scholars of Le Guin. Essays range over a variety
       of topics; they display "her gift for anecdote and meta-
       phor"; and are written in a "witty, urbane" style.

D519   ANON. Review of The Language of the Night. Cultural Informa-
       tion Service (4 June), p. 8.
           Responds favorably to her discussion of the fantasy
       genre and of specific fantasy writers.

D520   ANON. Review of The Language of the Night. Kirkus Reviews
       67, part II (15 February):240-41.
           Criticizes the editing. Judging by Levin's bibliography,
       reviewer believes Wood could have selected better essays:
       "she gives us much more of Le Guin the priggish deplorer of
       commercialism and masscult than of Le Guin the daring and
       unsentimental romantic."

D521   ANON. Review of Leese Webster. Kirkus Reviews 47 (1 Septem-
       ber):998.

Rates it "sound and expertly spun" but "not the brilliant parable" one would expect. Drawings help suspend reality.

D522   ANON. Review of Leese Webster. Publishers Weekly 216 (30 July):63.
       Notes her "poetic gifts" in constructing this "subtle allegory."

D523   ANON. Review of Malafrena. Kirkus Reviews 47, part I (15 August):951.
       Labels it her "masterpiece to date." Le Guin's qualities include "patience, lucidity, and the capacity to invest the ordinary pleasures of existence with a sort of luminous romanticism." The only criticism is that "what should be real moral exaltation here is sometimes merely facilely achieved sweetness-and-light."

D524   ANON. Review of Malafrena. Publishers Weekly 216 (27 August): 373-74.
       Praises the novel whose characters and plot make us remember "what words like liberty and nationalism meant when they were fresh and unsullied."

D525   ARBUR, ROSEMARIE. "Beyond Feminism, the Self Intact: Woman's Place in the Work of Ursula K. Le Guin." In Selected Proceedings of the 1978 Science Fiction Research Association National Conference. Edited by Thomas J. Remington. Cedar Falls: University of Northern Iowa.
       Rejects feminists' criticism of Le Guin's work, arguing that her portrayal of "things 'feminine'" usually transcends sex or gender stereotyping. She urges readers to recognize Le Guin's use of personae which are not identical to the author's own beliefs and values. She identifies and defines three categories of "gender-related" themes: traditional, feminist, postfeminist.
       She substantiates that Le Guin has passed through the first two stages to the third with examples from her poetry ("Song"), novels (Planet of Exile, The Left Hand of Darkness), and short stories ("Winter's King" and "Gwilan's Harp"). Develops three detailed discussions of Le Guin's work: the Earthsea trilogy, The Left Hand of Darkness and The Dispossessed, and "The Day Before the Revolution."

D526   BARBOUR, DOUGLAS. "The Early Hainish Novels." In Survey of Science Fiction Literature. Edited by Frank N. Magill. Vol. 2. Englewood Cliffs: Salem Press, pp. 681-86.
       Mentions previous future history series in science fiction and calls Le Guin's "one of the most imaginative, literate, and philosophically profound." He dates the three early novels in terms of League Years, assesses them

as clearly early works with the third being better than the
previous two. Each develops a traditional theme, but also
contains something unique. World is characterized as a
"science fantasy quest tale" in which Semley's quest is
ironically contrasted with Rocannon's. Planet is a
"'societal quest.'" City is the "conventionally paranoid
fantasy of the psychic superman who, beginning in ignorance,
eventually discovers his true identity and powers." It is
unusually complex. All three hold in common "linguistic,
imagistic, and thematic patterns" which appear in the later
and better Hainish novels.

D527   BARTTER, M.A. "By and About Ursula Le Guin." Democrat and
       Chronicle (Rochester, N.Y.), 25 November.
            Review of The Language of the Night and Ursula K.
       Le Guin, edited by Olander and Greenberg. Finds the second
       volume "a trifle repetitious and simplistic" for the serious
       scholar but good for the teacher and the student. Le Guin's
       essays are a better source for knowledge about the author.
       Not only are they "readable" and "charming," they range
       through topics from the nature of science fiction to the
       function of the artist.

D528   BEAGLE, PETER S. "A Beautiful Realm of Fantasy, Sci-Fi."
       San Francisco Chronicle World, 10 June, p. 49.
            Review of The Language of the Night. Admires her fic-
       tion and so welcomes this collection. It displays her wit,
       has no weak pieces, and includes "the definitive piece on
       fantasy"--"From Elfland to Poughkeepsie."

D529   BERGER, ALBERT I. "The Dispossessed." In Survey of Science
       Fiction Literature. Edited by Frank N. Magill. Vol. 2.
       Englewood Cliffs: Salem Press, pp. 548-53.
            Discusses the difficulty of and absence of utopian
       speculation in the twentieth century. Le Guin's novel is
       unique. It uses traditional science fiction elements ("an
       unconventional scientist whose work is rejected by his
       elders, the search for a faster-than-light spaceship drive,
       even the American myth of the frontier") yet avoids the
       "didactic sentimentality" of much utopian fiction and the
       "murderous nihilism" of the 1970s popular fiction. Its
       outstanding quality is the replacement of "technological
       determinism . . . with a vision of science and technology
       as varieties of human creativity existing in an environment
       of other varieties: art, music, love, and politics." His
       discussion focuses on the creativity of human politics,
       Shevek's growth and learning, and justification for the
       novel's circular structure.

D530   BISENICKS, DAINIS. "Children, Magic, and Choices." Mythlore
       6 (Winter):13-16.

Explores why character portrayal is significant in fantasy written for children. Uses Le Guin's A Wizard of Earthsea and Lloyd Alexander's Prydain books as examples of novels whose characters' choices rise out of themselves, not out of authorial manipulation for dramatic effect.

D531 BITTNER, JAMES W. "Approaches to the Fiction of Ursula K. Le Guin." Ph.D. dissertation, University of Wisconsin-Madison.

Because neither a work-by-work or encompassing discussion would fairly represent this author who is still producing, he selects as his theme what Le Guin herself has stated it is: "Marriage," which he defines as "any complementary, correlative, or interdependent relationship between what we may perceive as opposites or dualisms, but which are in reality aspects of a whole, or moments in a continuous process." Asserts that this "idea of complementarity, represented by the yin-yang circle . . . define[s] not only Le Guin's central theme, but also her fictional techniques, her modes of thought, and ultimately, her world view."

Chapter one discusses her "principal narrative tool for marrying opposites"--the literary form of the romance. Uses City of Illusions to demonstrate that "not only the form itself of Le Guin's stories--the poetics of the romance--but also the relationship she creates between her stories and their readers--the rhetoric of the romance--is their content." The importance of storytelling leads Bittner to a theoretical discussion of the romance, its purpose, pattern, and worldview.

Chapter two explores complementarity in the "realism and fantasy" in Orsinian Tales where Le Guin "marries history and art to create an imaginative reality that is and at the same time is not like our familiar world" [see D453].

Chapter three discusses the "complementarity of myth and science" by examining her sources. Considers three early stories in the Hainish and Earthsea development to show the complementarity of her science and her magic. Analyzes "Schrödinger's Cat" to show the combination of Greek myth and quantum mechanics to gain a new perspective.

Chapter four depicts the chronological development of the Hainish future history series and explores two levels of complementarity: "a dialectical interplay between the conventions of pulp science fiction on the one hand, and myth and anthropology on the other" [Asimov and A. Kroeber].

Chapter five analyzes Le Guin's philosophy, examining the "complementarity of yin and yang [Taoism], and her romance forms, suggesting that Le Guin's utopianism is a natural, perhaps even inevitable, result of the interplay." Sketches the basic Taoist beliefs and traces their imagery and attitudes in the first three novels.

Dissertation concludes with an appendix which is a "bib-

liographic guide to Taoism" and a full bibliography [see
D532].

This work is perceptive and dense with biographical and
literary discussion, and ample footnotes.

D532 _____. "Bibliography." In "Approaches to the Fiction of
Ursula K. Le Guin." Ph.D. dissertation, University of
Wisconsin-Madison, pp. 435-84.

Consists of three parts. Part One is "A Bibliographic
Checklist of the Works of Ursula K. Le Guin In English"
with Jeffrey H. Levin. It is divided into four sections,
each arranged chronologically: "Separate Publications,"
"Contributions to Periodicals and Anthologies" (divided
into six categories), "Interviews and Feature Articles Containing Interview Materials," and "Miscellaneous." Part
Two lists, in alphabetical order, works about Le Guin.
Part Three is a general bibliography of science fiction
literature and reference works, works on science, romanticism, religion, and philosophy."

D533 _____. "A Survey of Le Guin Criticism." In Ursula K. Le Guin:
Voyager to Inner Lands and to Outer Space. Edited by Joe
De Bolt. Port Washington, N.Y.: Kennikat, pp. 31-49, 200-
4.

Chronological account of critical attention, which began
with her fourth and fifth novels (A Wizard of Earthsea and
The Left Hand of Darkness). Demonstrates that foreign
criticism came first and continues to be significant.
Identifies the beginning of American "academic recognition"
with Robert Scholes's "The Good Witch of the West" [see
D204]. Contains clear, valuable assessments of the critical
trends. He encourages readings which compare Le Guin and
nonscience fiction works: readers, he says, may discover
that the "imaginary countries" of science fiction, fantasy,
and other literary modes "are all part of the same world."

D534 BRENNAN, JOHN B., and DOWNS, MICHAEL C. "Anarchism and
Utopian Tradition in The Dispossessed." In Ursula K.
Le Guin. Edited by Joseph D. Olander and Martin Harry
Greenberg. Writers of the 21st Century Series. New York:
Taplinger, pp. 116-52, 229-34.

Their thesis is that the novel participates in and
critiques both "the utopian tradition and the philosophy
of anarchism." It deserves to be examined as a "serious
inquiry into political ideals and experience." They list
seven characteristics of the utopian tradition, establishing
them with examples from Plato's Republic, More's Utopia,
Morris's News From Nowhere, and Skinner's Walden Two. They
detail the appearance of the characteristics on both Anarres
and Urras, concluding that "on nearly every point" Anarres
is "the model utopian society." Thus, in spite of the

novel's ambiguity, it does not advocate "a moral relativism."
Further, Anarres is utopian in being more advanced than
Urras in "political articulation." Essay marred by illogi-
cal divisions.

D535 BRIGG, PETER. "The Archetype of the Journey in Ursula K.
Le Guin's Fiction." In <u>Ursula K. Le Guin</u>. Edited by
Joseph D. Olander and Martin Harry Greenberg. Writers of
the 21st Century Series. New York: Taplinger, pp. 36-63,
225.
    The journey is Le Guin's major archetype. Using
<u>Rocannon's World</u>, <u>The Left Hand of Darkness</u>, and <u>The Dis-</u>
<u>possessed</u>, he discusses its prominence and its development
from being primarily physical to being inward as well.
Essay is divided into three sections: Destinations,
Travelers, and Landscapes.
    Rocannon moves toward a clear goal, but is unprepared
for its costs. Genly Ai quests for the situation that will
unite Gethen with the Ekumen, but discovers a new goal in
personal contact. Shevek quests but has no final goals.
The "destinations . . . become progressively more complex
and elusive, moving from the external and morally clear to
the internal and imprecise."
    The three travelers all partake of the journey that be-
comes "a metaphor of the loneliness of human existence,
stressing that man is constantly at risk, both physically
and morally." Shevek is the most complex because he knows
the importance of every action and because he is not a
trained envoy.
    All three must take into account the physical and polit-
ical landscapes of their worlds, with <u>The Dispossessed</u>
presenting a landscape closest to our own.
    One of the few essays tracing her development as an
artist which convincingly substantiates its claims.

D536 BROWN, ROBERT McAFEE. "Lenten Reading 1979: Looking in Some
New Directions." <u>Christian Century</u> 96 (14 March):282-86.
    Review of <u>Very Far Away From Anywhere Else</u>. Quotes
several reflective passages, explains the Owen-Natalie
relationship, and concludes that new kinds of communication
can mend damaged relationships, that "little deaths can be
the preludes to modest resurrections."

D537 BUDRYS, ALGIS [J.]. Review of <u>The Language of the Night</u>.
<u>Booklist</u> 75 (1 June):1474.
    Values it not only as a revelation of her intellect and
wit, but also as a contribution to the study of science
fiction "as a genre in transition toward conscious literary
excellence."

D538 CARTER, STEVEN. "Science Fiction." <u>English Journal</u> 68

(December):73-74.

One of several articles in a section titled, "Best of the Year 1979." Names The Eye of the Heron as one of several books which show the "vigor, imagination, versatility and star-reaching influence of the Women's Movement." Le Guin's theme is "the need for continuing evolution in individuals and societies."

D539 COGELL, ELIZABETH CUMMINS. "Taoist Configurations: The Dispossessed." In Ursula K. Le Guin: Voyager to Inner Lands and to Outer Space. Edited by Joe De Bolt. Port Washington, N.Y.: Kennikat, pp. 153-79, 207-9.

After surveying the extent to which Le Guin's work reflects the Taoist philosophy, she shows that this novel is "the culmination of Taoist philosophy in Le Guin's writing" and that Taoism affects the structure and content of the novel. Taoism is supportive of science; and Shevek's work in theoretical physics reflects the Taoist attitude toward unity and diversity, toward nature, and toward the mystical experience. Discusses three major principles of Taoism—following the model of nature, the theory of letting alone, and the eternality of change—and shows how each is reflected in the novel's elements of personal development, society, and government. Supports her argument with quotations from the novel and from Taoist books and commentaries.

D540 CROW, JOHN H., and ERLICH, RICHARD D. "Words of Binding: Patterns of Integration in the Earthsea Trilogy." In Ursula K. Le Guin. Edited by Joseph D. Olander and Martin Harry Greenberg. Writers of the 21st Century Series. New York: Taplinger, pp. 200-24, 236-39.

Their thesis is that an analysis of Earthsea, Le Guin's best work, "will reveal its own coherence, as well as the patterns and themes which reveal the unifying vision of her work, from Rocannon's World to The Dispossessed." Her fantasy "reveals the common heroism necessary to confront a world without a transcendent god, a world in which man is thrown back on his own finite existence." All her work stresses the primacy of the individual. The three basic patterns of development in the fantasy are named, discussed, and identified in her other works: the "movement from social disorder to social order"; the "process of individuation"; and the "theme of balance" developed in "a dialectical form." Her philosophical concepts come from existentialism and Jungian psychology. Lengthy discussion of the trilogy's concern with the "distinction between being and doing."

Last section continues discussing the trilogy but with numerous comparisons to her other work. Her view of reality, it is argued, is the foundation for "an epistemology, an ethics, and a political philosophy."

D541 CURREY, LLOYD W. "Ursula Kroeber Le Guin." In Science Fiction and Fantasy Authors: A Bibliography of First Printings
of Their Fiction. Boston: G.K. Hall, pp. 304-6.
A descriptive listing of fiction published as individual
volumes (novels, short story collections, pamphlets), edited
fiction, nonfiction (on fantasy only), and reference. Description makes possible the identification of first editions.

D542 De BOLT, JOE, ed. "A Selected Le Guin Bibliography." In
Ursula K. Le Guin: Voyager to Inner Lands and to Outer
Space. Port Washington, N.Y.: Kennikat, pp. 211-14.
Listing divided into three sections: Books, Selected
Shorter Fiction, Other Selected Works (essays and poems).
Entries are followed by brief note of identification, often
including awards the piece won. Headnote refers the reader
to the Bittner essay for critical works [see D533] and the
De Bolt biography for interviews [see D460].

D543 _____. Ursula K. Le Guin: Voyager to Inner Lands and to
Outer Space. Port Washington, N.Y.: Kennikat, 221 pp.
Contains an introduction by Barry Malzberg [see D579],
a biography and a bibliography by De Bolt [see D460 and
D542], and eight essays: James W. Bittner, "A Survey of
Le Guin Criticism"; Karen Sinclair, "Solitary Being: The
Hero as Anthropologist"; Peter T. Koper, "Science and
Rhetoric in the Fiction of Ursula Le Guin"; Rollin A.
Lasseter, "Four Letters About Le Guin"; John R. Pfeiffer,
"'But Dragons Have Keen Ears:' On Hearing 'Earthsea' with
Recollections of Beowulf"; Francis J. Molson, "The Earthsea
Trilogy: Ethical Fantasy for Children"; Elizabeth Cummins
Cogell, "Taoist Configurations: The Dispossessed"; Larry
L. Tifft and Dennis C. Sullivan, "Possessed Sociology and
Le Guin's Dispossessed: From Exile to Anarchism."

D544 DYER, RICHARD. "Le Guin Steps Out." Boston Globe, 11 December.
Review of Malafrena. This "historical novel in the 19th
century manner of Charles Reade" is perhaps her answer to
her own comment that the science fiction genre cannot include tragedy or "'coherent complexity.'" Praises the
"narrative power," multiple characterizations, excitement
of action and discussion, descriptive setting. Her "moral
universe" depicts "the way things really are"--"we must
suffer the same shatterings of illusion, and partial re-
building that her characters do."

D545 EDELHEIT, S.J. "The Language of Le Guin." New Boston Review
(September/October), 3 pp.
Review of The Language of the Night. Greatest value of
the collection is that it is like meeting her in person--

"a feisty, witty, extraordinarily sensible, tough, and
honest writer and woman." Reviewer quotes liberally from
the essays to discuss her major topics—criticizing the
ghettoizing of science fiction, and the need for the same
standards in science fiction as in other novels. Her fiction is distinguished by "the remarkable quality and power
of her imagination." Discusses the importance of the journey as a way to image the artist's inward look that is the
source of creativity. Le Guin is also very interested in
the external world, particularly the political realm. The
collection could have contained better, more substantial
essays, and the Levin bibliography is disconcerting—"the
dreary necessities of the scholar-industry" turned on
Le Guin.

D546 ELLIS, ABBY. "18th Century Rebel With Cause: Novel Studies
Intellectual." Denver Post, 7 November.
Review of Malafrena. Compares the novel to the works of
Herman Hesse but finds it "tends to be a ponderous journey."

D547 ERLICH, RICHARD D. "The Left Hand of Darkness." In Survey of
Science Fiction Literature. Edited by Frank N. Magill.
Vol. 3. Englewood Cliffs: Salem Press, pp. 1171-77.
Discusses the sections of the novel, particularly the
"interpolations" into Ai's "anthropological survey."
Lengthy discussion on the logical placement of the interpolations to show that each reflects back on the preceding
chapter and looks forward to a later event in the novel.
Chapters seven and seventeen are particularly important because "they interrupt the narrative at such crucial points
. . . [and] help set up the philosophical system by which
the action of the novel is to be judged."

D548 ESMONDE, MARGARET [P.]. "The Gift of Men: Death and Death-
lessness in Children's Fantasy." Fantasiae 7 (April):1,
8-11.
In light of the recent attention being given to the
teaching of children about death, she asserts that fantasy
literature "so often reviled as escapist, has always dealt
with the subject of death honestly and skillfully, shunning
neither the grief of the survivors nor the question of an
afterlife." Discusses Tolkien, E.B. White, Natalie Babbitt,
and Le Guin. The Earthsea trilogy contains "the greatest
and most moving examination of death."

D549 ESMONDE, MARGARET P. "The Master Pattern: The Psychological
Journey in the Earthsea Trilogy." In Ursula K. Le Guin.
Edited by Joseph D. Olander and Martin Harry Greenberg.
Writers of the 21st Century Series. New York: Taplinger,
pp. 16-35, 225.
Her thesis is that in Earthsea we can most clearly see

the major design of all her work, that is, the psychological journey ("the progression of an ego from uncertainty and self-doubt to assurance and fulfillment"). For support beyond the trilogy, she draws on Le Guin's "The Child and the Shadow" [C82] and Jung's writings.

Discussion of A Wizard of Earthsea is the least detailed. This novel traces Ged's process of individuation, aided by Ogion, the "wise old man" archetype. The shadow is his "dark self," as well as "the shadow of sexual desires, . . . desire for power, . . . of his own mortality."

Tombs traces a more passive achievement of individuation in the female. It draws on the Theseus and Ariadne myth, as well as the complex symbol of the apple. Novel uses subtle sexual symbolism of the staff, the labyrinth, the ring to portray Tenar's awakening womanhood.

Shore is the most complex in that it portrays "the psychological journey toward wholeness through acceptance of personal mortality." Le Guin must portray "metaphysical . . . experiences . . . in concrete images," but her use of Arren and the "heroic epic tradition" makes it easier for the reader to become involved. Concludes by briefly showing that all of Le Guin's protagonists experience the same "psychological journey through pain and fear to integration."

D550 FAERY, REBECCA BLEVINS. "The Earthsea Trilogy." In Survey of Science Fiction Literature. Edited by Frank N. Magill. Vol. 2. Englewood Cliffs: Salem Press, pp. 692-97.
Believes that the trilogy is "perhaps her greatest achievement." As a physical place, it is as "thoroughly imagined as C.S. Lewis's Narnia or J.R.R. Tolkien's Middle Earth." Its events are made of myth and its vision is of "harmony, integration, and balance." A Wizard of Earthsea depicts Ged's "coming of age" by dealing "with the mystic dimensions of human life." The Tombs of Atuan "is the story of Ged's discovery of sexual love, of his finding the woman who will complement and complete his life" and of Arha's coming of age. The Farthest Shore draws on "all the thematic threads of the first two stories." Asserts the trilogy is also about "art, and the making of art."

D551 FANZONE, JOSEPH, Jr. "Ursula K. Le Guin Imagines A Culture of Another Century." Baltimore Sun, 16 December.
Review of Malafrena. Finds the novel's themes and tones hard on the reader who dares to empathize with these characters. "The novel is rooted in an 'intense unchanging sadness' that admits of no facile truths, destroys cherished illusions." On the one hand, it is a bildungsroman of Itale Sorde. But it also presents empathic pictures of other characters. Its theme is "live free, or die" and its tension stems from "contending views on freedom, its nature,

its need, its relationship to responsibility." Reviewer
is reminded of his own experience of the sixties, his
activity in student strikes at Johns Hopkins contrasted
with the killings at Kent State and finds the novel very
"timely." Le Guin's resolution is tough: "Ideals will die
in reality's dry winter, but the souls from which they
spring may survive--and the hope of a future blossoming is
all we are given."

D552 FEKETE, JOHN. "The Dispossessed and Triton: Act and System
      in Utopian Science Fiction." Science-Fiction Studies 18
      (July):129-43.
          Argues that science fiction has the potential for modeling
      "possibilities and limits of social and individual life."
      Selects these two outstanding novels for discussion. They
      begin with the same criticism of alienation in contemporary
      life, offer anarchist models, differ greatly in their focus
      (Le Guin on "reconciliation," Delany on "dispersion"), but
      ultimately fail to present open systems.
          Analyzes and critiques The Dispossessed from point of
      view of social and political theory and practice--its
      images, view of history, political bias, landscape of
      scarcity. Although Le Guin recognizes many of the threats
      to individual and social freedom, many of her assumptions
      and solutions are "problematic" and reflect "our culture's
      illness." Ultimately, her view is also "totalitarian."
          After discussing Triton, he concludes with plaudits for
      science fiction as a resource for sophisticated social
      models.

D553 FINDSEN, OWEN. "Le Guin Needs Some Fantasy." Cincinnati
      Enquirer, 2 December.
          Review of Malafrena. Argues she uses the same theme of
      the necessity of returning home as in The Dispossessed, but
      does not develop it as well. Classifies it as "historical
      fiction."

D554 FITCH, ROBERT M., and SVENGALIS, CORDELL M. "Images of the
      Future Through Science Fiction." In Futures Unlimited:
      Teaching About Worlds To Come. National Council for the
      Social Studies--Bulletin No. 59, pp. 61-67.
          Explains the value of "'new wave' SF" ("oriented toward
      social criticism and experimentalism") in teaching about
      the future. Concludes with a listing of novels in fourteen
      categories. The Word for World is Forest and The Dis-
      possessed are cited.

D555 FITTING, PETER. "The Modern Anglo-American SF Novel: Utopian
      Longing and Capitalist Cooptation." Science-Fiction Studies
      6 (March):59-76.
          Discusses Le Guin's The Left Hand of Darkness and The

Dispossessed in an essay tracing "the interplay between
ideology and utopian longing in the modern SF novel." Works
of Le Guin and Russ are cited as examples of "the critique
of capitalism and specifically of sexism" in imagined
"utopian alternatives." *Left Hand*, although flawed in its
presentation of sexuality, is valued "for the range and
imagination with which the questions are posed." Compares
and contrasts *The Dispossessed* with Russ's *The Female Man*.
He calls their fiction "some of the most significant SF of
the last ten years."

D556 FLECK, LEONARD M. "Science Fiction as a Tool of Speculative
      Philosophy: A Philosophic Analysis of Selected Anarchistic
      and Utopian Themes in *The Dispossessed*." In *Selected Pro-*
      ceedings of the 1978 Science Fiction Research Association
      National Conference. Edited by Thomas J. Remington. Cedar
      Falls: University of Northern Iowa, pp. 113-43.
          First half of the article argues that utopian literature
      is philosophically valuable for investigating whether our
      choice of social forms and values can be rationally justi-
      fied. He cites three reasons: it is liberating, it func-
      tions as an empirical thought experiment for the philos-
      opher, it reveals how interrelated the values and the sys-
      tem are.
          The second half uses Le Guin's novel to illustrate the
      "symbiotic relationship" between philosophy and utopian
      literature. The novel examines the conditions under which
      the state can be discarded, and the relationship between
      individual freedom and the rules that preserve the society.
      The causes of the failure of Anarresti anarchism are very
      complex--"social, systemic, and moral." He concludes that
      utopian literature and philosophy do not reach final an-
      swers, but they do reach tentative answers which are
      liberating.

D557 FRANE, JEFF. Review of *Millennial Women*. *Unearth* (UK) 2
      (Winter):169-70, 172.
          Le Guin's novel is the climax of the anthology. Specu-
      lates that it shows the influence of her visit to Australia
      [in 1975]. Praises her choice of protagonists and use of
      language. Her characters are well motivated and heroic
      without becoming "Heroes."

D558 _____. "A Writer As Critic." *Locus* 12 (June):13. Reprinted
      in *Seattle Times Magazine* (1 July), 1979.
          Review of *The Language of the Night*. Values it both as
      a collection of essays by a good critic and as essays that
      reveal much about Le Guin. Three best essays are "The
      Child and the Shadow," "From Elfland to Poughkeepsie," and
      "Science Fiction and Mrs. Brown." Critical of the editing
      as the introductions by Wood are lifeless and the essays

selected result in some repetition.

D559 FULLER, EDMUND. "A Summer's List of Light Reading." <u>Wall
      Street Journal</u>, 12 July.
      Review of <u>The Language of the Night</u>. His summer reading
      list is selected from current books he has not found time
      to review. Calls Le Guin's book a "treasure" for anyone
      interested in science fiction, fantasy, or the "craft of
      writing." Delighted with her ability as an essayist--
      "wise" and "witty."

D560 GREEN, ROLAND. Review of <u>Malafrena</u>. <u>Booklist</u> 76 (1 December):
      540.
      Judges it to be "rich but not entirely satisfactory"
      because of its slow development, numerous characters, and
      over-elaborate style. On the other hand, characters are
      well drawn, ethics are clear and strong, and there is no
      "romantic nonsense" about revolutions.

D561 GUNEW, SNEJA. "Mythic Reversals: The Evaluation of the
      Shadow Motif." In <u>Ursula K. Le Guin</u>. Edited by Joseph D.
      Olander and Martin Harry Greenberg. Writers of the 21st
      Century Series. New York: Taplinger, pp. 178-99, 236.
      An extensive reworking of her 1976 article [see D329].
      She adds other novels and short stories to her original
      discussion and organizes them around a new principle: the
      spectrum of meanings which the shadow has. At one end of
      the spectrum is the shadow as "microcosmic image signify-
      ing individual chaos" which can either be death or the
      source of life and creativity. She illustrates both
      choices in Le Guin's work, using <u>The Left Hand of Darkness</u>,
      a poem, and especially the Earthsea trilogy as the most
      consistent development of the second.
      The middle of the spectrum consists of the shadow imaging
      "recognition of the other." Here also, there are two
      branches: the Jungian emphasizing the "suppressed self"
      and the Taoist emphasizing the polarities within each self.
      The second is best illustrated with <u>Left Hand</u>. The other
      end of the spectrum uses the shadow as image of the "dy-
      namic interaction of opposites," where <u>Left Hand</u> is again
      the best illustration and the trilogy also significant.
      Conclusion asserts that Le Guin has become more sure in
      "investing these traditional images with her own particular
      metaphorical implications."

D562 _____. "Signposts." <u>SF Commentary</u>, no. 57 (November), pp.
      7-8.
      Review of <u>Nebula Award Stories 11</u>. Comments on indi-
      vidual pieces, including Le Guin's introduction which she
      describes as gently enjoining writers to work with science
      fiction's questioning, open quality.

D563 GUNN, JAMES. The Road to Science Fiction #3: From Heinlein
      to Here. New York: New American Library, pp. 8, 575-77,
      passim.
          General introduction provides a publishing context for
      Le Guin; introduction to the excerpt from The Left Hand of
      Darkness discusses science fiction "as simile."

D564 HAYLES, N.B. "Androgyny, Ambivalence, and Assimilation in The
      Left Hand of Darkness." In Ursula K. Le Guin. Edited by
      Joseph D. Olander and Martin Harry Greenberg. Writers of
      the 21st Century Series. New York: Taplinger, pp. 97-
      115, 228-29.
          Examines the use of androgyny in order to show that
      Le Guin emphasizes its ambivalence just as myth and history
      have done and that this ambivalence provides the novel with
      its unity. Traditionally, androgyny has reflected a
      sought-after unity or a to-be-avoided alienness. Le Guin's
      Taoist base allows her to incorporate both senses: "Al-
      though the alien remains the other, once its otherness is
      admitted and understood, it can come into creative tension
      with the self, and from this tension a new wholeness can
      emerge."
          Discusses the development of this creative tension on
      two levels--within Gethenian culture and within the rela-
      tionship between Ai and Estraven. The various narrative
      accounts fit into one of two modes--mythic or objective.
      Both blend together, emphasizing similar experiences, so
      the narrative method reflects closure, the coming together
      of dualities. Le Guin in spite of having a strong vision
      to convey, never becomes dogmatic: "No truth is allowed
      to stand as the entire truth; every insight is presented ·
      as partial, subject to revision and another perspective."

D565 HENDERSON, DAN. "Masters of Form." Commercial Appeal
      (Memphis), 10 June.
          Review of The Language of the Night. Praises the essays
      for being as good as her fiction. Collection reveals she
      is one of "speculative fiction's . . . foremost apologists."
      Quotes from "Talking About Writing" to demonstrate Le
      Guin's concept of the inward nature of the artist.

D566 HERBERT, ROSEMARY. Review of Malafrena. Library Journal 104
      (15 October):2237.
          Recommends it as "a book about freedom and commitment."
      The imaginary country resembles Italy and the subject has
      a "Tolstoyesque flavor and grandeur."

D567 HERSHMAN, MARCIE. "Short Takes." Boston Sunday Globe, 27
      May, p. 45.
          Review of The Language of the Night. In spite of not
      reading science fiction except under "duress," reviewer

finds this collection praiseworthy. She has "a firm grip
on the realities of the fantastical" and writes essays that
are "lucid, light, delightful, perceptive."

D568   HOLYOKE, T.C. Review of Nebula Award Stories Eleven. Antioch
       Review 37 (Winter):122.
           "Le Guin and her essayists" try to critique science
       fiction, suggest its variety, and argue that some writers
       are taking "the ethical mode of literature" more seriously.
       The stories seem to illustrate these assertions.

D569   JOHNSON, MARK. "Fantasy Provides its own Critics." San Jose
       Mercury-News, 15 July.
           Review of The Language of the Night. Discusses her
       definition of fantasy, practical advice to writers, and her
       admission of the difficulties in balancing the familiar and
       the fantastic in one piece of fiction.

D570   KOPER, PETER T. "Science and Rhetoric in the Fiction of
       Ursula Le Guin." In Ursula K. Le Guin: Voyager to Inner
       Lands and to Outer Space. Edited by Joe De Bolt. Port
       Washington, N.Y.: Kennikat, pp. 66-86, 205-6.
           Finds Le Guin's fiction limited and flawed but argues
       she attracts readers because she has exploited her
       audience's sense of "the beleaguered self in the face of
       the challenge of science." The unifying element in her
       fiction is the opposition to scientific rhetoric, that is,
       those aspects of the scientific method (from Descartes and
       Bacon to their present supporters) that deny the self,
       subjectivity, personal opinion, and fantasy.
           Essay divided into four sections: (1) compares "April
       in Paris" and "The Masters" to "illustrate the complex
       tensions between self, culture, and knowledge" which are
       fundamental in her fiction; (2) discusses how "rhetorical
       criticism affects the interpretation of Le Guin's work";
       (3) enumerates "some characteristics of science as a mode
       of rhetoric and their consequences for the prototypical
       scientist"; and (4) examines her major works "to demonstrate
       the ways in which the dilemma of their protagonists mirror,
       in essence, the dilemmas of the scientist and hence of
       Le Guin's audience."

D571   LAMBE, DEAN R. Review of Malafrena. Science Fiction & Fan-
       tasy Book Review 1 (November):135.
           Questions whether Le Guin's move to mainstream is really
       necessary for this novel. Notes that the "socio-political
       themes" resemble those in The Dispossessed, and that the
       concerns with gender role were previously developed in The
       Left Hand of Darkness. Furthermore, the work seems too
       similar to that of past authors who wrote better novels
       (Pasternak, Dostoevsky, Malraux, Balzac, Voltaire).

D572 LASSETER, ROLLIN A. "Four Letters About Le Guin." In <u>Ursula K. Le Guin: Voyager to Inner Lands and to Outer Space</u>. Edited by Joe De Bolt. Port Washington, N.Y.: Kennikat, pp. 80-114, 206.

Sees the trilogy as a "watershed" in her fiction, delineating the dual nature of man, represented by man and shadow. Her resolution to what could be an opposition of forces is to accept the shadow as also part of the self, "embracing that otherness without capitulation or domination." His discussion of <u>A Wizard of Earthsea</u> is the clearest and most faithful to the novel. Ged must learn to accept suffering, to be responsible for his shadow. Views <u>The Tombs of Atuan</u> as a love story illustrating that feelings can be freed by "eros, love for another." <u>The Farthest Shore</u>, like her dystopias, depicts our world afflicted by a collective shadow and the necessity of acting despite despair. Arren is a more successful character that Shevek because Arren achieves the "resurrected vision."

D573 LEVIN, JEFF[REY H.]. "Bibliographic Checklist of the Works of Ursula K. Le Guin." In <u>The Language of the Night</u>. Edited by Susan Wood. New York: Putnam, pp. 237-70.

A full, accurate bibliography of primary works up to 1 October 1978. Titles are divided into six categories, then arranged alphabetically with subsequent editions, including translations, listed beneath each title. Some secondary works which include "original quotations" of Le Guin are included in the last section.

D574 LEVY, MICHAEL M. Review of <u>The Language of the Night</u>. Literata (<u>Minnesota Daily</u>), 18 June, 2 pp.

Le Guin's criticism grows out of her "desire to observe, to understand" fantasy. This leads her to be more critical of her own work and demand the same standards in science fiction and fantasy as in any literature. Discusses four essays: "From Elfland to Poughkeepsie" stresses the "importance of proper language in fantasy"; "Science Fiction and Mrs. Brown" emphasizes the importance of "character development"; "Is Gender Necessary?" illustrates her concern with women in science fiction; "Why Are Americans Afraid of Dragons?" explores the current "hostility to fantasy and, more generally, to literature."

D575 _____. Review of <u>Malafrena</u>. <u>Minnesota Daily</u>, 26 November.

Recounts her writing career as poet, essayist, science fiction and fantasy writer, observing that this successful novel shows "a major writer growing, expanding her art into new areas." Basically a <u>Bildungsroman</u> with clear depiction of major and minor characters. Minor criticisms of book's pacing.

D576 LYNN, RUTH NADELMAN. Fantasy for Children: An Annotated
      Checklist. New York: Bowker.
            Lists the three Earthsea novels and The Wind's Twelve
      Quarters.

D577 MacGREGOR, LOREN J. "Le Guin, the Essayist." Seattle, Wash.
      Post-Intelligencer, 23 September.
            Review of The Language of the Night. Praises her ability
      as an "essayist and critic." She writes insightfully of
      both science fiction and writing in general.

D578 MAGILL, FRANK N., ed. Survey of Science Fiction Literature.
      Vols. 2, 3, 5. Englewood Cliffs: Salem Press.
            Contains six "essay reviews" on Le Guin's work, each
      followed by skeletal bibliographies of book reviews and
      critical articles. [See D526, 529, 547, 550, 617, 644.]

D579 MALZBERG, BARRY N. "Introduction: Circumstance as Policy."
      In Ursula K. Le Guin: Voyager to Inner Lands and to Outer
      Space. Edited by Joe De Bolt. Port Washington, N.Y.:
      Kennikat, pp. 5-9.
            Declares the essay's purpose is "to assess the reasons
      for Le Guin's importance and success within contemporary
      science fiction." Distinguishes the "detailed and anthro-
      pological" nature of her work which, as used in The Dis-
      possessed, could only have been done as science fiction.
      Asserts that she represents the seventies postideological
      science fiction. Identifies himself as one with Ballard,
      Silverberg, Disch, and others who were writing polemical
      books in the sixties, looking toward a collapse and re-
      forming of the culture. Cultural institutions rejected
      that vision in the seventies, and Le Guin represents the
      predominance of culture: "the connection between individual
      and culture is seamless; and the character bears less re-
      sponsibility for his acts than he does in the fiction of
      these other writers." Although The Lathe of Heaven is
      essentially a failure, the message of The Word for World is
      Forest is clear: "its principals can take no action what-
      soever to alter the system." Predicts her future work will
      not be published as science fiction. Final evaluation is
      yet to come, but "she may be seen, some time from now, as
      less a perpetrator of visions than their mirror."

D580 MANDELL, STEPHEN. "An Alien Encounter: Ursula K. Le Guin's
      The Left Hand of Darkness." Connecticut Quarterly 1
      (June):40-49.
            Announces his thesis: "For Le Guin, the alien encounter
      is a metaphor for her own aesthetic encounter with the
      world." Genly Ai and Le Guin both "attempt to define a
      totally new reality with words" that are unavoidably anthro-
      pomorphic and that are "barriers to perception." Discusses

Ai's problems of perception on Gethen; he uses the story, an aesthetic mode, for his report, in order to capture the kind of truth he has learned. Similarly, the Ekumen "is a political entity that, like Plato's Republic, defines reality aesthetically."

D581 MARMOR, PAULA [K.]. Review of The Language of the Night. Fantasiae 7 (July):4.
    Finds Wood's introduction "illuminates and illustrates." Welcomes this collection of essays that show Le Guin's insights into science fiction and fantasy, as well as her development of "an ethic of fantasy." Best essay is "From Elfland to Poughkeepsie."

D582 MASON, MARJORIE. "Romantic Adventure Set in Revolution." Monitor (McAllen, Tex.), 30 December, p. 7F.
    Review of Malafrena. Labels it her "first mainstream novel." Finds the "slow-motion" pacing suitable for the mid-nineteenth century setting. Notes that crucial events are not explicitly protrayed in the novel—they happen "around the corner or across the city." Of all the characters, only Itale is believable.

D583 McALLESTER, DAVID P. "The Astonished Ethno-Muse." Ethno-musicology 23 (May):179-89.
    Describes the changes in the formalized study of ethno-musicology (twenty years old in 1978). In arguing for a recognition of the importance of music, he states: "it has been called '. . . the cooperative art, organic by definition, social, the noblest form of social behavior we're capable of,' by one of the best minds of our era, Ursula Le Guin." His observations on the nature of this art and of human culture are similar to Le Guin's especially in the emphasis on cultural relativity, dynamism, and delightful variety.

D584 MOLSON, FRANCIS J. "The Earthsea Trilogy: Ethical Fantasy for Children." In Ursula K. Le Guin: Voyager to Inner Lands and to Outer Space. Edited by Joe De Bolt. Port Washington, N.Y.: Kennikat, pp. 128-49, 207.
    Urges that the trilogy should be evaluated as children's literature, a significant critical category. As such, it should be categorized as "ethical fantasy," a term more descriptive than heroic, or high, or didactic fantasy. Ethical fantasy is not limited to the traditional concepts of heroism and myths, is not judgmental about high or low purposes, and does not use allegory to present a moral. Earthsea does not endorse a particular sect or religion, but it does endorse a humanistic ethic that children can respond to. Discusses each of the three novels to show three different versions of coming of age, all of which

involve accepting responsibility for self, actions, and relations with others.

D585 MOORE, LINDA. "Value of Fantasy in a 'Real World.'" Asheville Citizen-Times, 10 June.
Review of The Language of the Night. Values and recommends the collection, not only for its discussion of "the craft of fantasy fiction" but also for its revelation of her underlying "philosophy of life."

D586 MORNER, CLAUDIA J. Review of Malafrena. School Library Journal 26 (December):104.
Maintains it demonstrates Le Guin's mastery "of contrasts and irony" as she delineates characters with physical, economic, or political limitations on their freedom.

D587 NAHA, ED. "Future Dreams on Public TV." Future Life 2 (December):28-31, 57.
Review of PBS "The Lathe of Heaven." Recounts the background leading up to the production. The series was to focus on speculative fiction ("that branch of science fiction which places less emphasis on science and technology and more emphasis on human behavior and social evolution"). Includes description of the producer, David Loxton, meeting with Le Guin in Portland and the reactions of the actors to the novel. Quotes Le Guin's favorable response to the production. She is generally critical of science fiction films for being thirty to forty years behind what science fiction readers are now interested in--"'real thought . . . real feeling.'" She tries to avoid stating the film's message because that makes it too much like a "'fortune cookie.'" "'Let's say it's about what happens when the American dream becomes the American nightmare.'"

D588 NEWMAN, ROBERT S. "Le Guin's 'The Dispossessed' and Anarchism." Black Rose 2 (Summer):37-47.
Argues for the relevance and accuracy of Le Guin's double theme--the attractiveness of anarchism, yet its susceptibility to domination. He quotes Laurence Veysey (The Communal Experience) to describe Shevek's difficult role of trying "'to maintain an attitude of skepticism toward both the mainstream and radical alternative.'" Discusses the novel in two respects. First, Le Guin shows that by reorganizing society from the "bottom up," "a freer and more egalitarian life" is achieved and "the superiority of anarchist theorizing" is demonstrated. Not only does she treat the major issues of distribution of goods, maintenance of individual freedom and social harmony, human motivation, she recognizes that the desire to dominate is "intrinsic." Second, she criticizes anarchism "both as to the power-domination urges in people . . . and the corollary, maso-

chism–submission by which many people will accept other
people's assertions of power." Ultimately, Le Guin relates
her concept of anarchism to time and relativity: "You are
responsible only when you put your individual actions within the context of the past (psychological, social, historical) and the future, and only if, in so doing, you sur-
render notions of temporal stability or perfection."

D589   NICHOLLS, PETER, ed. "Le Guin, Ursula K." In The Science
       Fiction Encyclopedia. Garden City, N.Y.: Doubleday, pp.
       345–58, passim.
            After minimal biographical information, he traces her
       writing career. Discusses chronologically the Hainish
       series, commenting on individual works and stressing their
       common philosophy and literary techniques. Her mature
       works are The Left Hand of Darkness, "Vaster Than Empires
       and More Slow," and The Word for World is Forest which place
       "a greater value on the individual, and less on the harmony
       of the whole."
            The Dispossessed is a "remarkable and major work of art"
       for its political speculation, "study in the thought pro-
       cesses of a scientist," and ideas. Some readers find the
       "didactic dryness" removes them from the characters.
            Discusses two additional works––the Earthsea trilogy and
       The Lathe of Heaven.
            Concludes by inquiring whether she has been overly
       praised. She has made significant contributions to the
       genre. Her one weakness is "a paradoxical one, a kind of
       grave and demure certainty which could, perhaps, be leavened
       with a little more openness to the random and the unpre-
       dictable," but it may just be self-confidence.

D590   NILSEN, ALLEEN PACE. "1978 Books for Young Adults Book Poll."
       English Journal 68 (January):56.
            Includes Very Far Away From Anywhere Else in an annotated
       list of the most popular books among young adult readers;
       prepared by University of Iowa Books for Young Adults
       Program––G. Robert Carlsen, Elizabeth A. Belden, Anne S.
       Harker.

D591   OLANDER, JOSEPH D., and GREENBERG, MARTIN HARRY, eds. Intro-
       duction to Ursula K. Le Guin. Writers of the 21st Century
       Series. New York: Taplinger, pp. 11–13.
            Discusses six characteristics of Le Guin's work which
       set her apart from most science fiction authors.

D592   _____. Ursula K. Le Guin. Writers of the 21st Century Series.
       New York: Taplinger, 258 pp.
            Contains an introduction and biographical sketch (D515
       and 591), a bibliography by Tymn (D635), and nine essays:
       Margaret P. Esmonde, "The Master Pattern: The Psychological

Journey in the Earthsea Trilogy"; Peter Brigg, "The Archetype
of the Journey in Ursula K. Le Guin's Fiction"; Peter S.
Alterman, "Ursula K. Le Guin: Damsel with a Dulcimer";
Philip E. Smith II, "Unbuilding Walls: Human Nature and the
Nature of Evolutionary and Political Theory in The Dispos-
sessed"; N.B. Hayles, "Androgny, Ambivalence, and Assimila-
tion in The Left Hand of Darkness"; John P. Brennan and
Michael C. Downs, "Anarchism and Utopian Tradition in The
Dispossessed"; Thomas J. Remington, "The Other Side of
Suffering: Touch as Theme and Metaphor in Le Guin's Science
Fiction Novels"; Sneja Gunew, "Mythic Reversals: The Evolu-
tion of the Shadow Motif"; John H. Crow and Richard D.
Erlich, "Words of Binding: Patterns of Integration in the
Earthsea Trilogy"; Marshall B. Tymn, "Ursula K. Le Guin: A
Bibliography."

D593 PARRINDER, PATRICK. "The Alien Encounter: Or, Ms Brown and
Mrs Le Guin." Science-Fiction Studies 6 (March):46-57.
Reprinted in Science Fiction: A Critical Guide. Edited
by Patrick Parrinder. London: Longman, pp. 148-61.
  Examines the issue of characterization in science fiction by focusing on the motif of the alien encounter.
Connects the motif with the seventeenth and eighteenth
century satirists. Names the two basic theories of characterization: "the first doctrine holds that character-
creation is the fundamental purpose of the novel, while
the second holds that character is subordinate to plot."
Both have recently been restated for science fiction, the
first by Le Guin [see C136] and the second by Scott Sanders.
On a general level, Le Guin's theory is too limiting. "SF
describes a world transformed by some new element . . . ;
it is the new element, and not the need for a subtle and
rounded characterization, which determines the basic rules
of the genre." With regard to that literature in which
the alien is the new element, he urges that Le Guin's concept not be abandoned but be altered because it assumes
"that what is characterized most fully must always be the
autonomous human beings of liberal individualism."

D594 _____. "Delany Inspects the Word-Beast." Science-Fiction
Studies 6 (November):337-41.
  Review of The Jewel-Hinged Jaw, by Samuel R. Delany.
Singles out the essay on The Dispossessed for praise. Re-
constructs Delany's argument for criticizing the novel and
states his own, similar criticism. The novel displays an
"awkwardness" because it oscillates "between a conception
of character and environment that is realistic and one that
is largely symbolic."

D595 PARRINDER, PATRICK, ed. Science Fiction: A Critical Guide.
London: Longman, 238 pp.

In addition to the essays annotated separately [D593,
D596, D543, D648], there are passing references to Le Guin
in other essays.

D596 PARRINDER, PATRICK. "Science Fiction and the Scientific World-
View." In Science Fiction: A Critical Guide. London:
Longman, pp. 67-88.
      Analyzes the twentieth century "scientific world-view"
best exemplified in science fiction by H.G. Wells. Chronological analysis of its use and then rejection in modern
science fiction, concluding with a discussion of Lem and
Le Guin as authors whose fiction counteracts "the widespread fragmentation of the scientific world-view." Although Le Guin's earlier works endorse the classic scientific world-view, The Dispossessed "expose[s] the scientific outlook to psychological, epistemological, and
ideological scrutiny."

D597 PEARLMAN, EDITH. "Radcliffe Books." Radcliffe Quarterly 65
(December):44.
      Review of The Language of the Night. Praises the col-
lection because of its variety in type and subject of essay
and because it caused the reviewer to look for more Dunsany
and Le Guin to read. Finds "The Child and the Shadow" and
"From Elfland to Poughkeepsie" especially significant.

D598 PFEIFFER, JOHN R. "'But Dragons Have Keen Ears:' On Hearing
'Earthsea' with Recollections of Beowulf." In Ursula K.
Le Guin: Voyager to Inner Lands and to Outer Space.
Edited by Joe De Bolt. Port Washington, N.Y.: Kennikat,
pp. 115-27, 206-7.
      Asserts that the trilogy is generally like heroic fan-
tasy, particularly Beowulf in four ways: prominence of
the word "bright"; life-affirming cosmology; "subjects,
events, and scenes" from a common tradition; and use of
oral storytelling techniques. The last is the most significant, and he shows seven techniques that are similar in
the two works. The central theme of the trilogy emphasizes
the significance of the spoken word; not only does its
mastery create the self, it creates worlds.

D599 RABKIN, ERIC S. "Determinism, Free Will, and Point of View
in Le Guin's The Left Hand of Darkness." Extrapolation 20
(Spring):5-19.
      Argues that the novel uses point of view to bring about
a recognition that both determinism and free will are
operant but are subsumed to the concept that "'truth is a
matter of the imagination.'" Discusses the tactics Le Guin
uses to alter the reader's point of view, always noting
that the determinism of the novel is undercut by the
author's free will in constructing the novel. Extended

examples include the folk story about the place inside the
blizzard, the use of the word "traitor," and the mind-
hearing incident. Concludes with a discussion of the
parallels between this attitude and Taoism, a philosophy in
which differences also become irrelevant "by acknowledging
and accepting them as necessary for mutual fulfillment."

D600   _____. "Metalinguistics and Science Fiction." Critical
    Inquiry 6 (Autumn):79-97.
        Science fiction uses the "metalinguistic function of
    language" in three ways: it can treat language "as sub-
    ject, material, or context." Each way is "making a reality
    claim for the text that employs it." His discussion of the
    second function includes three examples drawn from Le Guin.
    First, The Left Hand of Darkness uses "transformed lan-
    guage" to help establish the validity of the created world,
    Second, it creates new words, "kemmer," for example, and
    thus, "Le Guin makes an implicit claim for the reality of
    her alternative world with its alternative values." Third,
    The Dispossessed is an example of a failure in language
    transformation. The language has no possessives; this is
    so discomforting to the reader that it does not help him/
    her accept the new ideology.

D601 REED, NANCY GAIL. "Woman's Place in Outer Space." Christian
    Science Monitor, 15 March, p. 18.
        Review of Millennial Women. Maintains it takes up
    "basic feminist themes" which are overworked. Praises
    Le Guin's writing and remarks that her protagonist finds
    love among what could be "the future descendants of the
    1960s student idealists." Criticizes her female character's
    sweeping statements about male nature.

D602 REGINALD, R. Science Fiction and Fantasy Literature: A
    Checklist, 1700-1974. Vol. 1. Detroit: Gale Research
    Co., pp. 314, 733, 736, 774.
        Includes a checklist of her published works, and entries
    in the Series Index and Awards Index. In the Statistical
    Tables, Le Guin is second only to Harlan Ellison in two
    tables, "Award Winners (Fiction) by Number of Awards" and
    "Award Winners in All Categories by Number."

D603   _____. "Ursula K. Le Guin." Science Fiction and Fantasy
    Literature: A Checklist 1700-1974. Vol. 2. Detroit:
    Gale Research Co., pp. 972-73.
        Biographical sketch is followed by quotations from a
    questionnaire Reginald sent out. Of particular interest is
    her selection and chronological ordering of the major
    Hainish works and her discussion of why she writes science
    fiction.

D604   REMINGTON, THOMAS J.   "The Other Side of Suffering: Touch as
       Theme and Metaphor in Le Guin's Science Fiction Novels."
       In Ursula K. Le Guin. Edited by Joseph D. Olander and
       Martin Harry Greenberg. Writers of the 21st Century Series.
       New York: Taplinger, pp. 153-77, 234-36.
            Argues that "the touch of isolated opposites is central
       to the expression of Le Guin's vision, both thematically
       and metaphorically." Traces the use of that imagery in
       her six science fiction novels and tries to show how it
       becomes more complex as Le Guin advances in her sense of
       her own artistry. Uses Rocannon's World, Planet of Exile,
       City of Illusions, The Left Hand of Darkness, The Lathe of
       Heaven, and The Dispossessed. The three early novels
       establish touch as a metaphor for connecting opposites.
       Left Hand shows the need to be willing to reach out. The
       Dispossessed uniquely shows the Hobbesian idea that shared
       pain is the fundamental human condition. Le Guin goes
       beyond Hobbes by suggesting that pain is necessary for the
       "initial" relationship but that love or brotherhood take
       one beyond shared pain into other kinds of relationships.
       Essay contains sound catalogs of the use of touch imagery,
       particularly hands touching. It is an extension of his
       discussion in D355.

D605   REVIEWING STAFF.   "Popular Reading: Light Romance." Booklist
       75 (15 February):928.
            Includes Very Far Away From Anywhere Else in a bibliog-
       raphy of light romance from the seventies compiled by the
       children's and young adult reviewing staff.

D606   RIDLEY, JIM.   "Highlights: Mary Stewart Tale, 'Saturday
       Night Live' and Le Guin Novel." Nashville Tennessean, 28
       October.
            Review of Malafrena. Identifies it as a "mainstream"
       novel and finds the storytelling excellent. Believes the
       editor should have corrected some of the weak prose.

D607   RIGGENBACH, JEFF.   "Ursula Le Guin: Novelist." Reason
       (December), p. 41.
            Review of The Language of the Night. Discusses her
       ideas about fiction, particularly that it speaks through
       metaphorical truth. Emphasizes the "alternative polity"
       metaphor which she uses in The Dispossessed, The Word for
       World is Forest, "The Diary of The Rose," "The Eye of the
       Heron." Although she appears to be a libertarian, she has
       rejected and criticized the category. Finds her criticism
       in "Stalin in the Soul" inconsistent with her insights in
       The Dispossessed. Welcomes the collection and the bib-
       liography but finds the Wood introductions too long.

D608   RUSS, JOANNA.   "Gentlemen." Science-Fiction Studies 6 (March):

178

117-18.
Response to Klein's article [see D409]. Castigates
Klein for sexist treatment of Le Guin. Points out that
male authors are analyzed by "their work and their class,"
but that Le Guin, the only female author treated, is analyzed by her sexual health and family relationships.

D609   ____. Review of Ursula K. Le Guin's Science Fiction Workshop: The Altered I. Fantasy and Science Fiction 57
(June):51-53.
Finds Le Guin's story "The Eye Altering," "interesting
but minor." Urges all authors to use the pronoun "she" so
as not to keep women "on the sidelines."

D610 SAGONA, PAUL. "Science Fiction Essays 'Interesting, Tedious.'"
State (Columbia, S.C.), 15 July.
Review of The Language of the Night. Although the
collection is not as good as it could be, he recommends it
for new writers and for readers who are unconvinced of the
value of science fiction. Criticizes the repetition, a
"chatty, too-cute style," and the lengthy bibliography.

D611 SANDERS, SCOTT. "Going Home with Le Guin, Struggling For
Freedom." Chicago Sun-Times, 4 November.
Review of Malafrena. Quality of the novel removes the
fantasy and science fiction label from Le Guin; now "she is
simply a writer, one of the best we have." Novel deals with
two major topics, "the search for home and the struggle for
freedom" which are interconnected. Both tasks are under-
taken by the male and female characters in a European
setting, 1825-1830.

D612 SARGENT, LYMAN TOWER. British and American Utopian Literature,
1516-1975: An Annotated Bibliography. Boston: G.K. Hall,
324 pp.
Includes The Left Hand of Darkness, "The Ones Who Walk
Away from Omelas," The Dispossessed, and "The New Atlantis."

D613 SCHECHTER, HAROLD. "Introduction: Focus on Myth and Popular
Art." Journal of American Culture 2:210-16.
Introduces a series of essays on myth and American popular culture by discussing the two major views that (1)
myths are secularized and appear in entertainment media or
(2) myths still hold religious meaning. Uses Le Guin's
"Myth and Archetype" as an example of criticism of pop art
myths and to raise the issue of aesthetic value.

D614 SCHLOBIN, ROGER C. "Preparing for Life's Passages: How Fantasy Literature Can Help." Media & Methods 16 (November):
26-27, 29, 50-51.
Argues for and illustrates the value of fantasy in the

classroom. "Fantasy deals with those issues that are
imminent in the lives of all people and that are especially
crucial for the growing student." Uses Le Guin's Earthsea
novels and stories as an extended example. Their key
issues include "the nature of language and speech," magic
(or "the ability to shape and change nature through the
force of will and ritual"), and "the rite of passage or
initiation."

D615 SCHLOBIN, ROGER C., ed. "Ursula K(roeber) Le Guin." In The
Literature of Fantasy: A Comprehensive Annotated Bibliog-
raphy of Modern Fantasy Fiction. New York: Garland, pp.
145-46.
Annotated entry lists The Wind's Twelve Quarters, three
Earthsea novels, and two bibliographical articles about
Le Guin.

D616 SCHWEITZER, DARRELL. "The Vivisector." Science-Fiction Review,
no. 29 (January-February), pp. 39-40.
Review of Millennial Women. Views the anthology as
a "marketing gimmick," a Le Guin novel " with frills at-
tached." Her novel is good because it lacks the polemics
of The Word for World is Forest, but it also lacks the
power of The Left Hand of Darkness and the complexity of
The Dispossessed. Its society, however, is more convincing
than that in The Dispossessed. Praises her detailed settings but wishes the characters were more developed.
Berates the dust jacket.

D617 SEIDEL, KATHRYN L. "The Lathe of Heaven." In Survey of
Science Fiction Literature. Edited by Frank N. Magill.
Vol. 3. Englewood Cliffs: Salem Press, pp. 1161-64.
Refers to her previous novels to show that this one is
of a different direction, experimenting with Earth in a
near present setting. Novel's theme is that we must all
"endure" reality. Orr is "one of the most fascinating and
original portraits of a hero in science fiction." Both he
and Lelache have characteristics opposite those of the
stereotyped male and female figure. Novel satirizes the
social reformer, present social conditions, and "today's
faith in the cure-all capacity of science and technology."
Le Guin's style is different from her preceding works:
"crisp, light" and is handled well.

D618 SELTZER, HARA L. Review of Lesse [sic] Webster. School
Library Journal (November), p. 66.
Compares the spider to Wilbur's Charlotte--"an anthro-
pomorphic, individualist spider of determined taste."
Notes the "poetic undertone" of the book.

D619 SHAW, MILDRED HART. Review of The Language of the Night.

Westworld (Grand Junction, Colo.), 12 August.
Praises her fine style, as well as her serious and
humorous discussions of her own writing, of the nature of
science fiction and fantasy, and of other authors, from
the Brontes to Philip K. Dick.

D620 ____. "The Truth About Freedom in Fiction." Westworld
(Grand Junction, Colo.), 11 November.
Review of Malafrena. Judges it to be "brilliantly
created and magically told" like her science fiction and
fantasy. Recognizes that "at one level this is a romantic
novel of the Ruritania stamp; at another it is an in-depth
examination of the meaning of freedom."

D621 SINCLAIR, KAREN. "The Solitary Being: The Hero as Anthropologist." In Ursula K. Le Guin: Voyager to Inner Lands
and to Outer Space. Edited by Joe De Bolt. Port Washington, N.Y.: Kennikat, pp. 50-65, 204-5.
Le Guin's protagonists "all seem to have characteristics
that separate them from the worlds in which they find themselves," either as "offworlders" or "skeptics and free-
thinkers in their native society." Marginality becomes a
metaphor. Quotes Levi-Strauss to illustrate the similarity
between her heroes' two-mindedness (critic of both his own
and alien societies) and the constant condition of being an
outsider. Ultimately, Le Guin is "not optimistic": "it can
be argued that her heroes' lack of success is due in fact
to the failures of society--a failure to examine, to re-
appraise, and to change." Examines five novels, describing
the hero/anthropologist, what he learns, the constant tension of marginality. The Word for World is Forest is the
clearest development of "the theme of hero as translator
and commentator." Tries to show that even though the hero
helps bring about order and unity, the hero increases his
sense of aloneness.

D622 SINKLER, REBECCA. "Best Books of the Year." Philadelphia
Inquirer, 25 November, p. 161.
Includes The Language of the Night in an annotated list
of the best books published in 1979. Books chosen were
those receiving the "most energetic and engaging responses"
from the reviewers.

D623 SLUSSER, GEORGE E.; GUFFEY, GEORGE R.; and ROSE, MARK, eds.
Bridges To Science Fiction. Carbondale and Edwardsville:
Southern Illinois University Press, 168 pp.
A collection of essays which "suggest connections be-
tween science fiction and other aspects of Western culture,"
presented at the First Eaton Conference on Science Fiction
and Fantasy Literature, University of California-Riverside.
Le Guin is most frequently mentioned in "Science Fiction

and the Gothic" by Thomas H. Keeling. Even though Le Guin
and others use "traditional gothic motifs," he demonstrates
that their novels do not have essential characteristics of
the gothic novel. Uses The Left Hand of Darkness and The
Dispossessed in his argument.

D624 SMITH, PHILIP E. II. "Unbuilding Walls: Human Nature and the
Nature of Evolutionary and Political Theory in The Dis-
possessed." In Ursula K. Le Guin. Edited by Joseph D.
Olander and Martin Harry Greenberg. Writers of the 21st
Century Series. New York: Taplinger, pp. 77-96, 226-28.
Effectively demonstrates the influence of Kropotkin's
philosophy of anarchism on Le Guin's The Dispossessed and
examines her use of the metaphor of the wall in developing
both the protagonist and the theme.
Both thinkers link together "human nature, evolutionary
theory, politics, and ultimately ethics" in anarchism.
Both begin from the analogy of the society to "a unified
natural organism." Both debate the advantages of this kind
of society based on the instincts of mutual aid over "cap-
italistic or socialistic states based on the impulse to
dominance." Conflict of novel develops out of Le Guin
going beyond Kropotkin.
Shevek first has to clarify his personal responsibility
before he can fulfill his social responsibility and bring
Anarres back to Odonianism. Breaking down both personal
and social barriers is imaged as breaking down the walls.
Smith traces the imagery through chapters in chronological
order, providing a fine catalog and discussion of how the
image in a particular chapter relates to Shevek's personal
and social development.

D625 SONDAK, NORMAN. "'Malafrena': A Society in Transition." San
Diego Union, 21 October, p. 7.
Review of Malafrena. Disappointed because the novel "is
complex in structure and ambitious in scope, but the characters and events lack a sense of immediacy and focus."
Her theme is relevant and her "narrative description"
strong.

D626 SPEARS, MONROE K. "Science Fiction's Queen of the Night."
Book World (Washington Post), 28 October, p. 6.
Review of The Language of the Night and Malafrena. Commends the collection as "the most attractive introduction
to science fiction yet to appear." Le Guin is "unpreten-
tious" and insightful, arguing primarily for the recognition that science fiction and fantasy are significant to
the "civilized and humane mind" and should not be separated
from the "wider world of fiction." Quotes from her essays
at length to show how well she has defined science fiction
and fantasy and set up critical standards for each.

Malafrena is not her best work. Neither mainstream nor science fiction, it is more like a "historical novel" except that it is not "interpreting characters and events." Correctly speculates that it is probably an early novel, "competent, intelligent, decent . . . but . . . not much more."

D627 STEEN, SARA JAYNE. Review of The Farthest Shores of Ursula K. Le Guin, by George Edgar Slusser. Extrapolation 19 (May): 138-39.
Judges the study to be "a contribution to our understanding of Le Guin's works, [but] it is seriously flawed." Major flaws are his contextual criticism, a "bias in favor of the introspective mainstream novel," and "factual inaccuracies." Best chapter is that which shows the relationship between the Earthsea novels and her other fiction. Recommends the study.

D628 STUMPF, EDNA. "From Extreme to Extreme in the Science Fiction World." Philadelphia Inquirer, 26 August.
Review of The Language of the Night. Discusses her high standing in the field where she has taught all her readers something "about Taoism and Jungianism and art." Recommends every essay as being worthwhile.

D629 _____. "An Unassuming Little Tale By a Master of Fantasy." Philadelphia Inquirer, 11 November.
Review of Malafrena. Labels it a "quiet," "psychological novel" with a "predictable" plot. It demonstrates qualities Le Guin is known for--geographical description, "meticulous prose," empathetic characters, and fine language. She suspects it is an early, heretofore unpublished novel and hopes Malafrena is not the country of her coming work. Erroneously identifies the setting as "early 1900s."

D630 STUTTAFORD, GENEVIEVE. Review of The Language of the Night. Publishers Weekly 215 (19 February):97.
Recommends the essays for both the "casual" and the serious reader because of their energy, wit, and wide range of topics.

D631 SUVIN, DARKO. Metamorphoses of Science Fiction: On the Poetics of a Literary Genre. New Haven, Conn.: Yale University Press, passim.
No extended analysis of her work, but frequent references to her.

D632 SYMONS, JULIAN. "The Heavy Fantastic." New York Review of Books 26 (27 September):48-50.
Review of The Language of the Night. Rationally analyzes Le Guin's statements about the nature of fantasy and finds

them implausible. Criticizes what he sees as a double
ethic--that she is an active "political liberal," in the
real world but her stories "explore the individual psyche
and not the external world." In his discussion of the
origins and nature of science fiction, he finds nothing
helpful in Le Guin's book and offers his own definitions:
"SF is about imagined futures while fantasy is about
imagined pasts." Digresses into a strong criticism of hard
science fiction and praises Le Guin's fiction because it
shows her concern with language, ethics, politics; and it
is "highly imaginative." However, her ideas "often fail to
carry her through to the end of a story." The Dispossessed
is her best work because it is about the real world and
would be notable among any kind of fiction of the past ten
years. Calls for real critical distinctions to be made in
science fiction, as in the detective story.

D633 TELEVISION LABORATORY, WNET/THIRTEEN (New York). Publicity
      packet for "The Lathe of Heaven."
         Folder contains four publicity releases, a five-page
      production credits list, and three photographs.

D634 TIFFT, LARRY L., and SULLIVAN, DENNIS C. "Possessed Sociology
      and Le Guin's Dispossessed: From Exile to Anarchism." In
      Ursula K. Le Guin: Voyager to Inner Lands and to Outer
      Space. Edited by Joe De Bolt. Port Washington, N.Y.:
      Kennikat, pp. 180-97, 210.
         Subjective response to the novel, detailing the readers'
      emotional experience of the novel. Strongly critical of
      Western sociologists for shutting themselves off from the
      experiences of themselves, others, and the community. This
      false isolation is treated in The Dispossessed. The reader,
      to break out of his/her own isolation, needs to experience
      the journey with Shevek--a "journey out of boundaries" which
      "negates the journey within" that sets up boundaries. Sum-
      marizes many of Shevek's experiences to show their similar-
      ity to Western man's isolation and need for wholeness. "The
      possessed life of the United States is our past, the dis-
      possessed life of anarchism is our future; in the creative
      joining of the two is our present, is our journey, is the
      invitation for us to be whole." Interesting essay, as an
      emotional response to Le Guin, but it fails to examine the
      reader response in depth.

D635 TYMN, MARSHALL B. "A Bibliography." In Ursula K. Le Guin.
      Edited by Joseph D. Olander and Martin Harry Greenberg.
      Writers of the 21st Century Series. New York: Taplinger,
      pp. 241-46.
         Labels it a "comprehensive" and "representative" listing
      of both primary and secondary works. It is divided into
      five sections: Books and Pamphlets, Short Fiction, Articles

and Essays, General, and Criticism. Listing is strong in
the pre-1976 period.

D636 TYMN, MARSHALL B.; ZAHORSKI, KENNETH J.; and BOYER, ROBERT H.,
Fantasy Literature: A Core Collection and Reference Guide.
New York: Bowker, pp. 110-13, passim.
"Core Collection" includes and annotates A Wizard of
Earthsea, The Tombs of Atuan, The Farthest Shore, and The
Wind's Twelve Quarters. Wizard is praised for its characterization of Ged and its "substantive psychological and
philosophical" content. Tombs is selected for its themes,
characterization, and "narrative structure." Shore carefully balances "theme and action"; the closing accounts of
dragons "are perhaps the most exciting, action-packed seg-
ments to be found in contemporary fantasy." Wind's contains
four fantasies ("April in Paris," "Darkness Box," "The Word
of Unbinding," and "The Rule of Names").
"Fantasy Scholarship" includes three essays by Le Guin:
"Dreams Must Explain Themselves," "From Elfland to Poughkeepsie," and "Why Are Americans Afraid of Dragons?".

D637 "Ursula K. Le Guin." In A Reader's Guide to Science Fiction:
A Comprehensive and Fascinating Source-Book for Every
Reader of Science Fiction. Edited by Baird Searles, Martin
Last, Beth Meacham, and Michael Franklin. New York: Avon,
pp. 102-4 [paper].
Her outstanding qualities are her "beautiful prose
style," "human detail," "plausible" science. Comments on
Rocannon's World, The Left Hand of Darkness, The Lathe of
Heaven, The Word for World is Forest, The Dispossessed, and
the Earthsea trilogy. To readers who enjoy Le Guin they
recommend Marta Randall, Frank Herbert, James Tiptree, Jr.,
and James Gunn.

D638 VAUGHN, ED. Review of The Language of the Night. Seattle,
Wash. Post-Intelligencer, 26 August.
Although she has not done for science fiction what E.M.
Forster did for the novel, she does explain how she writes.
Recommends the collection.

D639 WALKER, JEANNE MURRAY. "Myth, Exchange and History in The
Left Hand of Darkness." Science-Fiction Studies 6 (July):
180-89.
Argues that the function of myths in the novel can best
be understood by examining them in light of Levi-Strauss's
theories. He asserts that "myth incorporates in story form
pairs of images which represent contradictions lying at the
center of the society"; the narrative then resolves those
contradictions. In this novel, "the myths both anticipate
and act as ideal models for the 'historical' events." Most
of the myths concern kinship exchange, the basis for the

formation of society. Discusses four myths, first showing
how each comments on the necessity for social exchange and
how each reconciles opposites. Then discusses how the
myths illumine and comment on the events in the novel itself, as well as set up the ethics. Concludes with the
generalization that "the myths in Left Hand assert the
impossibility of retreating from history and from human
society."

D640 WENDELL, CAROLYN. "The Alien Species: A Study of Women
      Characters in the Nebula Award Winners, 1965-1973."
      Extrapolation 20 (Winter):343-54.
          Le Guin's The Left Hand of Darkness is the sole entry
      in the category, "A World without sex roles." Asserts that
      the reader cannot see the Gethenians as gender-free; they
      are male. Qualifies her assertion with the observation
      that because humans are "sexual beings, both born and bred,"
      our impulse is to see all beings as one sex or the other.
      [For response, see D703.]

D641 WHEATLEY, BARBARA. "Teaching Linguistics Through Science
      Fiction and Fantasy." Extrapolation 20 (Fall):205-13.
          Discusses the use of science fiction to introduce stu-
      dents to the questions of linguistics. Briefly recounts
      using the Earthsea trilogy to illustrate a past belief that
      "language is a gift from God" and to contrast this with
      current belief that "human language can have no power over
      external reality."

D642 WHITE, VIRGINIA L. "Bright the Hawk's Flight: The Journey
      of the Hero in Ursula Le Guin's Earthsea Trilogy." Ball
      State University Forum 20:34-45.
          Catalogs the parallels between Joseph Campbell's descrip-
      tion of "the classic journey of the mythic hero" and each
      volume of the trilogy as well as the trilogy as a whole.
      Everywhere is displayed the three-part structure of de-
      parture, initiation, and apotheosis/return.

D643 WINGROVE, DAVID. Review of Planet of Exile, The Lathe of
      Heaven, and Orsinian Tales. Vector 92 (March-April), pp.
      20-21.
          Appraises all three thus: "Each of these three books is
      about marriage: of minds, of ideals, and occasionally of
      a more literal kind." Characterization and writing quality
      are excellent. The first is a forerunner of The Left Hand
      of Darkness; he hypothesizes that the natives are based on
      the Amerind and the farborns "on some metaphysical vision
      of human possibility." Notes the style and structure of
      the second novel are very like Philip K. Dick's. Finds
      himself unable to be objective about the third book; rather
      he responds intellectually and emotionally to all that she

says, especially the significance of art.

D644   WOLFE, GARY K.   "The Word for World is Forest."   In Survey of
       Science Fiction Literature.   Edited by Frank N. Magill.
       Vol. 5.   Englewood Cliffs: Salem Press, pp. 2492-96.
          Pointing out that it is the significant Hainish piece
       published between The Left Hand of Darkness and The Dis-
       possessed, he notes that it continues her already established
       themes, adds the contemporary issue of the Vietnam War, and
       looks forward to the issues of The Dispossessed.   Novel
       strains to keep its two threads together: "to condemn the
       mentality of racist imperialism . . . [and] to explore the
       possibility of a psychology based on the union of the con-
       scious and unconscious through the deliberate control of
       dreams."   Story reveals that the two radically different
       cultures are both flawed.   Forest is the dominant image
       and "unites all the branches of her plot"--political, eco-
       logical, psychological.   The Forest represents both the
       "phenomenal world" and "the unconscious."   Notes the shift-
       ing style for descriptions of one culture or another, the
       lack of sentimentalizing.

D645   WOOD, SUSAN.   "Discovering Worlds: The Fiction of Ursula K.
       Le Guin."   In Voices For The Future: Essays on Major SF
       Writers.   Edited by Thomas D. Clareson.   Vol. 2.   Bowling
       Green, Oh.:   Bowling Green University Popular Press, pp.
       154-79, 204-5.
          Argues that the web imagery in her fiction describes the
       situation of the protagonist and of the artist: the work
       is a collection of independent words, important in them-
       selves, but also interconnected--"Life is a pattern or web,
       with individual points of life joined by lines of communi-
       cation."
          First half of the essay discusses Le Guin's "thematic
       and conceptual interdependence consistent with her philos-
       ophy," supported by cross-references to many of her novels,
       all of which depict protagonists searching for the "'real
       center' of their lives"--The Left Hand of Darkness, The
       Lathe of Heaven, and The Dispossessed.   The first one
       demonstrates the paradox of dualism and harmony through the
       "interplay of action, setting, metaphor and myth."   Lathe
       suggests the significance of the individual and the living
       of the life which involves finding the right way of accept-
       ing.   The last novel functions through its unifying symbol,
       the wall, the "rejection of freedom," explored by both the
       novel's characters and structure.   It is flawed in its
       didacticism where ideas are stated too frequently rather
       than (or sometimes even after) being shown.   Earthsea
       trilogy is her best fiction in which idea, character,
       structure, setting, and style support each other.

D646 WOOD, SUSAN, ed. <u>The Language of the Night: Essays on Fan-</u>
<u>tasy and Science Fiction by Ursula K. Le Guin.</u> New York:
Putnam, 270 pp.
Book contains six introductions by Wood. The first
introduces the collection, discussing the title and emphasizing throughout Le Guin's concept of fantasy (which includes science fiction) as translation of subjective perception into words. She asserts the value of the essays
and names the three major ideas: (1) that fantasy and
science fiction are "different branches of the same form of
writing"; (2) that the integrated individual results from
inward journeys such as fantasy provides; (3) that her
central concern is "with the ethics and aesthetics of art."
Groups Le Guin's essays thematically into five sections.
The introductions to each of these five sections include
the publishing history of the essays, a discussion of
Wood's arrangement, and sometimes notes on the interrela-
tionships among essays. [See C175.]

D647 WOODCOCK, JOHN. "Science Fiction and the Real Future."
<u>Alternative Futures</u> 2 (Spring):25-37.
Believes that writers, like Le Guin, who insist that
science fiction is not about the future, have not clearly
defined "future" and "falsely limit the interest of science
fiction." He defines the future psychologically, as "a
present expectation" and asserts that "imagining the future
is something we do all the time, an activity that helps us
maintain our identities and adjust our actions in a changing
environment." Science fiction literature's degree of
realism about the future can be demonstrated by three categories: "the fantastic, the moral-philosophical, and the
realistic." <u>The Left Hand of Darkness</u> is briefly discussed
as an example of the second category. Points out that
models for forecasting, designed by computers and futuro-
logists have had serious problems; science fiction, however,
combining knowledge and intuition, objectivity and subjectivity, is a worthwhile enterprise.

D648 WOODMAN, TOM. "Science Fiction, Religion and Transcendence."
In <u>Science Fiction: A Critical Guide.</u> Edited by Patrick
Parrinder. London: Longman, pp. 110-30.
Brief discussion of <u>The Lathe of Heaven</u> as "a thorough-
going attack on scientism," which earlier science fiction
writers had praised. Haber's attitude is associated with
"the Judaeo-Christian ethic."

D649 YONKE, DAVID. "Sci-fi Expert Turns Romantic." <u>Tampa Tribune-</u>
<u>Times</u>, 2 December.
Review of <u>Malafrena</u>. Notes that although the novel is
not science fiction, it is not far from it because Orsinia
is an imaginary country. The narrative pacing improves

once the story gets underway; novel is "masterfully written."

1980

D650 ANON. Review of The Beginning Place. Bulletin for the Center
for Children's Books 34 (September):14.
Praises the characterization, plot development, and
blending of "realism and fantasy."

D651 ANON. Review of Edges. Publishers Weekly 218 (3 October):65.
Favorable reaction to the editors' collection of stories
that are "experimental, sometimes even cryptic, certainly
not bound by conventions of the genre."

D652 ANON. Review of Hard Words and Other Poems. Publishers
Weekly 218 (26 December):56.
Describes the contents and judges that her "attention
to the sound of words and rhythmic sense is intriguing,
[but] many poems lack sufficient development of subject
matter and ideas."

D653 ANON. Review of Leese Webster. Children's Book Review Ser-
vice 8 (May):95.
Identifies it as an "animal fantasy for younger children"
which has a "nicely conceived moral."

D654 ANON. Review of Leese Webster. Bulletin for the Center for
Children's Books 34 (September):14.
A "quiet story" with a "poetic concept and style."

D655 ARBUR, ROSEMARIE. "Le Guin's 'Song' of Inmost Feminism."
Extrapolation 21 (Fall):223-26.
Shows that the poem is "a celebration and definition of
the deepest sort of feminism." Focuses on the dynamics of
the poem to argue that it is not dialectic (moving from
experiential to rational), but that it "imitate[s] verbally
the processes of growth toward mature womanhood." This
state is achieved by the "conscious acceptance of all that
the woman is," both the rational and the experiential.
[See D525 for Arbur's previous discussion of this poem.]

D656 ASIMOV, ISAAC. "A Pumpkin is Not a Spaceship." Horizon 23
(January):37.
Generally criticizes movie and television versions of
science fiction, as well as the people who watch them instead of reading the stories. Specifically criticizes the
choice of The Lathe of Heaven for a TV film. It attracts
because it includes spectacular destruction, offers a chance
for special effects, and can be passed off as the occult
rather than science.

D657 ATTEBERY, BRIAN. The Fantasy Tradition in American Literature:
From Irving to Le Guin. Bloomington: Indiana University
Press, pp. 161-86, passim.
    In discussing the successors of Tolkien, he concentrates
on Le Guin. Examines her other work before looking at the
trilogy in detail. Fantasy should be judged by "the clar-
ity and consistency with which it evokes our sense of the
numinous, a sense compounded of equal parts of wonder and
significance." Lengthy, careful description of Earthsea,
its society, history, geography, land of death, and a
stimulating discussion of her possible sources. Notes that
she avoids sentimentality that often accompanies a return
to a simpler time "by giving the people . . . problems
which are appropriate to their situation and also in some
way analogous to our own troubles." All three volumes depict the need for "the courage to understand and accept the
universe." Second and third volumes are "stronger," because
they deal with nearly irresolvable problems. Tombs treats
the "perversity of religion," Shore shows that "the anti-
thesis of every ill must also be its cure." Lists numerous
"paired images." Refers to several poems and poets whose
concerns parallel hers.

D658 _____. "On a Far Shore: The Myth of Earthsea." Extrapolation
21 (Fall):269-77.
    Announces that Theodore Roethke's poem, "In a Dark Time"
shares the same meaning as The Farthest Shore and that "by
reading the two works together, one can more clearly trace
the significant patterns that give meaning to both." He
explicates the poem line by line with the help of Roethke's
essay on the poem; then finds a corresponding element in
the novel. Both works are about self-discovery and use the
shadow archetype. Roethke, however, starkly describes a
state of mind while Le Guin draws a complete narrative with
setting, plot, and characterization.

D659 BAEN, JAMES, ed. Introduction to Galaxy: The Best of My
Years. New York: Ace, p. 26 [paper].
    Brief, behind-the-scenes accounting of literary agent's
and editors' reaction to the story, "The Day Before the
Revolution."

D660 BAILEY, EDGAR C., Jr. "Shadows in Earthsea: Le Guin's Use of
a Jungian Archetype." Extrapolation 21 (Fall):254-61.
    Catalogs the appearances of and references to the shadow
and points out their parallels in Jung's discussions. Her
ability to keep the "symbolic message" secondary to her
"captivating adventure story" makes this "great fantasy."
Adds no new information to the earlier essays on the
Jungian nature of the shadow.

Part D: Critical Studies

D661 BAIN, DENA C. "The Tao Te Ching as Background to the Novels
        of Ursula K. Le Guin." Extrapolation 21 (Fall):209-22.
            Purpose of the article is to give "some definition to
        the Taoist mythos that permeates" three novels--City of
        Illusions, The Left Hand of Darkness, and The Dispossessed.
        After an overview of Taoism, she discusses each novel to
        illustrate its Taoist ideas. The common threads are "the
        concepts of wholeness, of presence, of reconciling forces
        which appear totally opposed, but which, in the moment of
        complete reduction and return to the Uncarved Block, are
        invariably revealed to be necessary complements."

D662 BERGER, MATTHEW. Review of The Beginning Place. Best Sellers
        (April), pp. 12-13.
            Places it in the context of "'high fantasy' . . . fic-
        tion that deals with the concept of 'alternate realities'--
        parallels to our universe." Praises its style, story, and
        tough-minded message about the acceptance of reality.

D663 BIERMAN, JUDAH. "Futures Research and the Myth of Utopia."
        Alternative Futures 3 (Fall):92-99.
            In arguing that futures research partakes of the utopia
        myth, she briefly discusses The Dispossessed and Ecotopia
        (Callenbach). Although The Dispossessed is the superior
        novel, both convey a "subjective and holistic" alternative
        future.

D664 BISHOP, MICHAEL. "Books." Fantasy and Science Fiction 58
        (June):59-65.
            Review of Malafrena. Praises this novel which shows a
        greater debt to Tolstoy than to Tolkien. Comments on the
        similarities between Itale and Shevek in determination and
        in the journey and return. Believes Itale is "poised for
        a further foray into the world" at the novel's conclusion.
        Because of its concern with human values, he calls it a
        "noble book." In passing, notes that Maylita Kaine in "The
        Negation" by Christopher Priest appears to be partly modeled
        on Le Guin.

D665 BITTNER, JIM. Letter to the editor. WAM! (Women and Men)
        2 (October):44-45.
            Discusses Le Guin's use of homosexuality in Planet of
        Exile. Concludes that "Le Guin merely touched the subject
        and didn't develop it clearly."

D666 BRANTLINGER, PATRICK. "The Gothic Origins of Science Fiction."
        Novel: A Forum on Fiction 14 (Fall):30-43.
            Cites Le Guin's essays to support his criticism of
        Robert Scholes's concept that as science fiction approaches
        the "realism of the future," it will become a stronger
        rival of mainstream fiction. He argues instead that science

fiction, out of its gothic roots, is antirealist in being
its authors' subjective responses to experience. Asserts
that Le Guin's definition and support of fantasy "makes
much better critical sense."

D667 BRIGG, PETER. Review of The Language of the Night. Science
Fiction & Fantasy Book Review 2 (February):22.
     Praises Wood's introductions and selections. Finds the
repetition between essays inconsequential because Le Guin
"is always expanding, reconsidering, approaching her ideas
from new angles." Enjoys Le Guin's style and unassuming
tone; lists her topics of discussion.

D668 BROWN, BARBARA. "The Left Hand of Darkness: Androgyny,
Future, Present, and Past." Extrapolation 21 (Fall):227-35.
     Argues that the impact of androgyny in the novel stems
from its being explored on three levels: as a possible
future condition, as a reflection of the present condition,
and as a past myth. Defines mythic, literary, and contemporary discussions of androgyny, showing that the modern
"theory of androgyny affirms that we should develop a
mature sexuality in which an open system of all possible
behavior is accepted, the temperament of the individual and
the surrounding circumstances being the determining factors,
rather than gender." Novel leads us to accept androgyny in
a two-step development. Genly Ai experiences "the movement
from duality to unity on all levels" and becomes sensitive
to truth via "intuition and mystical awareness." He is
thus prepared to accept the androgynous nature of the
Gethenians. The reader is urged to accept "the archetypal
androgyny within us."

D669 BRYFONSKI, DEDRIA, ed. "Le Guin, Ursula K(roeber)." In Con-
temporary Literary Criticism. Vol. 13. Detroit: Gale
Research Co., pp. 345-52.
     After a brief biography, excerpts are given from D362,
D391, D457, D579, and D621.

D670 BUCKNALL, BARBARA [J.]. "Ursula K. Le Guin." In American
Women Writers: A Critical Reference Guide from Colonial
Times to the Present. Edited by Lina Mainiero. Vol. 2.
New York: Ungar, pp. 546-47.
     Claims her first three novels show both new wave and
sword and sorcery tendencies. Earthsea is her "most
unified work," blending form and content. Maintains that
Le Guin's main concern is with the freedom of the "creative
imagination." Bucknall gives a superficial definition of
her Taoism ("wholeness is reached through a dynamic balance
of opposites") and erroneously asserts that Le Guin labels
all the stories in The Wind's Twelve Quarters, "psychomyths." Assessment ends with 1976.

D671 BURG, VICTOR KANTOR. "Ever Want to be Somewhere Else?"
    Christian Science Monitor, 5 March, p. 17.
        Review of The Beginning Place. Praises the novel for its
    insight that in both worlds, the characters have to face
    the same fear and that they can "preserve" the fantasy
    world as well as "acquire the will to live without it."
    Finds the resolution flawed by an absence of the "patience
    which so firmly guides the majority of the narrative."

D672 CAMPBELL, PATTY. "The Young Adult Perplex." Wilson Library
    Bulletin 55 (September):56-57.
        Review of The Beginning Place. Welcomes it as an uncon-
    ventional love story which "moves beyond romantic love" to
    the reality of love based on mutual need and shared exper-
    ience."

D673 CARD, ORSON SCOTT. "You Got No Friends in This World: A Re-
    view of Short Fiction." Science Fiction Review 9 (February):
    55.
        Review of "The Pathways of Desire." Finds it disappoint-
    ing, merely "above average." The characters are strong and
    deserve more than the "sophomoric ending" that she provides.

D674 CHESTNUT, TONI. "Your Ass An' Ours." WAM! (Women and Men) 2
    (October):14-16. Reprinted from Plexus (January 1976).
        Review of The Dispossessed. Le Guin's vision is limited
    as evidenced by her choice of a male protagonist and her
    "monogamous heterosexuality" bias. In aspects other than
    sexuality, however, the book is stimulating and speculative.
    The article's title is a pun on "Urras and Anarres."

D675 CLARESON, THOMAS D. "Le Guin's Latest Novel: A New Beginning
    Place?" Extrapolation 21 (Fall):299-301.
        Quotes from several reviews of the novel and asserts
    none have noted that the two worlds "fuse together into a
    single complex symbolism which not only explores the nature
    of love but the fear and inadequacies that surround it
    everywhere." Discusses the development of the theme,
    slaying of the dragon is a "parody of the heroic quest and
    romantic love." Suggests novel may be her "beginning place
    for an ever more mature act of fiction."

D676 COSGRAVE, MARY SILVA. Review of The Beginning Place. Horn
    Book Magazine 56 (June):333-34.
        Notes the betrayal of the villagers who welcome Hugh as
    their hero and rescuer but in fact send "him and Irene
    forth as sacrificial victims in payment for the village's
    freedom." Identifies it as "a crisp contemporary fantasy."

D677 CUMMINGS, MICHAEL S. "Democratic Procedure and Community in
    Utopia." Alternative Futures 3 (Fall):35-57.

The Dispossessed is one of nine utopian models, all of
which are democratic and all of which are flawed in their
"inattention to democratic procedure." His discussion of
the general issue focuses on three questions: "(1) Why do
democratic utopians ignore questions of political procedure? (2) What problems are likely to result? (3) What
procedural revision of the utopian-democratic paradigm will
give us theoretically sound and practically workable solutions to these problems?" Le Guin has not sufficiently
detailed the issues of "political motivation, dissent, and
community solidarity."

D678 del REY, LESTER. The World of Science Fiction: 1926-1976:
      The History of A Subculture. New York: Garland, pp. 205,
      233, 243, 262, 337, 348, 387.
          Although it contains few comments on Le Guin, it pro-
      vides a context of publishing history for her work.

D679 DIXON, BUZZ. Review of PBS production of The Lathe of Heaven.
      Cinefantastique 10 (Summer):14.
          Applauds it as "one of the 10 best science fiction films
      of all time." Praises all who were involved, but especially
      Le Guin, "who wrote the original novel as a children's story
      and contributed much as technical advisor." [His claim that
      Lathe was once a children's story is unsubstantiated.]

D680 DOOLEY, PATRICIA. "Magic and Art in Ursula Le Guin's Earthsea
      Trilogy." In Children's Literature: Annual of The Modern
      Language Association Group on Children's Literature and The
      Children's Literature Assoc. Vol. 8. New Haven: Yale
      University Press, pp. 103-110.
          Uses Arnold Hauser's discussion of the three stages in
      the development of art and the presence of magic in each to
      help her identify and describe the three types of magic in
      the trilogy and to argue that "the central function of
      magic in the novels is as a metaphor for art." The three
      types of magic are use-magic, illusions, and art-magic.
      The latter is dominant and demonstrates the interconnected-
      ness of knowledge, power, and language. Le Guin's view of
      the world is based on Taoism and modern psychology, and
      stresses the "moral responsibility of the artist." "The
      heroic act is redefined as the recognition of one's whole
      self and its subsequent acceptance."
          Oversimplifies her description of the yin/yang balance
      and the relationship between man and nature.

D681 DUGUID, LINDSAY. "Prisoner of St. Lazar." Times Literary
      Supplement, 11 April, p. 416.
          Review of Malafrena. Announces it is "a remarkable feat
      of imagination," sound in characterization, narrative,
      setting, and minimalized "'period' writing." Her sharp

details remind the reader "that things are more complicated
than the hero's process might lead us to believe." Admits
the last sections, from the imprisonment on, are not as
"convincing" as the earlier sections.

D682 ELBOW, GARY S., and MARTINSON, TOM L. "Science Fiction For
Geographers: Selected Works." Journal of Geography 79
(January):23-27.
Discusses novels and themes of science fiction which can
be used in the geography classroom. Discussion is divided
into four sections; Le Guin's works are used to illustrate
the first two--"Invented terrestrial landscapes." Her work
is especially valuable in courses on cultural geography.

D683 GALBREATH, ROBERT. "Holism, Openness, and the Other: Le
Guin's Use of the Occult." Science Fiction Studies 7
(March):36-48.
Explores the "significant aesthetic and integrative
functions in her work" of the occult. Carefully defines
the general concept of the occult and compares it to
Le Guin's ideas, noting especially the "holistic tendency"
in both. Discusses four examples of the occult in her work
which occur at pivotal moments in the narrative: (1) Mind-
speech in The Left Hand of Darkness, (2) "Supernormal
empathy" in "Vaster Than Empires and More Slow," (3) Fore-
telling in Left Hand, and (4) the Atlantis myth in "The New
Atlantis." Concludes with a brief discussion of her "ironic
and paradoxical uses" of the occult to convey her vision of
"the peculiar coincidence of familiar and unfamiliar, open
and closed.

D684 _____. "Taoist Magic in the Earthsea Trilogy." Extrapolation
21 (Fall):262-68.
Discusses the paradox of Le Guin's Earthsea magic that
is sharply revealed in the climaxes of A Wizard of Earthsea
and The Farthest Shore: "The practice of magery requires a
person of exceptional will because paradoxically willful-
ness must be set aside: its power does not force, its
knowledge does not impose, its practitioner does not choose."
Opposed to this "antimagic or 'Taoist' magic" is Ged's mis-
use of magic and Cob's "coercive, Faustian magic which,
defying all limits, strives for domination over nature" as
well as for overcoming death. Discusses significance of
Ged's "integrative transformation" and the ways in which
this magic is Taoist.

D685 GEIS, RICHARD. Review of The Beginning Place. Science Fiction
Review 9 (May):26.
Asserts she seems to be "commenting on the binding fears
that hold us all in various ways and which rule us and im-
poverish us, and which can be shattered more easily than

imagined." Praises the characterization and "gritty realism."

D686 _____. Review of The Lathe of Heaven. Science Fiction Review 9 (May):28-29.
Her story is similar to a movie of the 1930s, The Man Who Could Work Miracles. This novel fails because it does not answer "the obvious questions: why does George Orr possess this power to alter the past and present to any extent, and how does this power operate?"

D687 _____. Review of Malafrena. Science Fiction Review 9 (February):35.
Criticizes it as an "intellectual's novel which ultimately seems "empty . . . and pointless." Although Itale is the main character, "the women in his life . . . are the real focus--their struggles, their development, their eventual triumphs." It shares with the nineteenth century style "an almost complete absence of sex and physical concerns."

D688 _____. Review of Millennial Women. Science Fiction Review 9 (February):33.
Rates it a "powerful" novel on Le Guin's special topic-- "the story of an oppressed people seeking freedom." Maintains it is not a "polemic," but allows the reader to "see both sides, all arguments."

D689 GILDEN, MEL. "Unsatisfactory Story of a Twilight Zone." Los Angeles Times, 11 May, The Book Review, p. 17.
Review of The Beginning Place. Novel fails because it has a "thin" plot; setting and characterization are strong. The problem in "the twilight land" is unclear, the "whys and wherefores" of the quest are unknown, and what the characters "find does not explain anything."

D690 GILSON, CHRISTOPHER. "Language, Music & Reality: Another Look at Magic in Middle-earth." Fantasiae 8 (October):8-9.
Response to Wallace's article contrasting the "roots of magic" in Tolkien and Le Guin [see D740]. Argues that their roots are the same; article primarily supports his assertions about the nature of Tolkien's magic. [For Wallace's reply, see D761.]

D691 GLENDINNING, VICTORIA. "The One Real Thing." Sunday Times (London), 20 April, p. 43e.
Review of Malafrena. Labels it a "fine Costume drama," but it is not as "portentous as her mythic imagination might have made it." Strong qualities are her sense of place and her "linguistic ingenuity" in making up a Romance language. Two of her themes are "the gap between ideals

and achievement" and "the tension between male and female," in which she explores the "19th century polarity between the sexes."

D692 GRAY, PAUL. "Worlds Enough and Time." Time, 11 February, pp. 86, 90.
   Review of The Beginning Place. Asserts Le Guin is clearly "as good as any contemporary at creating worlds, imaginary or our own." Praises her "narrative savy" and "quick, sharp description." The novel is a retelling of the "blissful garden" story but includes a snake. Review is mildly critical of the novel's modesty: "Although she assembles an array of epic material, Le Guin does not venture much past the borders of the lyrical."
   Following the review are four unsigned paragraphs of biographical and descriptive material based on the writer's visit to Le Guin's home in Portland. Le Guin is quoted on her writing habits, her reading of science fiction, and the limits/challenges of the science fiction genre.

D693 GREEN, ROLAND. Review of The Beginning Place. Booklist 76 (1 February):756-57.
   Praises the book for its "brisk pacing and a near-total absence of preaching or ill-timed introspection," as well as its style and characterization. Deems it "more accessible" than Malafrena.

D694 GRIGG, DAVID. "Truth Deeper Than Logic." SF Commentary, no. 59 (April), pp. 4-5.
   Review of The Language of the Night. Admits his favorable bias stems from having been one of the participants in her Australian SF Writers' Workshop (1975). Credits the collection for revealing the author's "lucid, entertaining, and convincing prose" and for emphasizing the human quality in science fiction. Claims no other writer except Lem has "done so much to expose lovingly the faults of" the genre "while unceasingly pointing the way to the right road."

D695 HERBERT, ROSEMARY. Review of Edges. Library Journal 105 (15 October):2236.
   Recommends the stories that present "unusual perspectives on experience" and commends Le Guin for her introduction.

D696 _____. Review of The Beginning Place. Library Journal 105 (15 January):227.
   Finds it demonstrates the same "high literary quality" as her previous works. Perhaps it should be classified as "allegorical rather than fantastic or science fictional."

D697 HEWISON, ROBERT. "Astounding Alternatives." Times Literary Supplement, 12 December, p. 1048d.

Review of Threshold. Finds that the real world in which Hugh and Irena live is more convincingly drawn than their fantasy world, "a William Morrisey land of folklorique folk" in a Tolkienized society. Story is a quest with strong roles for her male and female characters. Novel loses momentum at the end and the resolution is incomplete.

D698 JORY, TOM. "A 'Daring' Move in Science Fiction." San Francisco Chronicle, 7 January, p. 42.
Review of PBS production of The Lathe of Heaven. Recounts that Loxton used Le Guin's fiction because it contained "all of the best elements of what I wanted this thing to be." Loxton quotes Le Guin on the novel: "'This is about inner space, not outer space.'" Describes the careful attention to script revisions in order to retain the "consistency" of the novel.

D699 KELLER, DONALD G. "Television Review." Fantasiae 8 (March): 8.
Review of PBS production of The Lathe of Heaven. Although he finds the novel to be "fairly minor Le Guin," the TV adaptation was "successful." In spite of the ending of both versions being "fuzzy," he found setting, characterization, and visual detail impressive.

D700 _____. Review of Interfaces. Fantasiae 8 (March):7-8.
Finds the collection "disappointing"; all but one story (James Tiptree's "Slow Music") are "rather minor."

D701 KHOURI, NADIA. "The Dialectics of Power: Utopia in the SF of Le Guin, Jeury, and Piercy." Science-Fiction Studies 20 (March):49-60.
Utopian desire reflects a critique of the "historical moment," but it may be thwarted by the effect of the ideology of that same moment on the author. The Dispossessed is limited by Le Guin's inability to truly imagine a utopia beyond the political states of the present. Her underlying assumption that "economic abundance" is the "source of exploitation, selfishness, and greed" becomes the source of her ethics; thus "moral categories substitute themselves for economic phenomena." Shevek's key actions are not accounted for by the logic of the narrative but by the economically determined ethic. Further, her concentration on Shevek thwarts her imagining a utopia arising out of the conflicts between Urras and Anarres. Novel is ideologically and aesthetically weak.

D702 KIMMEL, ERIC A. "Beyond Death: Children's Books and the Hereafter." Horn Book Magazine 56 (June):265-73.
Discusses lack of attention to death and dying in children's literature, and analyzes four authors who have faced

the issue--Tolkien, Le Guin, Lindgren, and Nichols. The
Farthest Shore is "remarkable" for presenting, in its portrayal of Cob, three "views of death existing side by side"
--death of the body, death of the soul, and "utter extinc-
tion" which Ged denies by his actions. However, Kimmel
prefers Nichols's treatment of a series of reincarnations
which is "whole and hopeful."

D703 LaBAR, MARTIN. "The Left Hand of Sexism? Women as the Alien
Species on Gethen." Extrapolation 21 (Summer):187-89.
Response to Wendell's essay [see D640]. Finds Wendell's
implication of sexism in The Left Hand of Darkness unsub-
stantiated. Lists four charges by Wendell and argues
against each.

D704 LEVIN, JEFF[rey H.], and BITTNER, JIM. "Of The Open Hills: A
Poetic Bibliography of Ursula K. Le Guin." Anthology of
Speculative Poetry, no. 4, pp. 4-5.
A checklist containing thirty-two entries, arranged in
chronological order from 1959 to 1979. An accurate and
first bibliography of Le Guin's poetry.

D705 MANLOVE, C.N. "Conservatism in the Fantasy of Le Guin."
Extrapolation 21 (Fall):287-97.
As a conservative genre, fantasy "portrays the preserva-
tion of status quo, looks to the past to sustain the nature
and values of the present, and delights in the nature of
created things." Asserts that the Earthsea trilogy exempli-
fies all of these in its emphasis on "balance, moderation,
and the celebration of things as they are." Offers evidence
from the volumes, with greatest detail on the "theme of
balanced." Notes that her science fiction emphasizes
"altering the status quo." Concludes praising her ability
to convey her own delight in creation and in mixing the
real and the fantastic.

D706 MARMOR, PAULA K. "The Day Before the Revolution." Fantasiae
8 (March): 1, 9.
Review of Malafrena. Shows that the novel is in keeping
with Le Guin's other fiction. First, it is a "prologue"
which "explores the changes in people that lead them to
attempt changes in their world." Second, it "explores . . .
revolution." Itale learns that "freedom cannot be bought
for others with guns and knives and intrigue, but must be
won each for himself." The true revolutionary has "to try
to create change in the hearts and minds of others." The
pain of this way is illustrated by Estenskar. The novel,
as an early Le Guin piece, illustrates "how central is this
idea of the burden of the artist."

D707 _____. Review of The Beginning Place. Fantasiae 8 (April):11.

Calls the novel "an odd beast." It is like <u>Very Far Away From Anywhere Else</u> in dealing with the theme of "growing up misfit to our American culture" but unlike it in having a "strong fantasy element." Although there is the danger of making the novel simply a "morality play," its theme is "the conquest of fear."

D708 MARMOR, PAULA [K.], ed. "The Works of Ursula K. Le Guin" [special issue]. <u>Fantasiae</u> 8 (March).
        All but two articles are on Le Guin. Contents include Paula K. Marmor, "The Day Before the Revolution"; James P. Wallace, "The Power of Names--Magic in Earthsea"; Donald G. Keller, Review of <u>Interfaces</u>; Donald G. Keller, "Television Review"; Ian M. Slater, "The Day After the Revolution"; and a list of seven articles which have appeared in the magazine, 1973-1979. [Note: there have been eight.]

D709 MATZNER, ROSALIND. "Love, etc., in Young Adult Fiction, 1956-79." <u>Top of the News</u> 37 (Fall):55-65.
        Annotated bibliography of stories on heterosexual love for readers twelve to eighteen. Includes <u>Very Far Away From Anywhere Else</u> which is judged appealing for its theme of conformity and its male viewpoint.

D710 MAYER, ALLAN J. "Beyond the Freeway." <u>Newsweek</u> (1 September), pp. 74-75.
        Review of <u>The Beginning Place</u>. In the discussion over whether or not Le Guin has "gone mainstream," he states, "what she really does is write fables: splendidly intricate and hugely imaginative tales about such mundane concerns as life, death, love, and sex." On one level, the novel is "entertaining fantasy," but on another it is "an elegantly accurate parable of maturing adolescent sexuality." Le Guin is a "gifted" writer.

D711 MINK, ERIC. "Science Fiction Winner." <u>St. Louis Post-Dispatch</u>, 11 January, p. 10D.
        Review of PBS production of <u>The Lathe of Heaven</u>. Welcomes it as "intelligent, adult science fiction drama."

D712 MITCHELL, W.J.T. "Editor's Note: On Narrative." <u>Critical Inquiry</u> 7 (Autumn):1-4.
        Provides an overview of the symposium, "Narrative: The Illusion of Sequence" from which the essays in this issue come. His account of the debate concludes with praise for Le Guin's presentation [see C191], saying "if the story of the narrative symposium is to be found anywhere, it is the secret sequences of Le Guin's jocular and haunting tale."

D713 MONK, PATRICIA. "Frankenstein's Daughters: The Problems of the Feminine Image in Science Fiction." <u>Mosaic</u> 13 (Spring/

Summer):15-27.
Asserts that science fiction has been dominated by an
"androcentric mystique." Supports by discussing its appearance in science fiction written by men since the nineteenth
century and its continuation in choice of protagonist, type
of plot, and portrayal of females in science fiction by
women since the 1940s. The Left Hand of Darkness and The
Dispossessed are used as examples. While the male protagonist in Left Hand is justified, it is not in The Dispossessed. Furthermore, the women characters in the second
novel are used to develop the male protagonist.
Second half of the essay argues that recent science fiction is exploring "gynocentric concepts" that may "elimi-
nate" the androcentric mystique. Her underlying assumption
is that the primary issue for the woman science fiction
writer is "the nature of a woman's identity as a woman."
Using Le Guin's discussion of science fiction as a
heuristic experiment, she analyzes why the genre is particularly amenable to such exploration. Briefly discusses
three examples--The Left Hand of Darkness, Bradley's The
Ruins of Isis, and Russ's The Female Man. Concludes
praising the artistry and originality of the three.

D714 MOYLAN, TOM. "Beyond Negation: The Critical Utopias of
Ursula K. Le Guin and Samuel R. Delany." Extrapolation 21
(Fall):236-53.
Discusses The Dispossessed and Triton as representative
"critical" utopias, that is, literary works which "possess
a duality both in content and form which allows considera-
tion of the repressive reality as well as the utopian dream."
The Dispossessed shows not only the opposition between
Anarres and Urras but also the duality within Anarresti
society as the "revelationary initiative" subsides and the
society moves toward centralization. Criticizes novel's
"aesthetic weaknesses," especially "the subordination of
character and plot to the ideas."
Discusses Triton, contrasting it with The Dispossessed,
concluding that "although the utopian ideas may be clearer
in Le Guin's work, the relationship between utopian vision
and everyday life may ultimately be more evident, more
accessible, in Delany's." The two novels "constitute an
encompassing picture of the opposition vision within United
States culture in the 1970s."

D715 MULLER, AL, and SULLIVAN III, C.W. "Young Adult Literature:
Science Fiction and Fantasy Series Books." English Journal
69 (October):71-74.
Review and recommend eight series, including Le Guin's
Earthsea trilogy. Books are selected for being initiation
stories and well told.

D716 O'FLAHERTY, WENDY DONIGER. "Inside and Outside the Mouth of
God: The Boundary between Myth and Reality." <u>Daedalus</u>
109 (Spring):93-125.
A compelling study of mythology as "irrational truth."
Uses selected "Indian, Greek, and Shakespearean myths" to
show that myth is "a boundary line where fantasy and reality
meet." Myths have the power to "grow out of reality and to
<u>make</u> reality." Discussion is amenable to Le Guin's ideas
on myth in her essays and use of myth in her fiction. She
is quoted/cited four times.

D717 REES, DAVID. "Earthsea Revisited." In <u>The Marble in The</u>
<u>Water: Essays on Contemporary Writers of Fiction for Chil-</u>
<u>dren and Young Adults</u>. Boston: Horn Book, pp. 78-89,
passim.
Lists many of the mythic and historical allusions in
Earthsea, but concentrates on those elements that make her
unique among authors of children's books. He names such
concepts as her recognition that evil is within and cannot
be simply banished like St. George's dragon, her wise and
humble adults who have "standards," her rejection of the
contemporary belief that "man should do things just because
he has the capacity to do them," her depiction of human
responsibility to nature. He discusses her conservatism
in presenting a male world and the need for special education for the gifted, but praises her use of Tenar who discovers "her femininity as a great source of good rather than
evil." She is superior to the over-rated Tolkien, C.S.
Lewis, and Richard Adams.

D718 REMINGTON, THOMAS J. "A Time to Live and a Time to Die:
Cyclical Renewal in the Earthsea Trilogy." <u>Extrapolation</u>
21 (Fall):278-86.
Constructs his essay as a response to Shippey's [see
D437]. Provides strong evidence for seeing that Le Guin's
use of "the seasonal cycle" is significant to the meaning
of the trilogy. Proves that in the first two volumes,
Ged's successes are at the time of Sunreturn. Thus the
pattern recalls Frazer's "myths of the vegetation cycle,
the wasteland, and the dying King." Further, "freeing of
the waters" is associated with Ged's victories, as are the
"symbols of the grail and the lance" (i.e. the ring and
sword of Erreth-Akbe) at the end of the second volume.
third volume inverts the pattern with victory coming at the
"vernal equinox" in a dry land. Thus just as the first two
novels show "the triumph of life over death," the last insists on the balance by showing "that death and darkness
have their place in the scheme of things."

D719 RIDDLE, IRA LEE. Review of <u>Malafrena</u>. <u>Best Sellers</u> 39
(January):363-64.

A "disappointing" mainstream novel; it is too long and lacks any "real conclusion."

D720 ROLNICK, AMY. Review of The Beginning Place. School Library
Journal 26 (April):132.
Cites Le Guin's fine blending of "the real and the fantastic," but finds the book "too slow moving and atmos-
pherically grim" for most readers.

D721 ROSENBERG, JUDE. "The Dispossessed: A Review." WAM! (Women
and Men) 2 (October):6-10.
Applauds the novel for its blend of "emotions" and
"politics," "discussions on sexuality," and depiction of
"the effects of our social environment on our behavior."
Disappointed that her bias for heterosexuality and monogamy
have limited her "visions of sexuality in a utopian society"
and that the protagonist is male. However, reviewer so admires the other aspects of this society that she would
choose to live in Anarres. Examining the history of Odonianism, she feels Le Guin missed one step in the develop-
ment--for women, "a period of separation in which to develop
themselves as complete persons."

D722 RUSS, JOANNA. "Books." Fantasy & Science Fiction 58 (February):94-101.
Review of "The Pathways of Desire" and The Language of
the Night. Enthusiastic over the story's union of form and
content: "the story barely holds together and almost self-
destructs in mid-air, a virtuoso performance that exactly
suits the writer's theme."
Commends the "intelligent and novelistically graceful
essays," preferring those that are more spontaneous. "From
Elfland to Poughkeepsie" is an example of an essay in which
her "teacherly generosity keeps her at too elementary a
level." Overall flaw is her "passion for morality and how
that passion is likely to be misused by readers." Two
essays which avoid this are "The Modest One" and "The Child
and the Shadow." Ends with a discussion of American youth's
naivete about difficulty of moral choice.

D723 _____. "Crossing Inner Lands." Book World (Washington Post),
24 February, p. 7.
Review of The Beginning Place. Describes the novel's
locale as "the intrapsychic landscape of her earlier fantasies." An artistic advancement is the use of a "gray,
gritty, realistic style" for both the fantasy and the real
world. However, the novel leaves the two protagonists with
no place to go. Le Guin clearly (and sanely) shows they
cannot live in Elfland, but Poughkeepsie is so inconsis-
tently and untruthfully drawn, so unaffected by the changes
in Elfland, that their solution to go to the real world is
unbelievable.

D724 SHRAPNEL, NORMAN. "Would They Like It Here?" Guardian Weekly
      122 (25 May):22.
          Review of Malafrena. Novel is a surprising addition to
      two fields--historical fiction and Le Guin's fiction. Its
      outstanding quality is its "unearthly calm," thus avoiding
      "the hectic flush this sort of Byronic subject matter
      normally brings on."

D725 SHWARTZ, SUSAN M. Review of The Beginning Place. Science
      Fiction Review 9 (May):37-38.
          Categorizes it as one of Le Guin's "psychomyths," a
      "statement, divorced from our own world, or the values we
      long to find in it." Le Guin varies her style to fit
      Hugh's thoughts or the quest. Likens it to Marge Piercy's
      Woman on the Edge of Time and Andre Norton's Year of The
      Unicorn, but Le Guin is less didactic and a better stylist.

D726 SIMMS, WILLARD. "Old Wine in an Old Bottle From Le Guin."
      Los Angeles Times, 17 February, The Book Review, p. 9.
          Review of Malafrena. Dismisses her novel because "she's
      captured all the froth and foam of the old masters and left
      out most of the substance." It is an entertaining novel
      without any serious theme; she has succumbed to the tempta-
      tion to escape to a simpler time--without "Darwin, Freud,
      Marx, two world wars, the atomic bomb."

D727 SLATER, IAN M. "The Day After the Revolution." Fantasiae 8
      (March):9-11.
          Surveys nonfictional, comparative studies of revolutions,
      a group to which Malafrena, apart from its literary nature,
      belongs. Names books and summarizes the views of thirteen
      authors, from the eighteenth century to the present, noting
      their relevance to Le Guin's novel. A helpful overview
      which includes information on the paperback editions of the
      works discussed.

D728 SPENCER, KATHLEEN. "Exiles and Envoys: The SF of Ursula K.
      Le Guin." Foundation, no. 20 (October), pp. 32-43.
          Draws on Victor Turner's analysis of liminality and its
      functions in society to understand "the pattern in Le Guin's
      fiction of the solitary hero reaching out to the alien."
      Society is a dialectical process between structure (i.e.
      statuses and roles, the norm) and communitas ("the affirma-
      tion of the connectedness of all human beings"). Change
      occurs when the communitas affects the structure. Members
      of it are outsiders, isolated. "They . . . stand outside
      the system and formulate alternative arrangements, to fit
      new phenomena into established systems of knowledge, to
      modify the structure as no one within the structure can do."
          Le Guin's characters are always outsiders and "liminality
      is the essential precondition for communication between

self and other." She discusses its use in "Nine Lives,"
The Left Hand of Darkness, and "The Eye of the Heron." In
all of Le Guin's work, the same message emerges: "shared
loneliness and mutual vulnerability--the fundamental human
condition, if we can only admit it--is the only ground in
which communication, friendship, love can flourish."

D729 STEELE, COLIN. "Beginnings of Le Guin." SF Commentary, nos.
      60/61 (October), p. 23.
          Review of Rocannon's World. Points out that Harper &
      Row corrected errors of previous printings but Gollancz did
      not. Responds favorably to its "colourfulness and romanti-
      cism," especially when compared to The Dispossessed. Feels
      she "has lost some of her early driving narrative and sense
      of wonder, although of course gaining much in the depth of
      exploration of concepts and character and the juxtaposition
      of themes."

D730 STEWART, ROBERT. "Filmedia: Crossings In Mist." Starship 17
      (Summer):34-35.
          Review of PBS production of The Lathe of Heaven. Pleased
      with the successful adaptation. Cites an example of the
      film's imagery which heightened the effect of a passage
      from the novel. The production "is proof of what can
      happen when filmmakers go beyond thinking about a 'property,'
      have some respect for the printed pages and go out of their
      way to involve the original creator of the material."

D731 STUEWE, PAUL. Review of The Beginning Place. Quill & Quire
      [Canada] 46 (August):34.
          Novel breaks out of the literary categories, as befits
      this writer who "is actually more speculative than scientif-
      ic and more fantasy-oriented than futurological."

D732 TAVORMINA, M. TERESA. "Physics as Metaphors: The General
      Temporal Theory in The Dispossessed." Mosaic 13 (Spring/
      Summer):51-62.
          To assess the function of the key event in the novel,
      Shevek's breakthrough that establishes the General Temporal
      theory, she discusses two issues. First, she amasses all
      references and hints in the novel in order to understand
      the theory "as a piece of science," pointing out where it
      resembles and differs from Terran science. Second, she
      answers the question, "How can a theory of time cast light
      on human action, and what light does Shevek's theory cast?"
      The time theory is a metaphor, significant because "the novel
      defines human responsibility as a temporal relationship."
      "By memory we bind the past to the present; by intention,
      we bind the present to the future." The novel's structure
      and ideas of human and social responsibility depend on the
      unity of concepts of sequence and simultaneity, "being and

becoming, duration and creation, stability and flux, eter-
nity and evolution, unity and plurality." The theory makes
possible the ansible, that is, accepting responsibility
which makes possible "a truly human community." It also
contains the concept of openness, or the necessary freedom
of a "healthy society."

D733 TOOMEY, PHILIPPA. "Stacks of Historicals." Times (London),
30 May, p. IId.
  Review of Malafrena. Labels it "first rate" and notes
the ambiguity of the resolution--was Itale's work "a romantic dream of youth" or will he become "their true leader?"

D734 UNGER, ARTHUR. "Television Previews." Christian Science
Monitor, 7 January, p. 15.
  Review of PBS production of The Lathe of Heaven. Unfavorable review because the meaning of the story is ultimately "obscure," including the quotation from which the
novel's title comes.

D735 UPDIKE, JOHN. "Imaginary Things." New Yorker (23 June), pp.
94, 96-97.
  Review of The Beginning Place. Describes her fiction as
always having "had a mainstream tact, color, and intelligence, combined with the requisite sci-fi expertise and
appetite for coining new worlds and languages." Places
this novel in the context of the "vaguely medieval never-
never land" which began with Malory, reappeared in Tennyson
and Morris, and was made modern by Tolkien. Praises her
description of settings.
  On the one hand, the novel can be read "as a metaphor of
sexuality emerging from masturbatory solitude into the
perilous challenge and exchange of heterosexual encounter."
On the other hand, many of her episodes "command belief
without an equation, gathering their own weight within a
fairyland that never seems too remote from actual states of
mind." Refers to her skillful handling of doubles--the
fantasy land within suburbia, the double personae of each
protagonist, and the reversal of the two worlds so that
suburbia becomes "the true beginning place." Her credibility
falters "only when it presses its moral too earnestly and
starts to sound like a marriage manual."

D736 Van GELDER, LINDSY. Review of The Beginning Place. Ms. 9
(July):30.
  Summarizes it as "pop-psych stuff" which has been turned
into "an absorbing tale."

D737 VAUGHAN, STEPHEN. "Wedlock and Disruptions." Observer (London), 20 April, p. 39.
  Review of Malafrena. Praises her first nonscience fiction

novel. "It glows with a quiet sense of time and place, love and loyalties at the healing point of despair."

D738   WALKER, JEANNE MURRAY. "Rites of Passage Today: The Cultural Significance of A Wizard of Earthsea." Mosaic 13 (Spring/Summer):179-91.

Argues that this novel and high fantasy, in general, "perform certain tasks for modern adolescents which in other societies are dramatized by rites of passage." Defines rite of passage, and perceptively asserts that the initiation rite described at the end of chapter one contains the thesis and action of the novel. Furthermore, the experience of reading the novel becomes a rite of passage for the adolescent. Discusses in detail the themes and action of the novel--"the necessity of the social order," the necessity of isolation which symbolizes the death of the old identity, and the fear of spending life caught in the gap between the old and new identity. Thus the novel also "convince[s] the reader of the social theory which makes rites of passage meaningful."

D739   _____. "Reciprocity and Exchange in Science Fiction." Essays in Arts and Sciences 9 (August):145-56.

Argues for a nonideological approach to science fiction criticism which will emphasize how it is like other literature. This approach reveals that science fiction, "like myth, articulates by analogy the primary patterns evident in society." The principle pattern in myth and science fiction is "exchange." "Exchange is a metaphor which, cutting across the distinction between historical and a-historical reality, allows the critic to accept each work of art in its own cultural setting with its own ideological premises."

Concludes discussing The Left Hand of Darkness and Canticle for Leibowitz. Summarizes her argument in D639 that "kinship exchange" is the foundation of the myths and Gethenian society and that it supports "a dynamic, flexible social structure."

D740   WALLACE, JAMES P. "Riastradh: The Power of Names--Magic in Earthsea." Fantasiae 8 (March):3.

Argues that, in spite of the similarities between Tolkien's fantasy and Le Guin's, their "roots of magic" are different--"Archipelagan magic is based on language rather than spirit." In Earthsea, language is the enabling link with magic whereas in Middle-earth, magic is "a part of the being of each living creature." Discusses the dynamism of naming and the various powers of Earthsea--wizards, Old Powers, dragons. [For response, see D690.]

D741   WATT, DONALD. "New Worlds Through Old Forms: Some Traditional

Critical Tools for Science Fiction." Essays in Arts and Sciences 9 (August):131-37.
 Concludes his argument for the validity of using some of the "historical and formalist modes of criticism" with a brief look at The Left Hand of Darkness. Asserts the novel is a "showcase of traditional techniques" and can be "rewardingly approached through textual, formalist, and psychological criticism."

D742 WOOD, SUSAN. "Worlds out of Words." Starship 17 (Spring):42.
 Review of Leese Webster and Malafrena. Recommends the first book, a "charming fable about art and life" for both children and adults. The second is a continuation of "the debate on freedom and responsibility, love and duty" from The Dispossessed and "The Eye of the Heron." Although a good novel of ideas, it is "oddly theoretical, at a bit of a distance."

D743 YOKE, CARL. "Precious Metal in White Clay." Extrapolation 21 (Fall):197-208.
 Maintains the widespread recognition of Le Guin's fiction is due to three factors: the moral complexity, allusions to "current and familiar history," and her ability to convince the reader of the "validity" of her created worlds and characters. Essay explores how she achieves the last quality, illustrating with The Word for World is Forest and "The Day Before The Revolution."
 World creation is explored in Word; he catalogs various areas which complicate and enrich the central metaphor of the forest. However, Yoke's liberal use of "creechies" for the Athsheans and his comparison of them to apes seems to mitigate against the theme of the story. Discusses Don Davidson and Laia Odo as examples of Le Guin's fine characterization.
 Concludes with an overview of the special issue which was occasioned by the editors receiving numerous "excellent articles" on Le Guin.

D744 YOKE, CARL, ed. "Special Ursula K. Le Guin Issue." Extrapolation 21 (Fall).
 Contains ten articles: Carl Yoke, "Precious Metal in White Clay"; Dena C. Bain, "The Tao Te Ching as Background to the Novels of Ursula K. Le Guin"; Rosemarie Arbur, "Le Guin's 'Song' of Inmost Feminism"; Barbara Brown, "The Left Hand of Darkness: Androgyny, Future, Present, and Past"; Tom Moylan, "Beyond Negation: The Critical Utopias of Ursula K. Le Guin and Samuel R. Delany"; Edgar C. Bailey, Jr., "Shadows in Earthsea: Le Guin's Use of a Jungian Archetype"; Robert Galbreath, "Taoist Magic in the Earthsea Trilogy"; Brian Attebery, "On a Far Shore: The Myth of Earthsea"; Thomas J. Remington, "A Time to Live and a Time

to Die: Cyclical Renewal in the Earthsea Trilogy"; C.N.
Manlove, "Conservatism in the Fantasy of Le Guin." Includes
one book review: Thomas D. Clareson, "Le Guin's Latest
Novel: A New Beginning Place?" With the exception of
Galbreath and Remington, edition is marred by lack of attention to previous Le Guin scholarship (possibly caused by
manuscripts being held some time before publication) and an
inattention to the correct version of Le Guin's name:
Ursula K. Le Guin.

D745 ZALESKI, PHILIP. Review of <u>Malafrena</u>, <u>The Beginning Place</u>,
and <u>Leese Webster</u>. <u>Parabola</u> 5 (May):118-20.
Places Le Guin in the context of modern science where
"paradigms" change overnight, and acknowledges her ability
that "weaves old myths and new science" into new art. All
three works are similar in focusing on protagonists at "the
moment between childhood and adulthood when home becomes a
prison" and in leading them to the discovery of themselves.
The first two are Taoist novels, without villains and without Le Guin taking sides in the tensions. The last is less
intense, a children's story about "the sources of creativity
in experimentation and courage." The PBS production of <u>The
Lathe of Heaven</u> will give Le Guin a wider audience; he
hopes they will turn to her books.

1981

D746 ANON. Review of <u>Hard Words and Other Poems</u>. <u>Kirkus Reviews</u>
49 (part 1, 15 January):133-34.
Finds her to be an "inept poet"; rarely does her usual
good writing appear in the poetry. Most of the poems use
"glib nursery rhymes and a mythopoeic beat."

D747 BRASWELL, LAUREL. "The Visionary Voyage in Science Fiction
and Medieval Allegory." <u>Mosaic</u> 14 (Winter):125-42.
Notes and discusses the themes and techniques shared by
science fiction and medieval allegory. Both use story form
to make an abstract idea concrete, and both use the journey
as a metaphor for progress toward "a vision of higher
truth." Consistently used as examples are <u>The Left Hand of
Darkness</u>, Zelazny's <u>Isle of The Dead</u> and Delany's <u>Babel-17</u>.
The voyage often takes the form of the "redemptive jour-
ney," as in <u>Left Hand</u>. Technical similarities include the
use of "qualitative names"; "associative iconography of
landscape"; and the use of authority figures and myths to
aid the hero.
All three novels show, like medieval allegory, a self-
consciousness about the form so that the goal of the quest
is often not the clear victory of which the traveler had
dreamed. Thus, modern science fiction may be speaking to

the limitations of human vision.

D748   BUCKNALL, BARBARA J. Ursula K. Le Guin. New York: Unger.
      After a brief biography, she devotes five chapters to a
      discussion, approximately in order of publication, of
      Le Guin's novels and novellas and one chapter to her short
      stories. Chapters contain solid plot summaries and identi-
      fication of some literary and scientific sources for specific
      works. Most original work is on The Left Hand of Darkness
      where she argues that incest is the primary theme [an ex-
      pansion of D457].
      Concludes with a summary of the common features in her
      novels (the outer journey; the inner journey; concern with
      love, friendship, and fidelity/betrayal; hatred of oppres-
      sion and love of freedom; use of romanticism and realism).
      Includes a select bibliography.

D749   DICK, PHILIP K. Letter to the editor. Science Fiction Review
      10 (Summer):31-32.
      Quotes a letter from Michael Bishop which paraphrases
      Le Guin's concerns over his new novel, Valis. Dick speaks
      directly to her to reassure her of his sanity. Discusses
      the theme and techniques of his novel. [For Le Guin's
      reply, see C203.]

D750   ESMONDE, MARGARET P. "The Good Witch of the West." Children's
      Literature: Annual of The Modern Language Association
      Group on Children's Literature and The Children's Litera-
      ture Assoc. Vol. 9. New Haven: Yale University Press,
      pp. 185-90.
      Review of Ursula K. Le Guin: Voyager to Inner Lands and
      to Outer Space, The Language of the Night, Ursula K.
      Le Guin, Structural Fabulation, and The Farthest Shores of
      Ursula K. Le Guin. Surveys the critical reception of the
      three Earthsea volumes and then annotates the books in order
      of publication, commenting on the essays about Le Guin's
      fantasy. Praises Scholes's early attention to Le Guin and
      his contrast of her to C.S. Lewis, but notes his analysis
      is primarily limited to A Wizard of Earthsea. Therefore,
      she finds Slusser's full treatment "more satisfying." Finds
      the Earthsea essays in both the De Bolt and Olander/
      Greenberg volumes helpful, but asserts that Le Guin's own
      collection of essays is the "most valuable."

D751   FEKETE, JOHN. "Circumnavigating Ursula Le Guin." Science-
      Fiction Studies 8 (March):91-98.
      Review of Ursula K. Le Guin: Voyager to Inner Lands and
      to Outer Space. Using the title of the collection as an
      indication of its theme, he criticizes the volume for not
      maintaining "a clear focus on the large crucibles within
      which the self is formed nor" the relationship between the

self and "a given historical-cosmic reality." Classifies
it as a "celebratory volume" for the "general educated
reader," and praises its variety.

Discusses the Earthsea essays and Le Guin's own statements on fantasy, noting that the issues raised by her own
essays are not critically treated in this collection. Although individual essays are clear, the book overall is
"limited by the relative lack of theoretical depth and
range."

Concludes by listing five critical methods which should
be applied to her work and six issues in her work that "are
endemic to our society and its current blockage and
struggles."

D752   GEIS, RICHARD E. Review of SF Commentary 60/61. Science Fic-
        tion Review 10 (Spring):31.
        He summarizes Le Guin's letter in that issue as saying
        she does not "read science fiction anymore." [For Le Guin's
        correction, see C204.]

D753   GREENLAND, COLIN. Review of The Language of the Night.
        Foundation, no. 21, pp. 104-5.
        Accepts Wood's selection of essays, but objects to two
        factors: the arrangement of essays by theme because it
        "obscures growth and change in the writer's ideas"; and the
        arrangement of Levin's bibliography in several "alphabetical
        lists" rather than by chronology. He recommends the essays,
        but warns that her discussions of the source of creativity
        and her literary criticism are not very analytical. The
        book is valuable as "self-description and diplomacy."

D754   _____. Review of The Beginning Place. Foundation, no. 21,
        pp. 77-79.
        Judges it to be "rich, and deft, and humorous, and wise,
        and beautiful." It is to be compared to Alan Garner's
        writing and her own Orsinian fiction, as well as The Far-
        thest Shore. It continues many of her themes, but also
        tries something new. As in her other works, she is inter-
        ested in "coupled contraries," "empty-handed" heroes, "dis-
        possession." Her new style is "a blurring of description
        by a drifting, appositional syntax, not everywhere, but
        especially where Le Guin is trying for an effect," which is
        not always meaningful.

D755   KLEINER, ART. Review of The Language of the Night. CoEvolu-
        tion Quarterly, no. 29 (Spring), p. 54.
        Recommends it as even "more inspiring" than her fiction.
        Valuable for its practical advice to writers and readers,
        insights on specific novels and literature, its depiction
        of imaginary literature as playing "out the conflicts that
        brew hidden in our collective imagination."

D756 LaBAR, MARTIN. "Refiner's Fire: Slipping the Truth in Edge-
wise." Christianity Today 25 (27 March):38-39.
Discusses the contents of Earthsea, noting Le Guin's
Taoism and quoting from her NBA speech and "Dreams Must
Explain Themselves." Her subjects are those common to
fantasy, "love, the meaning of life, coming of age, the
meaning of personhood, death"; and one uncommon subject,
"the role of man as a species." Regrets her lack of Christianity because although the books describe, they do "not
always properly prescribe" for the soul.

D757 LAKE, DAVID J. "Le Guin's Twofold Vision: Contrary Image-
Sets in The Left Hand of Darkness." Science-Fiction
Studies 8 (July):156-64.
Discusses the two image-sets to show "the nation of
Orgoreyn with its Yomesh cult is not so much the Contrary
as the Negation of Karhide with its Handdara religion; and
the implied author of the narrative is not neutral," but
favors Karhide. The image-set associated with Orgoreyn is
cold-light-white-ice-pale liquids-left symbolizing "ration-
alism, certain knowledge, tyranny, isolation, betrayal,
death." The image-set associated with Karhide is warmth-
darkness-red-earth-blood-light symbolizing "intuition,
ignorance, freedom, relationship, fidelity, life." Offers
supporting evidence, occasionally drawing on Blake's The
Marriage of Heaven and Hell for additional explanation.
Concludes Le Guin is "less optimistic than Blake" and her
contraries are not fully integrated.

D758 MILLER, FRED D. Jr., and SMITH, NICHOLAS D. Thought Probes:
Philosophy Through Science Fiction. Englewood Cliffs, N.J.:
Prentice-Hall, pp. 319-25, passim.
In a chapter, "Is Politics Necessary?" they contrast
Heinlein's The Moon Is a Harsh Mistress and Le Guin's The
Dispossessed as heuristic experiments about anarchism. The
novels differ on the issues of individualism, economic sys-
tem, and centralization.

D759 ROTTENSTEINER, FRANZ. "Le Guin's Fantasy." Science-Fiction
Studies 8 (March):87-90.
Review of The Language of the Night. Acknowledging that
her fantasy and her essays are based on the same principles,
he identifies her main topics as "the twin poles of beauty
and truth, aesthetics and ethics."
Challenges her assertion that science fiction ought to
be a literature of characterization. Le Guin is, ultimately,
not a "great writer"; her work is full of "human warmth"
but it fails to "face the full consequences and implica-
tions" of issues, characters, and situations.
Disagrees with her assessment that fantasy is ignored
and that the reason is our technological environment.

Actually, fantasy is possible and popular only as a reaction
against an industrial society.
   He does not believe that the myths of fantasy are alive
and relevant to modern times. Even though Le Guin is
better than Tolkien, she is "illusionistic and lacking the
courage and the insight to perceive the true state of
things."

D760 SPIVACK, CHARLOTTE. "The Perilous Realm: Phantasy As Liter-
      ature." Centennial Review 25 (Spring):133-49.
         After justifying the name "phantasy" for the genre, she
      characterizes it, drawing on Lewis, Tolkien, and Le Guin.
      "Fantasy," from Aristotelian thought, is suspect and not
      confirmed by the senses. "Phantasy," from Platonic thought,
      is literature "based on a vision of non-empirical reality."
      Discusses its origin in the Renaissance, its relationship
      to the romance, and its double quest of outward and inward
      movement toward a goal. The best modern phantasies are
      Narnia, Middle Earth, and Earthsea. Le Guin's differs from
      the other two in "mood and tone."

D761 WALLACE, JAMES P. "Riastradh." Fantasiae 9 (February):6.
         Reply to Gilson's article which disagreed with Wallace
      about the nature of magic in Middle-earth and Earthsea.
      Repeats his assertion that the roots of magic are different
      and clarifies his position. [See D690 and D740.]

Indexes

I: Writings by Le Guin
(Parts A, B, C)

References are to entry numbers, not pages.   Titles are shortened.
Selected subject headings are included.

Abstract, C183
Adaptation, B103, B142-144, B146-
   147
Afterword, C39, C115
"All about Anne," C128
"Amazed," B93, B96, B104
"American SF and the Other,"
   C111, C122, C175
"An die Musik," A1, A58
"Anger, The," B27, B40
"Announcing the O'Melas Contest,"
   C134
Anthology, edited, A65, A86, A89
"April in Paris," A2, A41, C96
"Arboreal," B27, B45
"Archaeology of the Renaissance,"
   B27, B34
"Ars Lunga," B27, B41
"Aspects of Death," C2
"At a Quarter to Fifty," B104,
   B128
"At the Sci-Fi Summit," C89
"At Three Rivers," B104, B113
Aussiecon Tapes, B63
Australian Writers Workshop,
   A55-A56, A71, B141, C117-118.
   See also C113.
"Author Broke into Print," C44
"Author of the Acacia Seeds,
   The," A38
"Author's Introduction," C160,
   C175
Autobiography, C50

Barbour, Douglas, B140
Barlowe, Wayne Douglas, B145
"Barrow, The," A57-58
Beginning Place, The, A84-85
"Bems Scarce," C20
"Book Bin, The," C35
"Book Bites Back, The," C42
"Books Remembered," C163
"Botticelli," B11
"Brothers and Sisters," A49, A58
Buckley, Kathy, B141

"Cake and Ice Cream," A27
"California: For Lowry Pei," B77
"Carmagnole," B81, B85, B104
"Cavaliers," B104, B131
"Central Park South," B104, B119
"Child and the Shadow, The," C82,
   C175
"Child on the Shore, The," B104,
   B129
Children's fiction, A53, A79
"Citizen of Mondath, A," C50,
   C175
City of Illusions, A12, A73, C168
"Coast," B104, B117
Collection, A40-41, A58, A66, A73,
   B27, B81, B93, B101, B104,
   C92, C175
"Coming of Age," B12, B27, B29
Comment and headnote, C8, C51,
   C55, C64, C69, C95-110, C119,
   C138

II: Writings about Le Guin
(Part D)

References are to entry numbers, not pages. Entries include authors, editors, and titles of critical works; titles by Le Guin which are reviewed or referenced; people whose names or works are mentioned in the annotations. Some titles are shortened.

More, Sir Thomas, D534
Morner, Claudia J., D485, D586
Morris, William, D154, D534,
 D697, D735
Moylan, Tom, D714, D744
Muir, Edwin, D60
Mullen, R.D., D169, D222-223,
 D244-245, D251, D260, D263,
 D279-281, D285, D290, D352,
 D409, D425
Muller, Al, D715
"Muse of SF, The," D354
Myers, Alan G., D260
"Myth and Archetype," D613
"Myth, Exchange and History,"
 D639
"Mythic Reversals: The Evalua-
 tion of the Shadow," D561
"Mythology of Control," D242
"Myths of anti-climax," D74
"My Trip Through Science Fiction,"
 D383

Naha, Ed, D587
Nash, Les, D486
Nasso, Christine, D419
"National Book Award Acceptance,"
 D153, D756
"Naumburg-Winning Jubal Trio,"
 D474
Nebula Award Stories 11, D297,
 D390, D415, D432, D439, D562,
 D568
Nelson, Alix, D349
"New Atlantis, The," D281, D362,
 D612, D683
"Newbery Honor Books," D75
"Newbery Medalist Susan Cooper,"
 D316
"New High for Sci-Fi," D172
Newman, Robert S., D588
"New SF: ESP, ZPG, etc., " D103
"New Utopian Novel, A," D325
"New World for Women," D490
"New Worlds for Old?," D224
New Worlds for Old, D188. See
 also David Ketterer.
"New Worlds, New Words," D446
"New Worlds Through Old Forms,"
 D741
Nicholls, Peter, D196, D322, D589
Nichols, Ruth, D702

Nicol, Charles, D420
Nilsen, Alleen Pace, D421, D590
"Nine Lives," D40, D84, D215, D274,
 D287, D293, D330, D342, D347,
 D355, D358, D479, D728
"1978 Books for Young Adults,"
 D590
"1969, West-Coast Nebula Awards,
 The," D63
Niven, Larry, D324
Nixon, Peter, D197
"No More Nannies," D343
Norton, Andre, D1, D8, D36, D106,
 D226, D725
"Notable Children's Books of
 1971," D81
"Notable Children's Books of
 1968," D12
"Notes on 'Teaching' A Wizard of
 Earthsea," D137
"Novels of Ursula K. Le Guin,
 The," D19
Novitski, Paul David, D422
Nowell, Robert, D198
Nudelman, Refail, D260, D279
Nye, Robert, D150-151, D199

O'Brien, Dennis, D423
O'Donnell, Gus, D261
Offutt, Andrew, D424-425
O'Flaherty, Wendy Doniger, D716
"Of Love and Sex and Death," D488
"Of The Open Hills," D704
"Of Things to Come," D246
Olander, Joseph D., D512, D515,
 D527, D534-535, D540, D549,
 D561, D564, D591-592, D604,
 D624, D635, D750
"Old Favourite, An," D401
"'Oldie' Ahead of Its Time," D505
"Old Wine in an Old Bottle," D726
Olsen, Tillie, D310
"On a Far Shore," D658
"On Barbour on Le Guin," D400
"On David Ketterer's New Worlds,"
 D262
"One Real Thing, The," D691
"Ones Who Walk Away from Omelas,
 The," D293, D317, D378, D612
Ones Who Walk Away from Omelas,
 The, D345
"On Le Guin's 'American SF,'" D324

D512
"Ursula K. Le Guin: The Earth-
sea Trilogy," D489
"Ursula K. Le Guin Imagines,"
D551
"Ursula K. Le Guin's 'Nine
Lives,'" D479
"Ursula K. Le Guin: The New
Atlantis," D388
"Ursula K. Le Guin: 'Using The
Language,'" D414
Ursula K. Le Guin: Voyager,
D543, D750, D751
"Ursula K. Le Guin Wins," D124
"Ursula Kroeber Le Guin," D382,
D454, D503, D541
"Ursula K(roeber) Le Guin," D502,
D615
"Ursula Le Guin: Explorer,"
D237
"Ursula Le Guin Giving a Les-
son," D41
"Ursula Le Guin: Novelist,"
D607
"Ursula Le Guin: Science Fic-
tion," D249
"Ursula Le Guin Wins All the
Marbles," D340
"Ursula Major: A Minor Review,"
D178
"Utopia and Science Fiction,"
D506
"Utopia, Where the Traffic Prob-
lem is," D174

"Value of Fantasy," D585
"Value The 'Other,'" D190
Van Gelder, Lindsy, D736
"Vaster Than Empires and More
Slow," D279, D289, D354-355,
D512, D589, D683
Vaughn, Ed, D638
Vaughan, Stephen, D737
Verne, Jules, D36
Very Far Away From Anywhere
Else, D300-301, D316, D328,
D331, D343, D349, D357, D367,
D374-375, D385, D394, D402,
D407, D413, D421, D438, D445,
D462-463, D488, D536, D590,
D605, D707, D709

Very Long Way From Anywhere Else,
A. See Very Far Away
Veysey, Laurence, D588
Viguers, Ruth H., D24
Vinson, James, D363
Virgil, D436
"Virgin Territory: The Bonds and
Boundaries," D404
"Virgin Territory: Women and
Sex," D87
"Visionary Voyage in Science Fic-
tion, The," D747
"Visions of Reality," D351
Visual Encyclopedia of Science
Fiction, The, D377
"Vivisector, The," D435, D616
Voltaire, Francois, D571
Vonnegut, Kurt, D175, D181, D513
"Vote to Keep the Prize, A," D134

Waggoner, Diana, D504
Walker, Jeanne, D639, D738-739
Walter, Paul, D69, D211, D492
Wallace, Doreen, D212
Wallace, James P., D708, D740,
D761
Ward, Jonathan, D153, D276
Warwick, Mal, D213
"Water is Wide, The," D422
Watson, Ian, D279, D289-291, D368
Watson, James D., D358
Watt, Donald, D741
Webb, Kaye, D214
"Wedlock and Disruptions," D737
"Week in the Country, A," D353
Weinbaum, Stanley, D427
Weiser, Norman, D339
Wells, H.G., D200, D596
Wendell, Carolyn, D640, D703
"West Coast Nebula Banquet," D254
Whaley, Stephen V., D215
"What Do you Want--The Moon?,"
D291
"What If?," D107
"What Women Want," D496
"What's New From Venus?," D230
Wheatley, Barbara, D641
White, E.B., D548, D618
White, Luise, D277
White, T.H., D60
White, Ted, D23, D25, D43, D117
White, Virginia L., D642